exploring
LIFE
DRAWING

Harold Stone

THOMSON

DELMAR LEARNING ™ Australia Canada Mexico Singapore Spain United Kingdom United States

THOMSON

DELMAR LEARNING

Exploring Life Drawing
Harold Stone

Vice President, Technology and Trades ABU:
David Garza

Director of Learning Solutions:
Sandy Clark

Managing Editor:
Larry Main

Acquisitions Editor:
James Gish

Marketing Director:
Deborah S. Yarnell

Director of Production:
Patty Stephan

Production Manager:
Stacy Masucci

Product Manager:
Molly Belmont

Content Project Manager:
Nicole Stagg

Technology Project Manager:
Kevin Smith

Editorial Assistant:
Niamh Matthews

Cover Image:
Harold Stone

Library of Congress Cataloging-in-Publication Data

Stone, Harold B.
   Exploring life drawing / Harold Stone.
       p. cm.
   Includes index.
   ISBN-13: 978-1-4018-9697-3
   ISBN-10: 1-4018-9697-9
   1. Figure drawing--Technique. I. Title.
   NC765.S84 2007
   743.4--dc22
                       2007003299

ISBN-13: 978-1-4018-9697-3
ISBN-10: 1-4018-9697-9

NOTICE TO THE READER

Dedication

For Ann

contents

modeling 134

Modeling drawing is often used as a vehicle for abstracting the figure, and it is also the traditional drawing technique used by Michelangelo and Raphael. It is an analytical method of studying and rendering the forms of the figure. This chapter will provide an opportunity to work with traditional modeling, and with two contemporary modeling techniques.

proportion 160

Proportion is the relationship of the elements of a drawing with respect to size. Proportion as it is used in life drawing can be complex because its application depends on the intent of the artist. Classical, objective and empirical proportions are all used in figurative art. This chapter give 12 methods of establishing and checking empirical proportions.

the figure—ground relationship 192

The figure-ground relationship is a process created by the artist and maintained by the drawing. It is one of the benchmarks of accomplished drawing and of a personal drawing style. Create a dynamic figure-ground relationship with contrast reversals, edge effects, and positive/negative space interactions.

composition 220

Composition issues in life drawing must be understood in the context of a life drawing's has a natural center of focus. Figurative artists will usually be more interested in the figure, or in the picture plane. An artist can combine illusionistic space with a considered surface treatment to create a spatial dialog in a drawing.

the finished drawing 244

A finished drawing is different from an exercise in that it is an ambitious work which meets the artist's highest personal quality standards. To create finished drawings, an artist must practice, and think about the practices. It isn't always easy for an artist to know how to create the best art possible, but by reflecting on past work to identify strengths and interests, and considering how to use devices such as narrative and abstraction, it is possible to identify some places to start.

CONTENTS

v

H. Stone, *Quick Studies*, black crayon on Rives
BFK paper, 22" × 30", 2000.

PREFACE

| *preface* |

INTENDED AUDIENCE

Exploring Life Drawing is an introduction to the art of drawing the human figure from observation. It emphasizes building skills, identifying figurative art issues of personal relevance, and constructing an individual drawing style. *Exploring Life Drawing* is intended as a textbook for an introductory-level college life-drawing course, but it would also be useful as a self-study guide for independent artists. It was written to be compatible with online course delivery.

The book starts with the premise that the most basic goal of any life drawing is to describe the three-dimensional forms of the human body. Instead of advocating one particular school of thought about how this should be accomplished, it offers a variety of structured exercises designed to help students apply this standard while making drawings consistent with their own interests. Each exercise focuses on developing a single skill and starts by discussing possible ways of addressing the problem, with examples from other artists. After listing the procedures, it includes a detailed, step-by-step demonstration of the assignment and ends with specific guidelines for assessing the results.

EMERGING TRENDS

Life drawing has been enjoying resurgence as an intellectual discipline and a career skill. Local drawing groups, online communities, and Web-based education have created new opportunities for image sharing and figurative art discourse. With the emergence of digital modeling and animation, animé, and new forms of comic book art, employment opportunities have expanded as well. Life-drawing practice has never been more diverse. Academic artists adapt traditional skills to express contemporary concerns, and contemporary artists strive to invent new ways of describing the human form. They have in common an interest in a rigorous art, requiring commitment and practice, and centered on the idea that other people are important.

BACKGROUND OF THIS TEXT

I wrote this book to help art students and independent learners find their own ways of expressing meaning through drawing the human figure. In addition to helping them develop skills, I want them to understand the set of premises and procedures that have been constant through life drawing's history: its common themes and its methods of making visible an artist's intentions. This is the consensus that makes life drawing central to the humanities and ensures its enduring relevance to artists.

In writing this book, it was my intention to teach specific, demonstrable skills and show how they can be used in a method of intellectual inquiry. I wanted to use plain language to explain the sometimes complex ideas related to the human figure in art and connect them to the daily practice of life drawing. *Exploring Life Drawing* is informed by the 30 years I have spent drawing the figure, more than 20 years as a college art instructor, and discussions I have had with artists, models, and other teachers.

My plan was to write a book that would be helpful to serious artists, but which would also fairly represent life drawing to someone whose involvement with it extends no further than a single survey course. Although any drawing skills are helpful while learning life drawing, it is not necessary for a student to have had previous instruction in drawing in order to productively use this book.

TEXTBOOK ORGANIZATION

Chapter 1 is an overview of learning how to draw the human figure, and Chapter 2, Chapter 3, and Chapter 4 each focus on developing one life-drawing skill. Chapter 5 and Chapter 6 work on integrating these skills and some new ones to make balanced, articulate drawings. Chapter 7 through Chapter 10 address proportion, integrating the figure into the space, and various strategies for composing pictures.

Chapter 1 gives instructions for creating a baseline drawing and describes the two major schools of thought about life drawing. In addition, it discusses drawing materials, criteria for evaluating the quality of life drawings, and practices for efficient learning.

Chapter 2 specializes in contour lines. It explains how a contour line differs from a contour and contrasts contour line drawing with value drawing. This chapter contains a detailed look at the blind contour exercise, along with a variation of it that will allow the student to immediately make competent line drawings. The chapter also covers evaluating the quality of a contour line and shows how lines can communicate subjectively, apart from their descriptive function.

Chapter 3 is a detailed look at value as it is used to describe the human form. It defines terms related to value, explains the three-value exercise, and shows two ways to do it. This chapter also encourages experimentation with various ways of applying drawing media and provides an opportunity for the student to practice them by using hatching lines in a four-value exercise.

Chapter 4 is an exploration of gesture in life drawing. It contains a discussion of the metaphor of balance in Western art and relates it to gesture drawing as an empathetic response to the movement in the pose. The chapter gives some variations of the gesture exercise and concludes with a gestural abstraction project.

In Chapter 5, the student uses quick studies to integrate contour line, value, and gesture, with the emphasis on creating a cooperative dialog between line and value. The chapter covers quick-contour drawing, the balanced quick study, and developing a gesture drawing into a finished picture.

Chapter 6 is an in-depth exploration into modeling drawing. It starts by connecting modeling to a drawing's use of structure and continues with a technical discussion of traditional modeling and a traditional modeling assignment. The theme of modeling as a manifestation of the drawing's structure is continued with an exercise in improvising with modeling and another one in which the theory of modeling is used to create a figurative abstraction.

Chapter 7 is dedicated to the complexities of proportion. It discusses classical, objective, empirical and internal proportions, and how they are applied in life drawing. The chapter gives twelve methods of measuring and verifying empirical proportions, relates proportion to the body's structure, and shows some common proportional errors.

The phrase "figure–ground relationship" is a common one in a life-drawing class. Chapter 8 explains in detail what the figure–ground relationship is and how figure–ground choices help communicate the artist's intentions. It includes exercises in edge effects, contrast reversal, and creating a dynamic figure–ground relationship.

Chapter 9 deals with the compositional issues unique to figurative art. It defines picture-plane–based composition and compares it to figure-based composition, explains how a spatial dialog can make drawings more interesting, and concludes with a project that develops an integrated deep-space composition.

In Chapter 10, students reflect on the skills they acquired during this course of instruction to recognize their own drawing styles and create finished, complete works of art. It starts with a discussion of how a finished drawing is different from a drawing exercise and guides students through an inventory of their drawings in order to identify the life-drawing strengths and interests they have developed during the course. This chapter shows some ways narrative and abstraction can be used in a finished drawing, has a structured exercise in drawing a finished portrait, and concludes with a step-by-step exercise in which students will create a finished drawing consistent with their own intentions, ambitions, and standards.

E.RESOURCE

This guide on CD was developed to assist instructors in planning and implementing their instructional programs. It includes sample syllabi for using this book in either an eleven- or fifteen-week semester. It also provides chapter review questions and answers, exercises, PowerPoint slides highlighting the main topics, and additional instructor resources.

ISBN: 1418014222

ABOUT THE AUTHOR

Harold B. Stone has been an artist specializing in life drawing for 30 years and has taught at the college level for more than 20 years. He has a B.S. from Texas A&M University, an M.A. and M.F.A. from the University of Tulsa, and has taught studio art for 24 years. In 1995 he founded the Minneapolis Drawing Workshop, an arts organization dedicated to exhibiting figurative drawings and paintings and presenting drawing workshops, marathons, and cooperative drawing sessions. He is also a founding member of Traffic Zone Center for Visual Art. He is a freelance art curriculum writer, specializing in Web-based instruction, and a web designer.

ACKNOWLEDGMENTS

I would like to thank my wife and son for the support they gave me while I wrote this book. I would also like to thank the people I think of as my life-drawing brain trust for their enthusiasm about drawing and the happy and productive hours we have spent making art together: Chad Balster, Lisa Colwell, Krystal Leehy, Joan Martin, Jules Meyer, Jeff Nygaard, Lisa Pfeiffer, David Rich, Dave Sandberg, and Mary Sandberg. I am also grateful to the Minneapolis Institute of Art, and particularly Kristen Lenaburg, for allowing me access to the Institute's drawing collection and for helping me with information and photography. Anne Majusiak is due high honors for heroic work tracking down obscure master drawings and getting permission to use them. I am very grateful to Jim Gish, at Thomson Delmar Learning, for giving me the opportunity to write this book, and to Jaimie Weiss and Molly Belmont for their guidance while I wrote it. Finally, I would like to thank my mother, Joy Walker Stone, for showing me how to make art and for letting me look at the naked people in her art books.

Thomson Delmar Learning and the authors would also like to thank the following reviewers for their valuable suggestions and expertise:

Gil Rocha
Art Department
Richland Community College
Richland, IL

Alberto Meza
Fine Arts Department
Miami-Dade College
Miami, FL

JoAnna Almasude
Game Art & Design
The Art Institute of Pittsburgh Online
Pittsburgh, PA

Howard Katz
Arts & Humanities/Illustration
Art Institute of Fort Lauderdale
Fort Lauderdale, FL

Heidi Neilson
Visual Communications
Katherine Gibbs School
New York, NY

Robert Clements
Visual Communications
International Academy of Design & Technology Pittsburgh, PA

Rebecca Gallagher and Andrea Moore Paldy
2006

QUESTIONS AND FEEDBACK

Thomson Delmar Learning and the authors welcome your questions and feedback. If you have suggestions that you think others would benefit from, please let us know and we will try to include them in the next edition.

To send us your questions and/or feedback, you can contact the publisher at:

Thomson Delmar Learning
Executive Woods
5 Maxwell Drive
Clifton Park, NY 12065
Attn: Media Arts & Design Team
800-998-7498

Or the author at:

hstone@drawingworkshop.com

H. Stone, *Untitled*, compressed charcoal on
Rives BFK paper, 22" × 30", 2004.

CHAPTER 1

objectives

- Define life drawing and describe its two schools of thought.
- Create a baseline life drawing.
- Know the primary goal of any life drawing, as well as some other common quality standards.
- Know some practices that help life-drawing students learn better.
- Know the common materials used in life drawing.
- Know where to find people to draw and how to treat them.

introduction

Take a scorched twig, and use it to draw someone in their human uniform. What kind of art can you make with these limited means? This is a problem that cannot be outsmarted. Every artist starts with the same set of facts, and the life of each drawing is visible in the finished piece. Salesmanship will not make a drawing good, and ridicule will not make it bad. A life-drawing studio is a place set aside, where vanity and pretense have no portfolio.

If drawing another person is easy for you, you are not working hard enough. The human body is complex and subtle, and the more you look at it, the more structures, and their interrelationships, you see. With practice, you will see more than you do now. Knowing how to see wisely is more difficult. There is another person in your picture. What do you have in common with that person? How much of the drawing is that person, and how much is you? What is the interpersonal chemistry that gives you great drawings with one model and memorable learning experiences with another?

The drawings we make are a lens through which others see us more clearly than they see the model. Life drawing confounds us when it makes our vulnerabilities into art, but it can also place clarity and grace literally in our hand. The deeper subject of a life drawing is our shared humanity.

You have a blank piece of paper in front of you. Are you ready to start?

Exercise 1-1: Baseline Drawing

Before you learn any more, you will make this drawing as a record of your current skill level. You can compare it with drawings you make in the future to assess your progress.

Materials

- Vine charcoal or compressed charcoal.
- An eraser or two.
- A piece of paper, at least 18" × 24".

Procedures

1. Draw a live human for thirty minutes.
2. Use any techniques you want.
3. Put the date on the drawing.
4. Store it in a safe place.

WHAT IS LIFE DRAWING?

Life drawing, also called **figure drawing**, is monochromatically rendering another person from direct observation. Life drawing as we practice it started over 500 years ago, during the

visual | 1-1 |

Jean Henri Cless (fl. 1795–1811), *The Studio of Jacques Louis David (1748–1825),* pen and ink on paper (b/w photo), 18.2" × 23", circa nineteenth century. *Musee de la Ville de Paris, Musee Carnavalet, Paris, France / Lauros / Giraudon / The Bridgeman Art Library*

Italian Renaissance. By tradition, it takes place in a studio where artists focus their attention on an unclothed or classically draped model, as shown in Jean Henri Cless's picture of a life-drawing class 200 years ago (Visual 1–1). Modern students dress less formally and come from a variety of backgrounds, but in other respects it hasn't changed much. If any of us could step into that class, or one from a century or two earlier, we would know just what to do.

What is the enduring appeal of life drawing? The life-drawing studio is a place to inquire into questions fundamental to the humanities: Who am I? Who are you? How are we alike? How are we different? Art and culture change, technology advances, and visual art theories come and go, but these concerns remain constant. To explore them, life drawing starts with a premise we all hold in common—that we are physical beings, interested in one another.

Classicism, Portraiture, and Judgment Day

People who obsessively draw the figure tend to assemble themselves into two schools of thought about their work, which loosely correspond to the art historical traditions of Classicism and portraiture. Classicists look for the nobility and beauty in their subjects, and the people in their drawings are likely to be exemplary in their proportions and features. If a life drawing is ever described as "in good taste," it was probably made by a Classicist. Raphael Sanzio, one of the inventors of life drawing, demonstrates the style in Visual 1–2. Instead of showing us the model's human personality, Raphael has cast her as a goddess: Venus, the personification of beauty. She doesn't need clothes because she lives in a better place than we do, outside the reach of human vanity. The drawing is a parable of transcendent qualities possessed by the individual.

Artists who approach life drawing as portraiture are interested in the particular rather than the exemplary. Their mission is to show how someone is unique. Visual 1–3 is a portrait-based life drawing that I drew in 1995. The subject is a professional model whom I had been drawing for twelve years, and my intention was simply to draw her as she was on that day. She doesn't inhabit a heavenly plane; she was in a basement with several other artists and me, collaborating with us to make some drawings. I will let you construct your own

H. Stone,
Portrait, graphite
on paper,
30" × 22", 1995.

meaning for the portrait school of life drawing, given that you will practice it in some of the exercises in this book.

These two conceptions of the discipline of life drawing represent two different motivations for drawing the figure, and two ways of assessing the finished work. The two frames of reference can cause some misunderstandings on judgment day, when the group critique takes place. When one form of drawing is evaluated by the standards of the other, feedback can be unconstructive. Adding another potential source of conflict to this meeting, most artists do not work purely in a single mode, so figuring out the strengths and weakness of a particular drawing can call for some subtle thinking.

Why is it important for us to look critically at a drawing? Is it so that we can decide how faithful it is to its artistic lineage? No, neither of these drawing traditions needs our protection, and judging an artist worthy of it is not in anyone's job description. The only reason to evaluate a life drawing is to help us get better at drawing the figure. We cannot make a valid observation about drawing skill unless we know something about the artist's intentions. In other words, in order to assess how well we are doing and make improvements, we need to know what we are trying to accomplish.

What Are We Trying to Accomplish?

The most basic goal of any life drawing is to describe the three-dimensional forms of the human body on the two-dimensional surface of the paper. Nothing that happens by accident will make a drawing do this better. The traditional way to assess how well a drawing achieves this is to ask the question, "Could a sculptor use this drawing to make an accurate model of the figure?" If the answer is yes, then the drawing meets the minimum **formal** objective of life drawing.

Shared Quality Standards

Beyond how well a drawing defines the body's forms, life drawing's oral tradition has produced a few other generally accepted quality standards. Do not treat these as inflexible requirements for every drawing; think of them as things to notice and nurture in your own work as you learn to draw the figure:

- Are the proportions plausible? The industry standard here is a drawing without glaring errors in proportion. Nonstandard human proportions don't by themselves seriously compromise a drawing unless they stand out as inconsistent with the drawing's intentions.

- Could someone recognize the model from this drawing? If you are interested in the portrait element of life drawing, you may want to work particularly toward this goal.

- Does the drawing imply a definite point of view? In other words, does the drawing communicate the sense that we are in the same space as the model, at a given distance and eye level?

- How much structure does the drawing show? This refers to not only how much detail is visible in the drawing but also how well it shows the relationships between the body's parts. Does the figure have a convincing weight distribution? Does the pose seem logical and complete?

- Is there a figure–ground interaction? The figure–ground relationship describes the integration of the figure into the drawing's composition. For example, a small figure floating on a white sheet of paper has no figure–ground interaction.

- Does the drawing manifest a personal voice? This is a subjective judgment about the truthfulness, integrity, and conviction visible in the drawing. The drawing's voice is the artist's presence, visible in the drawing's technique and construction.

Let's test-drive these standards on a drawing by Augustus John, entitled *Lady Standing* (Visual 1–4). Are the body's forms well defined in this drawing? Yes, they are. Enough information is present that we could make a clay model of this woman, using the drawing as a reference. The arms and torso are particularly well defined. The drawing has met its most basic objective and is therefore successful.

There is one conspicuous error in the figure's proportions; the woman's head is too small. It looks like the artist may have drawn the body first and didn't have room to draw the head at the right size. It is usually considered preferable to let a properly scaled head run off the paper rather than downsize it to fit, but if the artist had done that, the drawing may not have been as successful as a portrait. The drawing communicates a likeness well enough that we can tentatively identify the model as Dorothy McNeill, a frequent subject for this artist. The small head also contributes to the sense that we are looking at her from a low vantage point.

visual | 1–4 |

Augustus E.
John, A.R.A.,
English,
1878–1961,
Lady Standing,
graphite on
paper, 19.875"
× 13.875".
*Minneapolis
Institute of Arts,
John DeLaittre
Memorial
Collection. Gift
of funds from
Mrs. Horace
Ropes*

John does a great job of describing the model's structure. Her right hip is higher than the left, so we know that leg is straight. The shoulders tilt the opposite way, to balance the torso, with the angle moderated by the leverage of the extended right arm. There is a subtle twist to the torso that holds the model's left shoulder a little farther back than the right, and the tilt of the head right and forward counterbalances it.

The figure–ground interaction consists of a soft edge along the bottom of the dress and background shapes formed by the positioning of the figure.

The lines are confident and articulate, with no evasions or simplifications of the forms. The execution is straightforward and matter-of-fact. Is there anything in the drawing extraneous to the task of describing the model? What do these things tell you about the artist?

These quality criteria can also be applied to less conventional life drawings, such as Ann Piper's self-portrait, *Fishbelly* (Visual 1–5). For example, we could make an interesting clay model of the

visual | 1–5 |

Ann Piper,
Fishbelly,
charcoal,
30" × 22", 2003.
*Courtesy of Ann
Piper*

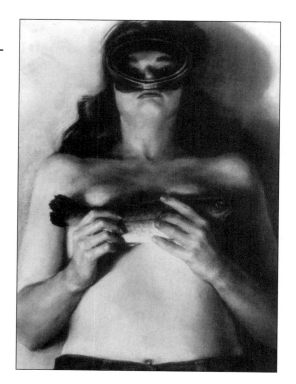

woman, her mask, and the fish in this drawing from the information it gives us. Because the forms in this piece are defined without any major areas of ambiguity, we can declare it successful as a life drawing. This is a value drawing, which consists entirely of masses of gray, with no use of **contour lines**. You have an opportunity to practice value drawing in Chapter 3.

LEARNING TO DRAW THE FIGURE

I remember the first time I knew I could do this. I was in a life-drawing class, and I had spent the morning doing standard exercises, generating one murky drawing after another. I wasn't the only student operating in conditions of poor visibility that day, but there were a couple of people who could draw with such lucidity that they might as well have been magicians. After the break, we began again with short poses. We were doing the quick-contour exercise, which is a line drawing executed at high speed (see Chapter 5), in poses lasting between two and five minutes. I don't remember the first drawing that had a spark, but I can recall what it felt like when, in a process as inevitable as a new tooth coming in, the line began to obey. In one drawing and then another, the line woke up, until, in one very short pose, I found a still place where I could draw a line with deliberate care. When that quick drawing was done, I looked at it and thought, well, that isn't too bad. I learned something important that day. Magic is just something you don't know how to do yet.

Building Skills

Life drawing is a continuing process of building skills. First, you learn how to draw a person, and then you learn how to draw a particular person; finally, you seek the best way to draw a particular person. Every person you draw is a new subject, unlike any other, and each successful life drawing you create is good in its own way. Life drawing is a form of inquiry: a method of discovering and evaluating facts, and assigning them meaning. It cannot be done well in a complacent state of mind.

Think and Learn to Draw

Life drawing is more a cognitive skill than a physical one. Learning how to do it is learning new ways of seeing and thinking. It is developing new software for your brain.

- The ability to draw the human figure is not a gift, it is a skill acquired through practice.
- Drawing is learned more quickly in structured exercises.
- A life drawing can be evaluated objectively according to agreed-upon standards.
- Skill in life drawing does not depend on good vision or coordination.
- In life drawing, everything good comes from practice. The main reason people are not as good at life drawing as they want to be is a lack of quality practice.

Practice Smart

Unlike other forms of studio art, life drawing has built-in time limits. Unless you have an unusually accommodating life partner, your time drawing the model will be confined to group drawing sessions. You can take steps to make sure that time is productive:

- Look at every drawing you can. This includes the work of the people you draw with and drawings by famous artists. Check out a couple of books of drawings from the library and look at them a little every day. You don't need to analyze these drawings, just relax and soak them in.

- Each exercise is a practice rather than a performance test. The only important thing about an exercise drawing is the skills you develop in doing that drawing.

- Most of the exercises are means to an end, so don't judge them by the standards of balanced, complete figure drawing. Work through them, and look for improvements in your drawing on the other side.

- Keep every drawing you do. This will help you accept what you do, suspend judgment about your work, and concentrate on learning. If you put a date on each drawing, you can review them (Exercise 1-1) and assess your progress.

- Always briefly look at your drawings soon after you do them. Note where the drawing is unsuccessful, and work on those issues in the next piece.

- Go into each drawing session with a specific point of technique to work on. This may come from the exercise or from the previous session.

- If you are physically able to, draw standing up to better calibrate your proprioceptive sense. This trains your innate sense of proportion.

- If you see the need for a correction, go ahead and make it, without worrying about its effect on the drawing.

- Don't get discouraged when things don't seem to be going well. Your feelings about how well you are doing are not always a reliable indicator of your progress. Trust the exercises.

Impasses

Over the course of learning how to draw the figure, it is typical to see gradual improvement over time, with the occasional thrilling breakthrough. Sometimes, though, it will seem that your drawing ability is getting worse, rather than better. You will handle your media ineptly, and doing your best won't help. You may develop the conviction that it isn't your day. When this happens, be encouraged. This is an impasse that most people who do life drawings experience from time to time. It means that you are about to experience a breakthrough.

It is always frustrating when you feel your skills have deteriorated, but don't give in to the temptation to call it a day. When you are at an impasse, when will power won't make your drawing improve, keep working until your breakthrough happens. It won't take long. If you walk away, you will never learn how to do the next thing.

MATERIALS AND SUPPLIES

To draw the human figure, you need something to draw with, usually some allotrope of carbon, and something flat to draw on. Life drawing uses a more limited range of materials than most visual art forms, but they aren't interchangeable. You probably will find that you do better work with some materials than with others. For best results, get an assortment, and experiment with them in different combinations until you find the one you are most articulate in.

Drawing Media

When you are learning to draw, don't get fancy with colored media. A drawing made from old-master style red chalk can look great, but its range of light to dark will be limited. Drawing with anything but black media is like playing piano with only half the keyboard. You will develop a more sensitive touch and learn how to balance values better if you stay with carbon.

Charcoal

Charcoal is the traditional material for life drawing, and there is much to recommend it. It can be applied throughout a range of grays to black. It is suitable for drawing fine, careful lines, or quickly covering large areas in a mass of black. It comes in different sizes and grades of hardness, and it isn't toxic. There are three kinds of drawing charcoal (Visual 1–6): vine, compressed, and powdered. Vine charcoal does not apply as freely as compressed charcoal, but it is easier to blend and remove. It excels in detail work. Compressed charcoal works well for large areas and deep, velvety blacks. Charcoal powder is not strictly necessary if you have the other two, but it can be useful for quickly applying large, flat areas of gray.

Vine charcoal (Visual 1–7) is made by heating sticks in an absence of air until all of its volatile components boil away. It preserves the grain of the wood it was made from, which helps it resist crumbling and allows it to ring when it is dropped. Willow charcoal has the finest grain and is considered to be the best variety. Vine charcoal is graded by hardness, but the grade may or may not correspond to how hard the stick actually is; run your thumb across it before you buy to make sure it is not too hard for you.

Compressed charcoal (Visual 1–8) is vine charcoal that has been crushed into a fine, dark powder, refined, and pressed into sticks. Compressed charcoal is more reliably graded than vine charcoal, its texture is more uniform, and it can be considerably softer. You can draw faster with compressed charcoal than vine charcoal, but it is a more sensitive medium that can require some time to learn to handle felicitously.

A charcoal pencil is a stick of compressed charcoal encased in wood or wrapped in paper. It requires sharpening, which can interfere with the pace of the drawing, but it can be useful in areas of detail such as eyes, ears, and mouths. Some artists use charcoal pencils to help keep their hands clean, but if this is important to you, disposable plastic gloves or **barrier cream** are better solutions.

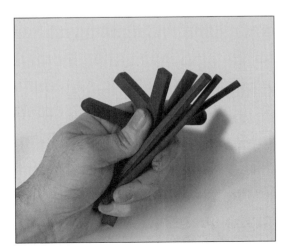

visual | 1–6 |

A fistful of charcoal. The three sticks on the left are compressed charcoal, and the rest are vine charcoal.

Artist charcoal varies a great deal in price and quality, and the most expensive medium is not necessarily the best. The first time you go shopping, buy a little of each of the cheaper grades. While you are drawing, keep track of what you are using, share information with your fellow artists, and stock up later on the products you like best.

Crayons

A crayon is a drawing stick composed of pigment, a binder, and sometimes chalk. Pastels, Conté crayons, oil pastels, oil sticks, grease pencils, and Nupastel® are types of crayons. A pastel is a crayon with a dry binder; other crayons have a varying amount of oil or wax. Most crayons are less messy than charcoal, but also less sensitive, and they are usually harder to make corrections to. For these reasons, crayons aren't as useful as charcoal for learning life drawing.

visual | 1–7 |

visual | 1–8 |

A portrait in vine charcoal. Vine charcoal is usually harder than compressed charcoal, which allows it to be sharpened enough to draw fine lines, such as the one that defines the model's chin. It also contains impurities that can impart a warm or cool tone, or make it flaky or slightly shiny. H. Stone, *Portrait*, vine charcoal, 14" × 17", 2001.

A portrait in compressed charcoal. Compressed charcoal is darker than vine charcoal, and its color is a neutral black. Contour lines drawn in compressed charcoal seldom have the crispness of lines in vine charcoal, but they are darker and more sensitive to hand movements. The loose strand of hair near the model's forehead is an example. H. Stone, *Portrait*, compressed charcoal, 14" × 17", 2001.

Graphite

Graphite is crystalline carbon, more closely related to diamond than it is to charcoal. It is a versatile drawing medium, neat, forgiving, and easy to use. It is shiny and slippery rather than crumbly, and more brittle than charcoal. It is not as black as charcoal, and it develops a slight metallic sheen when it is applied heavily, which can prevent it from being photographed as accurately as charcoal. It is commonly available in thirteen grades of hardness, with 6H the hardest, HB in the middle, and 6B the softest. Graphite for drawing is sold either encased in a pencil or as a solid stick (Visual 1–9).

visual | 1–9 |

A dream come true: pencils, a graphite holder, and graphite sticks.

The pencil (Visual 1–10) is the duct tape of life-drawing materials. It has a thousand uses, and it is always there for you when you run out of ideas. Soft pencils are good for general use, you can make crisp lines with harder ones, and the very hardest ones are good for people who collect pencils. 4B, 5B, and 6B are the soft grades, and there is little difference between them. Shop around and buy a dozen 6Bs, and go into your drawing session with all of them sharp, so you can draw without interruption. A B pencil is hard enough to hold a sharp point and draw a dark line without breaking, so get a couple of these, and they will probably outlast your set of 6Bs. The very soft pencils are not the best choice for sketchbook drawing because their graphite rubs off easily. For working on visual journals, the HB, otherwise known as the number two pencil, is made to order. If you aren't sentimental, mechanical pencils and lead holders are great for life drawing because, unlike a wood pencil, the instrument is always the same length. The refills also cost less than pencils. Be sure to get a system that accommodates 6B graphite because the soft grades are larger in diameter than the hard ones.

visual | 1–10 |

A portrait in pencil. H. Stone, *Untitled*, pencil on Rives BFK paper, 30" × 22", 1995.

A stick of graphite looks either like a small plank, with a square or rectangular cross section, or a cylinder the size of a regular pencil. It is more durable than a pencil and much cheaper for the amount of drawing you can do with it (Visual 1–11). I like the stick with the rectangular cross section best because it has enough mass that a 6B grade is strong enough to draw dark lines without breaking, and you can use its side to cover larger areas. To prepare a graphite stick to make fine lines, use a knife, a razor, or a small saw to cut it on the bias (Visual 1–12). If you choose to do this operation, do it safely: use a small vise to hold the stick while you are working on it, and wear eye protection.

Erasers, Blenders, and Smudgers

Before erasers, the correction device was a loaf of bread. The artist would break it open, pull some out, roll it into a ball, and use it to rub out mistakes. Nowadays we can correct our drawings without wasting food.

- A white polymer eraser, sometimes called a white plastic eraser, is the best one for completely removing charcoal or graphite. There are several kinds, but I like the dense, shiny ones used for drafting (Visual 1–13). Softer ones are available for fine art drawing, and they

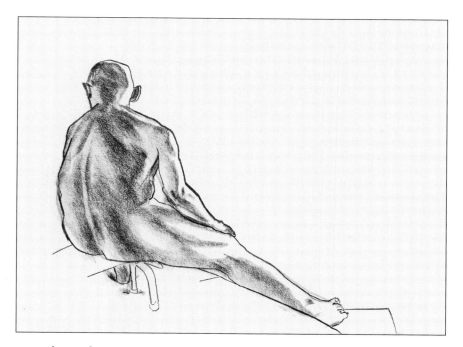

visual | 1–11 |

A portrait in graphite stick. An advantage of graphite stick is that you can immediately switch from drawing lines to drawing grays. It will generate the same variable line that you get from a stick of charcoal, but it is more durable. H. Stone, *Untitled*, 6B graphite stick, 22" × 30", 2002.

visual | 1–12 |

A graphite stick cut on the bias.

visual | 1–13 |

Five clean, new erasers. From left to right: a very soft gum eraser, a soft white eraser, a harder drafting eraser, a kneaded eraser, and a cheap pink eraser.

are good general-purpose erasers. Rubber erasers are good for lightening an area, although they do not always remove marks completely.

- The pink eraser is a good all-around tool for erasing, blending, and generating a **painterly** surface, and it is cheap enough that you can afford to buy as many as you want. It abrades the paper's surface and leaves a residue when used to erase very dark media, but sometimes that will be exactly what you are looking for.

- A kneaded eraser can be squeezed, flattened, and pulled into a point to use in small areas. Because it works by sticking to the medium and lifting it off the paper, you can use it like a rubber stamp to lighten an area without rubbing it. Its disadvantage is that it does not work when it is saturated with grime, and it gets saturated quickly in life drawing. If you rely on kneaded erasers, always keep a new one on hand.

- A gum eraser is a very soft, slightly sticky eraser most useful on finished pencil drawings. This kind of eraser can remove pencil cleanly, without abrading the paper's surface, but it crumbles and leaves plenty of residue. It is too soft for day-to-day life-drawing exercises.

In addition to using kneaded erasers for detail work, you can use solid erasers sharpened into a blade (Visual 1–14). When I am drawing, I keep a pocketknife on hand to make emergency eraser modifications.

Erasers can be used for blending, but a small cotton rag can be used to blend charcoal without lightening it very much. For fine blending, the traditional tool is the blending-stump (Visual 1–15), which is a small, tightly rolled paper cylinder sharpened on both ends. Stumps and similar instruments called *tortillons* are used to create very smooth surface blends in tiny

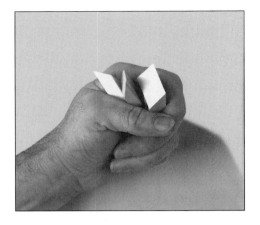

Erasers sharpened for detail work. The shiny drafting eraser is on the left, the cheap ink eraser is in the middle, and the soft white one is on the right.

Stumps and *tortillons*. Stumps are larger, denser, and pointed at both ends.

areas. They are of limited usefulness in day-to-day life-drawing exercises, but helpful in making very refined finished drawings.

To keep erasers and stumps clean, rub them on an abrasive surface such as sandpaper or the back of a drawing board.

Ink

There are two types of ink used for life drawing: dye-based and pigment-based. Dye-based inks are used in fountain pens, technical pens, and felt-tip pens. Because dye-based ink dries quickly, these instruments are ideal for drawing in journals or sketchbooks. Pigment-based inks are composed mostly of soot suspended in water and are applied with steel nibs, bamboo pens, reed pens, and brushes. Pigment-based inks are very dense, black, and permanent, and are used to make art to exhibit or reproduce (Visual 1-17). India ink and sumi ink are both pigment-based inks.

A steel nib, sometimes called a lettering or calligraphy nib, is a stainless-steel pen point that is loaded by dipping it into India ink. Steel nibs come in an assortment of sizes and shapes (Visual 1–16), to make lines of different thicknesses and variability. A crow quill is a small, very fine steel nib. You will need a pen holder for each nib you are using.

From left to right: Two new steel nibs in pen holders, a nib in use, a new crow quill, a #10 watercolor brush with synthetic fibers, a rigger with synthetic fibers, and a sable rigger.

If you are interested in drawing cartoons or comic books, you may want to try some of the exercises in this book using watercolor brushes and India ink. I recommend a #10 round and a #4 rigger, which can make a long, uninterrupted line (Visual 1–18). Get the cheaper brushes with synthetic bristles, and don't ever use them for watercolor after you have used them to apply India ink.

In Chapter 4, we work some with sumi ink, a very black ink used in Asian calligraphy. The process of using a calligraphy brush and bamboo pen (Visual 4–5) to apply the ink is called *sumi-e*. The exercise in Chapter 4 is specialized, but *sumi-e* is also a good medium for learning life drawing because the brush bristles lack the resilience of a Western watercolor brush. This characteristic makes the *sumi-e* brush less responsive to fine movements of the hand and encourages the artist to use the entire arm to draw. *Sumi* ink is used in washes (Visual 1–19) as well as full strength. If you use *sumi* ink, get the liquid version instead of the ink sticks.

Fixatives

A fixative is a type of varnish used to keep drawings from smudging. It is applied as an aerosol spray, traditionally out in the hall, where it annoys the whole building with its ill-smelling and often toxic vapors. A fixative affects the tonal balance of the drawing, and many varieties will,

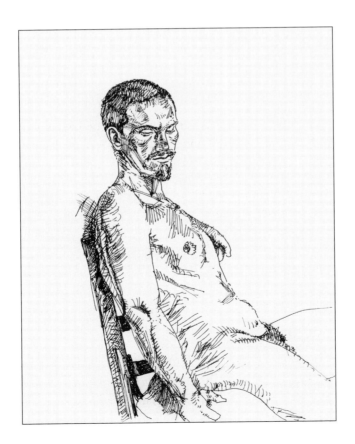

visual | 1–17 |

A life drawing made with a steel nib and India ink. H. Stone, *Untitled*, India ink, 17" × 14", 1997.

Two models
drawn with a
rigger and India
ink. H. Stone,
Untitled, India
ink, 14" × 17",
1998.

after only a few years, impart a yellow tint to the areas in which they have been applied. They are no more than marginally effective for their intended purpose, unless sprayed on very heavily. Some artists use the cheapest hairspray available to fix their drawings, and this is a very bad idea.

Save money, stay safe, keep your drawings pure, and do not use fixatives.

Drawing Board

Life drawing sometimes demands physical engagement: digging in, pushing hard, rubbing, and scraping. Always use a drawing board and clips to support your paper through this passion and turmoil. You can buy ⅛" hardboard drawing boards in art supply stores, but you can get a sturdier board and save a little money by purchasing a 24" × 48", ¼" hardboard from the home improvement store, and have it cut to 24"× 30". This will give you an 18" × 24" board for your pads and a larger one for sheets of premium rag paper. Get a few binder clips from the office supply store and you are in business.

Papers

For learning to draw the figure, a white or very pale paper is best. You will need a daily grade paper for exercises, and a good grade paper for finished drawings. Both grades need to be permanent. The factor most affecting the permanence of paper is its acid content. The cheapest paper is made from wood pulp, is very acidic, and will yellow and disintegrate relatively quickly. The very best paper is made from cotton rag, is acid-neutral, and will keep indefinitely if properly stored.

A life drawing made with a *sumi-e* brush and ink. H. Stone, *Untitled, sumi* ink, 24" × 18", 2000.

The Daily Paper

Newsprint is the traditional material for life drawing, but I think it is time for all of us to upgrade. Newsprint is a very acidic wood-pulp paper, and it is so flimsy that an eraser quickly wears a hole in it. It damages better papers it is stored with, and ink bleeds through it. It costs half as much as a minimally acceptable drawing paper, but it is not a bargain because using it ensures a short life for any drawing made on it. Newsprint is the only art material we buy with the understanding that it will be substandard.

For your daily work, get an 18"× 24" pad of general-purpose, acid-neutral drawing paper, and replace it as necessary.

Fine Paper

It is a pleasure to work on 100% rag, handmade paper. The sheet is sturdy and looks handsome before you even start drawing on it. Your blacks will be very black, and they will erase easily if necessary. It loves drawing media, and it is very, very permanent. The Arches paper mill was founded in 1492, and I would not be surprised if there were some drawings still around from that year. Unfortunately, premium paper is also expensive. Use it for drawings you would exhibit or that you plan to spend several hours on.

This kind of paper is sold by the sheet. A usual size is 22" × 30", and it is a good size for an ambitious life drawing. You can save money if you shop around and order with other artists, buying cartons of 25 or 100 sheets.

Storing Drawings

If we don't use fixative, how can we keep a charcoal drawing from deteriorating? The best way is to keep it in the pad. All charcoal drawings shed some loose particles, but they are not in danger unless the surface is smeared. They will remain stable if they are carefully stacked front to back and the sheets are not allowed to slide across each other. Leaving them in the pad, and leaving the pad flat, meets these conditions.

Loose sheets can receive the same treatment, except they will be safer if they are secured between two sheets of acid-free foam core. They will be protected even better if you place archival interleaving paper between the sheets. This is either glassine, a very thin, slippery translucent paper

visual | 1–20 |

Archival storage of 22" × 30" drawings. From the top down is the lid of the archival storage box, a sheet of buffered archival interleaving, a drawing, and the bottom of the box.

that does not attract charcoal particles, or a thin white rag paper. Interleaving can be found at a well-stocked art supply store or a library supply store.

If you produce more than a few drawings on premium paper, you may want to invest in an archival storage box (Visual 1–20). This box is made of acid-free materials, so using it with archival interleaving will keep your drawings safe indefinitely, in an acid-free environment.

THE PEOPLE YOU DRAW

The speed at which your drawing improves depends on how many hours per week you can spend practicing. The core of your practice, with the highest demands, the most structure, and the most support, is your weekly drawing group. Peer drawing is a very helpful supplement to the weekly studio. If you also draw in a sketchbook, you will make new friends, get ideas for art, and produce drawings that will make you happy.

Finding Someone to Draw

Where can you find people to draw? A structured learning program, such as the one in this book, requires a drawing session once or twice a week. A life-drawing class will provide this, but if one isn't available, find a drawing group, also called a drawing cooperative. Most towns of any size have at least one group of people who get together, hire a model, and draw. A large city will have several. To find one, ask other artists, check the Internet, or look at bulletin boards at art schools and art supply stores. Drawing co-ops vary quite a bit in the length of the poses and general environment. For example, some groups allow talking, and others prefer silence. Some play music; others do not. If you are not comfortable with the first one you try, shop around.

Peer Drawing

One of the best general drawing workouts I have done is to draw another artist while that artist is drawing me. We set up easels facing each other, and draw portraits (Visual 1–21). This is also a good activity if the model calls in sick.

A similar drawing structure is to take turns being drawn. This works well in a small group as well as with one other artist. It is good experience for several reasons but particularly because it will help you to understand the model's side of the life-drawing partnership. If you do this in your class, be patient with one another, take frequent breaks, and do not plan on being able to sit as still as a pro.

In peer-drawing activities, it is acceptable for everyone to keep their clothes on.

Sketchbook Drawing

A sketchbook is any drawing pad that is small enough to carry around. Sketchbook drawing is informal in that the subjects are not intentionally posing for you. Although this develops a different set of skills than drawing in the studio, if you can draw this way for a couple of hours a week while you are learning, your studio drawing will improve faster and be more consistent. For sketchbook drawing:

- Draw the people and animals you live with.
- Draw in public places, such as coffee shops or the airport.
- Draw yourself, either your hands and feet through direct observation, or a self-portrait using a mirror.
- Draw your friends when you are socializing. In my experience, this almost never works out.

visual | 1–21 |

H. Stone, *Partner Drawing*, graphite stick on Rives BFK, 22" × 30", 1996.

Working with Models

Drawing a living model is not a neutral act. The model is a partner in the studio environment, the learning process, and the art. The presence of another person places responsibilities on the artist that would not apply if the subject were a bowl of fruit or the interior of a soul. A set of standards have evolved to keep the models' workplace pleasant and to keep the session running smoothly:

1. Do not ever touch a model.

2. This is a collaboration. You are working together to create art. Instructions to the model should be in the context of that understanding.

3. Do not presume that you may take photos. A drawing group isn't a photography group, and in any case you would need written permission from the model before using a camera.

4. Do not assume that the model is not modest. Many models are comfortable being naked in a drawing class, but not when the door is left open, or strangers are allowed to come in.

5. Be conscious of the model's safety, and do not ask them to do anything that might injure them. No lights or other assemblies should loom over them, no unsecured power cords should be on the stage, and the floor should be freshly swept for splinters, shards of glass, tacks and staples. Halogen lamps should be kept at a distance, with their safety shields in place. The model stand should be padded, and padding should be available to make adjustments to the pose.

6. The model gets a veto power over the poses. Of course, if too many standard poses get vetoed, you might want to find another model.

7. The models need a secure place to change and store their clothes while they are working.

8. This is a workplace, and harassment laws apply. If you tend to make comments that others find offensive, err on the side of caution, and let someone else talk to the model.

Fortunately, there is one policy that will reliably guide you through most situations: respect the model.

Drawing from Photographs

Edgar Degas used photographs as sources for some of his drawings, and in some art forms, such as self-portraiture, it can be a necessity. It is a standard and accepted way of doing figurative art, and if you become an artist, there is a good chance you will use it. When you are learning life drawing, though, studio time in front of a model is irreplaceable and cannot be exchanged for drawing from photographs.

A photograph has a different meaning than a drawing. A camera makes an image by sampling reality; life drawing makes one by transcribing experience. A drawing communicates meaning through the way the image is made. When an artist transcribes a photograph of a person into a drawing, the static point of view of the photograph replaces the complex experience of the model. Drawing from photographs is a valid form of practice, and doing it will help you grow as an artist, but it develops different skills than drawing from a live model. When you are learning to draw the figure, it is best to draw from another person, rather than from a photograph.

THIS BOOK

This book is intended to help you build skills and to learn how to make figurative art you are happy with. Some of the exercises are traditional, and others are original exercises that students have found helpful. The goal is to present you with various ways of drawing the figure, so you can find your own way of making art that is meaningful to you.

This book is based on observational drawing, not anatomical drawing or drawing systems using primitive forms such as spheres, cones, and squares. If you are interested in human anatomy, an anatomical reference manual would be a good complement to this book, but you do not need to have a technical knowledge of anatomy to draw the figure well.

Finally, life drawing is a form of art, and as such it is not always compatible with rules and policies. When I make a sweeping statement, it is intended to help you better understand life drawing; it is not to be taken as absolute truth. There will probably be many exceptions to it. Think for yourself, and let your drawing guide you.

Thanks for reading this book!

H. Stone

CHAPTER SUMMARY

Life drawing is the art of drawing the human figure. The practice of life drawing originated approximately 500 years ago, during the Italian Renaissance. Artists who specialize in life drawing tend to be either Classicists, interested in drawing perfect-looking humans, or portraitists, who like to draw the individual features of particular people.

The most basic goal of a life drawing is to describe the three-dimensional forms of the human body on the two-dimensional surface of the paper. In addition, there are other common standards for figure drawings, such as correct proportions, the figure–ground interaction, and the presence of the artist's voice. The ability to draw the figure is not a gift; it is a cognitive skill that improves with practice, and there is a direct relationship between the amount of practice and the rate of improvement.

The materials used to draw the figure have not changed much since the discipline got started. All that is required is charcoal or graphite, paper, and an eraser. There are many places to find people to draw; all drawing subjects have in common a need for respect.

▶ *chapter questions*

Multiple Choice

1. Life drawing:
    a. Is difficult when done properly.
    b. Is best when done from photographs.
    c. Will be better if accompanied by the right explanations.
    d. Is an art form and therefore has no use for logic.

2. Life drawing:
    a. Cannot be judged by objective standards.
    b. Is different from portraiture.
    c. Has a set of common quality standards that apply to every drawing.
    d. Inquires into questions fundamental to the humanities.

3. Why is it important for us to look critically at a drawing?
    a. To place it in a historical context.
    b. To help us get better at drawing the figure.
    c. To protect a cultural idea of beauty.
    d. To expose impostors.

4. The common standard for proportion is:
    a. Every human figure should be 8 heads tall.
    b. Nonstandard proportions are always a serious flaw in a drawing.
    c. They are no longer important.
    d. A drawing should have no glaring errors in proportion.

5. When you are learning to draw:
    a. You should keep every drawing you do.
    b. If you are having a bad drawing day, you should quit early and come back when you can draw better.
    c. Correct an error only when doing so will make the drawing better.
    d. All of the above.

6. Vine charcoal:

   a. Is toxic and must be handled with care.

   b. Is made from vines.

   c. Rings when it is dropped.

   d. Is good for quickly covering large areas.

7. Graphite:

   a. Is made from the same chemical element as charcoal.

   b. Photographs more accurately than charcoal.

   c. Was originally used to draw graphs.

   d. Is harder and more brittle than pencil lead.

8. Charcoal drawings:

   a. Require the use of fixative to be stable.

   b. Are best protected if they are stacked with archival interleaving between the sheets.

   c. Should be drawn on newsprint.

   d. Will fade if not stored properly.

9. Two figurative artists are maligning each other's work. One of them says, "The face on that drawing looks pretty watered-down." The speaker is a:

   a. Classicist.

   b. Portraitist.

10. The artists' unkind remarks start a chain reaction in the studio, and soon another artist is heard saying about a different drawing, "Why would anyone want to draw a figure as ugly as that?" The speaker is a:

   a. Classicist.

   b. Portraitist.

Michelangelo Buonarroti, *Figure of a Woman Seated*, pen and brown ink over black and red chalk, 13" × 10.14", 1525. *© The Trustees of the British Museum. All rights reserved.*

CHAPTER 2

objectives

- Define a contour line, and describe how it differs from a contour.
- Understand how contour lines are used to define the three-dimensional forms of the human body.
- Study examples of how contour lines communicate subjectively apart from their descriptive function.
- Practice the blind contour exercise.
- Practice the semiblind contour exercise.
- Apply criteria for evaluating the quality of a contour line.

introduction

Ask someone without training in art to draw a person, and you will almost always get a **contour line** drawing. Your drawing volunteer will probably start by making a line around the outside of the figure and then add details such as eyes and a nose. The head or hands may get their own outlines. By demonstrating where the edges of the forms are, the lines are able to suggest, to one degree or another, what the subject looks like. Another term for the edge of a form is **contour**, so a drawing that uses a line to describe an edge is called a contour line drawing, or **contour drawing** (Visual 2–1). Contour drawing is an art form common to many cultures, and line drawings, created over a span of millennia, can be seen all over the world as petroglyphs (Visual 2–2). You find contour drawings wherever people draw unselfconsciously. In this chapter, you will learn how to use contour lines to draw the human figure.

visual | 2–1 |

Wayne Thiebaud, *Woman reading, page 14 in the book The Physiology of Taste*, drawings printed with photopolymer plates, 13¾" × 10¼", 1994. *Fine Arts Museums of San Francisco, Gift of George Hellyer in honor of Ira Yeager, 1999.137.42.1. © Wayne Thiebaud / Licensed by VAGA, New York, NY.*

visual | 2–2 |

Unknown artist, Ancient Pueblo people, *Kokopelli figure*, petroglyph, 24" × 24", circa 1000–1300.

THE ATTENTIVE LINE

It is interesting that people produce contour lines so naturally, without prompting, because a contour line does not exist in nature as we see it. We are able to see a form not because it has a line going around its edge but because it is lighter or darker than its background. A life drawing that closely reproduces exactly what our eyes see consists of light and dark shapes, rather than a set of contour lines. A contour line is a fiction.

visual | 2–3 |

Thomas Eakins, *Study of a Seated Nude Woman Wearing a Mask*, charcoal and crayon with stumping on paper, 24¼" × 18⅜", 1863–1866. The model's face was covered because of the shame associated with being unclothed.

Visual 2–3, by Thomas Eakins, is a charcoal drawing constructed the way that we see, with lights and darks. The artist created the image by reproducing as closely as possible the shapes of gray, black, and white, and the softness or hardness of their edges, as he saw them. No contour lines are present. The level of light and dark in a region of a drawing is called its **value**, or **tone**, and a drawing such as Eakins', which defines its forms with light and darks as they appear to the artist, is called a **value drawing**.

A value drawing addresses the basic formal objective of life drawing, giving a sense of the three-dimensional form of the model, by drawing as closely as possible what the eye sees. If the shapes of the forms and their relative levels of gray are correct, the figure will be clearly and articulately described, and this objective will have been accomplished.

I drew Visual 2–4 using a contour line instead of values to describe the figure. Relationships of light and dark, which

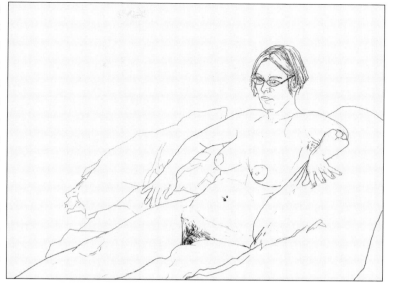

visual | 2–4 |

H. Stone, *Contour Drawing*, pencil on paper, 18" × 24", 2001.

our eyes see with great nuance, I ignored, concentrating instead on making lines the same shape as the forms I could see. Because the lines are the right shape, the subject is recognizable.

Which drawing method is more accurate? In life drawing, the basic standard of accuracy is how precisely the drawing defines the three-dimensional shapes of its subject. By that standard, both of these drawings are accurate because a sculptor could produce a clay model using either drawing as a guide. Both types of drawing can be highly descriptive; an experienced artist could be expected to create a specific and recognizable likeness using either method.

A value drawing isn't necessarily an objective description of what the artist sees, but the technique is compatible with a journalistic, emotionally neutral stance. This may be because most of the images we see are mass-produced value studies made by cameras, rendered by printing presses and video monitors, and exhibited to us as representing, on some level, objective truth. Because a camera and a human eye work pretty much the same way, an artist's judgments of light and dark can be corroborated, at least to a degree, by photographic processes. If we believe that a photograph is truthful, we may also be predisposed to see visual truthfulness in a value drawing.

An artist drawing with line may be committed to creating as neutrally descriptive an image as possible, but a contour line is an analogy, rather than a literal representation of visual reality. Subjectivity intrudes into the drawing as soon as the artist starts drawing. As the line spools out onto the paper, it leaves a distinctive trace of its maker's state of mind. The line is a graph of the artist's attentive process. The speed at which the line is produced, the confidence behind the strokes, and the consistency of the artist's focus are visible in the completed drawing.

A capable artist is able to draw a contour line with characteristics that add meaning to a drawing. The line may establish an emotional tone in the drawing, express a particular attitude

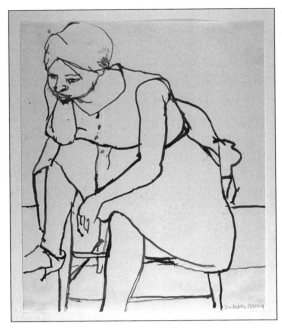

toward the subject, or be interesting for its own sake. An effective contour line is persuasive as well as descriptive; it suggests, provokes, and humors the viewer into agreeing with the artist that the form is present.

Visual 2–5 is a drawing of a woman sitting on a chair. She is drawn with a solid, black contour line that gets thin and breaks in some places, starts and stops, and is supplemented with spots, blotches, and smears. The artist obviously feels that a lack of refinement is acceptable in this drawing. What is he telling us by making the drawing this way?

Diebenkorn's drawing makes visible the process that created it. The solidity of the line shows that it was applied quickly, with a confident hand. The line communicates the momentum with which it was made. The spots and other artifacts of speedy pen work confirm that a direct, unaffected line was more important to the artist than a polished finished product. What can we learn from contemplating a drawing that challenges us to accept it the way it is?

A contour line is a device whose authority, like that of music, is perceived through both the feelings and the intellect. An honest line manifests the same sense of possibility as all successful art: it will speak truthfully to different people in different ways.

Exercise 2-1: The Blind Contour Drawing

Basic life-drawing skill is largely an ability to see another person without preconceptions. Without training, people usually attempt to draw what they think their subject looks like rather than what their eye specifically tells them. In other words, the idea of how the model looks interferes with objectively seeing the forms. Because blind contour drawing bypasses thoughts about the model in favor of developing the connection between the hand and the eye, it is the most useful drawing exercise. Some kinds of drawing practice will yield little or no visible progress until a breakthrough occurs, but this exercise will pay off in improved drawing skills every time you do it correctly.

Blind contour drawing is a cognitive exercise. In doing it, you are developing new software for your brain; the procedures are simple, but the exercise requires active, constructive thinking for its entire duration. Disregard how the drawing is developing as you work. We all want our drawings to turn out well, but during this activity, concern with how the drawing will look can interfere with the quality of your attention. During blind contour sessions, you are banking drawing skills that you will learn to apply later, so don't worry about the product.

Materials

- One fine-point fiber-tip permanent marker.
- A supply of your daily grade of paper, 18" × 24".

Procedures

1. Place the tip of your pen on the paper.

2. Study the model for a few seconds in order to locate a starting point on the outer edge of the figure.

3. Imagine that the tip of your pen is resting on the starting point you have selected, rather than on your paper. Take as much time as you need to visualize this.

4. When you are able to feel that the pen is touching the model, rather than the paper, start drawing, as slowly as you can.

5. Move your eye along the figure's edge, and move your hand with it, in perfect synchronization, for the duration of the exercise.

6. Do not lift the pen from the paper.

7. Do not look at the drawing until the time is up.

This exercise is most productive when undertaken in a relaxed, contemplative mood. If you find yourself starting to speed through it, slow down, and be scrupulous in drawing every form you are able to see. If you start clenching the pen in your hand, relax. In this exercise, it is always acceptable to slow down.

Welcome the opportunity to draw difficult areas. The human body is very complex, and it is easy to be intimidated by detailed structures such as the face, the hands, or the feet. When you get to complex areas, trust the exercise, let your hand and eye move in harmony, and the structures that you see will tell you what you need to know. If you want to move to a different place on the figure while you are drawing, get there by drawing a line across the figure. Just continue to visualize that your pen is on the model's skin, drawing across the surface of the form. The line that you will get from doing this is called a cross-contour line, sometimes called an **ant trail**.

You may draw any form as often as you want to.

Exercise Schedule

1. For the next four weeks, do this exercise once every time you draw from the figure.

2. Do a fifteen-minute version of the exercise the first few times you try it.

3. When your endurance and ability to see the details of the forms start to improve, increase the time span to twenty minutes.

4. Increase the time to thirty minutes when you feel that you are ready. Doing a blind contour drawing at the beginning of a drawing session is a great way to warm up, and it will sensitize you so that you will do better drawings all day.

5. You never will reach a level of drawing skill at which the blind contour exercise will no longer help you. If your drawing abilities ever get rusty, this is the fastest way to get them back up to speed; if you are having an off day, do this exercise to get back on track.

Demonstration 2–1: The Blind Contour Exercise

I like to use a fiber-tip permanent marker for this exercise for a couple of reasons. First, it will prevent the drawing I produce from ever being exhibited, so it forces me to think of it solely as an exercise. Second, this kind of marker bleeds into the paper, so I can see where I stopped to think. Knowing this will not make me draw better, but it is interesting. Whatever mood I am in, I take the first part of this exercise seriously. I relax, slow my thinking down, and look at the model. I visualize the point of my pen being somewhere on an edge of the model's form. This minute or so is the most important part of the drawing session because it affects the quality of everything I draw afterward. When this relationship feels real to me, I start moving my hand slowly, keeping my hand and eye moving together as mechanically as possible. I did this exercise for thirty minutes, and I started at the model's hairline (Visual 2–6). When you see hair, hands, or other regions of fine detail, slow down and savor them. The goal of this exercise is to spend the full time in intense concentration, so it doesn't matter how many yards of line you end up with. The important things are all happening in your head.

visual | 2–6 |

H. Stone, *Blind Contour Exercise*, Step 1.

Step 2 (Visual 2–7) shows how I followed the contour of the model's hair over the top of the head and down the other side. Notice that some forms are angular, and some are rounded. The succession of round and angular forms in a contour line brings the line to life. Don't speed through this exercise and miss it.

You can see the two kinds of forms more clearly in Step 3 (Visual 2–8). The contour line continues along the hairline until it reaches the ear. It moves down the ear to the neck, and then to the shoulder. Notice the little kink where the neck and shoulder meet. It is the only corner in an area of gentle curves, and it is the relationship between the two kinds of forms that makes that structure recognizable. The same relationship is happening in the model's left hand. It is easy to be a little intimidated by the complexity

H. Stone, *Blind Contour Exercise, Step 2.*

of the hand, but go ahead and draw it, every time, for better or worse. With practice, you will draw hands of every description. You will also start to feel superior to artists who often draw arms with no hands on the end of them.

Step 4 (Visual 2–9) shows how I addressed the common problem of running off the edge of the paper. After I had finished the arm and was drawing some of the drapery the model was sitting on, my line fell off the bottom of the page. You can see where I started again if you divide the

picture in vertical and horizontal thirds, so that you have an imaginary rectangle in the center. I started the new line at the upper left-hand corner of that imaginary rectangle. If you have taken a photography course, you may recognize this application of **rule of thirds**. I didn't use it intentionally; I was just trying to get going again as soon as possible.

Follow the new line from its stating point, and you can see it move down the

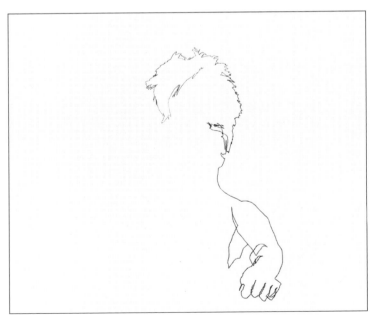

H. Stone, *Blind Contour Exercise, Step 3.*

H. Stone, *Blind Contour Exercise, Step 4.*

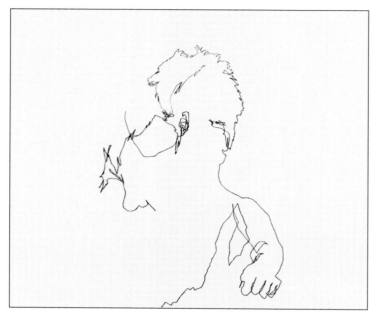

jaw line, to the box-like chin, and back up to the ear, which I drew for a second time. I followed the hairline over to the other side of the head and moved down into the face. Visual 2–10 shows how well the exercise worked when I used it to draw the face. If you look closely, you may see some forms suggesting an expressionistic interpretation of a scowling man.

I drew Visual 2–11 from the same pose so you could see what I was looking at. I used Exercise 2-2, the semi-blind contour exercise, to make this drawing.

Look at the Drawing

When you look at your first blind contour drawing, you may be unimpressed. It will probably seem disorganized, or even chaotic, and the proportions will almost certainly be inconsistent. As you study the drawing, you will most likely begin to see some redeeming qualities. The drawing may be successful as a caricature, or the way the line is drawn may be interesting in itself. You will

H. Stone, *Blind Contour Exercise, final version,* fiber-point marker on paper, 22" × 30", 2006.

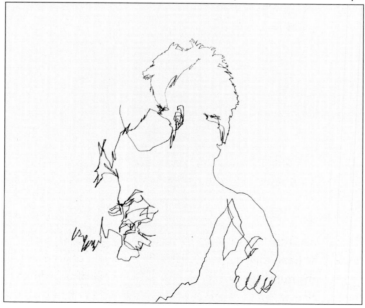

see some passages that are recognizable as part of the model, and others which will be a mystery. Take note of areas that feel right. If the line is familiar to you, or seems like something you discovered rather than created, it means that you have developed new skills, and they are visible at that place. In time, you will be able to apply those skills to create drawings that please you.

H. Stone, *Blind Contour Exercise Reference Drawing*, fiber-point marker on paper, 22" × 20", 2006.

When we evaluate the quality of a blind contour exercise, we can be thankful that creating a good likeness of the model in a well-organized, balanced drawing is outside the scope of the project. A blind contour drawing is evaluated solely on how precisely the line defines the edges of the forms. Look at your drawing and use this criterion to assess the quality of your concentration and how consistently you were able to maintain it. The line will tell you where you were attentive and where your concentration lapsed. If you were on track in the areas of detail, such as the face or hair, they will probably be much bigger than the other parts of the drawing.

In this drawing, we are looking for:

- A single, steady, controlled contour line.
- Recognizable anatomical structures in some places.
- Some areas of dense detail.
- Some errors in proportion. An accurately proportioned figure almost always means that the artist was looking at the paper from time to time. We won't use the word cheating.

We are not looking for:

- Any line that is not single and unadorned. For example, the line in Visual 2–12 was made with a reciprocating motion of the hand that cannot possibly be the result of accepting the eye's lead. This line attempts to substitute busyness for the accurate details of the contour. If we could plug this line into a speaker, it would generate white noise instead of a clear tone.

An awful line.

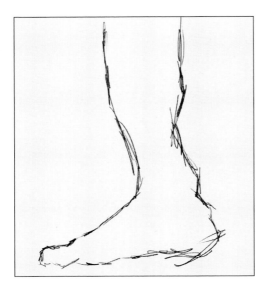

- An oversimplified line. This is a line that is oblivious to the details of the contour, or which makes the same forms over and over. In other words, it lacks either angular forms or round forms.

- Improvised lines, or other lines that do not correspond to anything actually seen in nature. For example, sometimes an artist becomes frustrated and draws a network of generic lines in the hair, instead of continuing to draw details.

- Any use of value or shading techniques.

- Any attempts to erase the line.

Some Student Blind Contour Exercises

It is always interesting to look at the way that others do this exercise because of the personality that each artist brings to the line. The next three drawings were made by students in their first drawing course, in their first or second day of line exercises.

The drawing in Visual 2–13 is a good example of a properly drawn blind contour exercise. The artist started at the top of the head, with the line moving down the model's left edge, then up

visual | 2–13 |

RoAnne Elliott, *Student Blind Contour Exercise*, ink on paper, 30" × 22", 2004.

the inside of the leg and down again, and back up to the head again. From there, she drew down the face, and then the body's **midline**. If you look closely, you may be able to see the spot at the beginning of the line. This shows us that the artist left her point still while she focused her attention. She restarted her line in a few places, and the spots are visible there, too. This initial moment of visualization paid off with a detailed, well-crafted line.

The exercise shown in Visual 2–14 is also a good, closely observed drawing. It has the dislocated proportions we expect to see in a blind contour exercise, and it excels in capturing both angular and round forms. You can see these in the transitions between the head and shoulders. The artist didn't chicken out when she got to the chair. We can see how its predominantly vertical and horizontal forms are different from those of the model. The presence of two kinds of forms in the same drawing shows us that the artist goes where her eye leads her.

Visual 2–15 shows a blind contour drawing created with vine charcoal. Like the previous drawing, it uses both curves and angles in its contour line. The hand and wrist near the center of the drawing (Visual 2–16) show how careful observation of these two kinds of forms can create a sense of anatomical structure. We are looking at the outline of the bottom edge of the right hand. This is the part that strikes the villain when you deliver a karate chop. The hand is bent back, supporting the model's chin. The bend in the line at *A* is caused by a protrusion called the pisiform bone, which is a small, knob-like bone in the wrist that gives leverage to the two muscles that are anchored to it. You can easily find your own pisiform bone by touching the edge of your hand where it connects to your wrist.

The human body has many of these visible protrusions of bone, and they are a subtle life-drawing problem. If you can draw one of them accurately, it will clarify the structure of the joint it works with, but if you draw it flabbily, nothing else you do will make the joint look right. Look at the drawing again and think about how it would be different if the bend in the line was a gentle curve, or a sharp angle. Would it still communicate the way that solid bone looks under a layer of skin? The bend at *B* is a curve interrupted by the creases where the skin on the back of the hand is wrinkled. *C* shows three bent places in the line, which suggest the structure of the fingers. Notice how each one is unique in the angle and sharpness of the bend. This is an attentive line.

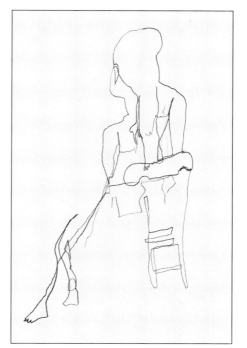

visual | 2–14 |

Eleanor L. Harris, *Student Blind Contour Exercise*, ink on paper, 30" × 22", 2004.

visual | 2–15 |

Eleanor L. Harris, *Student Blind Contour Exercise*, charcoal on paper, 30" × 22", 2004.

visual | 2–16 |

Eleanor L. Harris, *Student Blind Contour Exercise*, charcoal on paper, 30" × 22", 2004, detail.

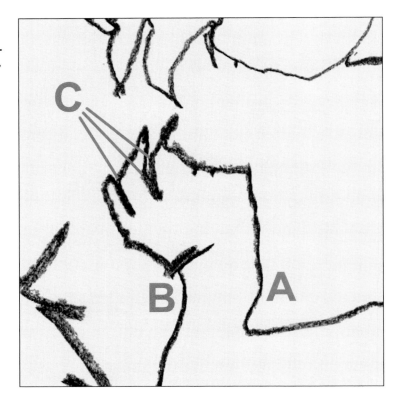

THE PERSUASIVE LINE

A good contour line does more than define the body's forms; it also persuades the viewer to make a sympathetic connection to the drawing. You can probably think of times when a drawing persuaded you that it held something important. It may have conjured a complex form with a few simple marks, or maybe it engaged you subjectively, like music: taut and sober, lyrical, or aggressive.

If you keep practicing, you will develop a repertoire of expressive contour lines that grow from your temperament and moods. When you have reached this level of skill, the most demanding line you can make will still be the thin, articulate line you learn in the next exercise. This line does not carry the viewer along on a tide of passion or shout the viewer down with emphatic strokes. This line is persuasive through reason and quiet logic. Because this is a contour line reduced to its most basic state, laziness or ineptitude cannot hide in it. Every inch of it shows the quality of the observation that generated it.

Eleanor Dickinson's drawing of a couple (Visual 2–17) uses a thin, eloquent line. She doesn't make a line for every structure she can see, but because her lines are so specific, we can see many forms in the drawing that the line only implies. For example, the woman's mouth is drawn simply, with a wavy line where the lips meet, a shorter line bracketing the lower lip, and a very small curved line to indicate the philtrum, the oddly-named dent between the mouth and nose. A very short straight line below the lower lip shows the lip's fullness and the chin's convexity. These few lines sensitively show us the complex form of the mouth. In the same way, only the bottom of the nose is actually drawn, but the entire nose is present in the drawing. She doesn't draw every eyelash or hair on the model's head, but the few she draws are accurate enough to stand in for the rest. If you imagine drawing a line down the midline of her face, across her skin, from the hairline to the chin, you can see how clearly Dickinson's lines define the face's three-dimensional shape.

visual | 2–17 |

Eleanor
Dickinson,
*Untitled (figure
drawing)*, black
ink, 32.99" ×
33.89", 1972.
© *Eleanor
Dickinson, 2007.
Courtesy of the
Fine Arts
Museums of San
Francisco, Gift of
William Stanton
Picher, 1978.2.16.*

Ben Schonzeit's *Syrena* (Visual 2–18) is also drawn with a thin contour line, but the mood of his drawing is different. Dickinson's drawing is a double portrait that focuses on the figures' faces and hands; Schonzeit's places the figure in an environment, using a consistent line to render the figure, the surface she is sitting on, the vegetation that surrounds her, and the horizon. The line is relaxed, but it is not carelessly drawn. The figure's structure, position, and proportions are

visual | 2–18 |

Benjamin
Schonzeit,
Syrena, pen and
black ink, 11.22"
× 14.96", 1985.
*Fine Arts
Museums of
San Francisco,
Gift of the artist,
1987.2.115.*
© *Benjamin
Schonzeit.
Courtesy of the
artist.*

accurate, and her face is a portrait. One reason this drawing sustains our interest is the control the artist is able to bring to this calm, matter-of-fact line.

One of the lessons of the contour exercises is that there are a few wrong ways to make a contour line. The good news is that there are a great many ways of doing the job right. A contour line has done the minimum when it describes the figure's forms. A harder-working line will be interesting to look at, and it may attach some emotional connotations to the drawing. Great contour lines have force of personality. Such lines are often described as being confident, assured, or possessing authority. In other words, not only are the artist's intentions made clear in the application of the line, but the lines are able to persuade you that the drawing is a product of experience, wisdom, and emotional depth.

Exercise 4: The Semiblind Contour Exercise

I regret that I haven't been able to think up a more euphonious name for this exercise, but this one at least keeps the focus on the idea that this activity is very similar to the blind contour exercise. If you do this exercise properly, you will soon be surprised at how well you are able to make a competent line drawing. Practice with the exercise leads you to an individual drawing style that you can use as a springboard for more adventurous drawing experiments.

This exercise does not flow smoothly at first. Its staccato movement may seem incompatible with the felicity and grace that are normally associated with classical figure drawing. The process of alternating your attention between the model and the paper, starting or stopping your hand each time, can be unsatisfying. Persist, and you will find that your eye will gain the ability to flicker between the model and paper, and you will, increasingly, be able to keep track of what is happening in both places at once. This kind of complex attention probably has precedents in your experience. For example, consider how, if you drive a car, you are able to monitor not only where the car is going, but its speed, the view in the mirrors, and the music you are listening to, all at the same time. Be patient, concentrate on using the exercise to make the best drawing you can, and your process will smooth out soon enough. In time, with practice, you will no longer be doing a semiblind contour exercise; you will be doing a line drawing. You will be able to keep track of the figure and the paper at the same time, and the exercise will have evolved into your own contour line technique.

Materials

- One fine- or medium-point fiber-tip permanent marker.
- A few sticks of vine charcoal.
- A supply of inexpensive paper, at least 18" × 24".

Procedures

1. The semiblind contour exercise is exactly like the blind contour exercise in almost all respects: pause before starting in order to visualize that your drawing instrument is on the model, rather than on the paper; move your hand slowly; and keep your hand and eye moving together in perfect synchronization. As you draw, continue to imagine that your pen point is actually on the model, rather than on the paper.

2. In this exercise, you may look down at the paper and check the position of your pen point, as long as you stop your hand when you do it.

3. You may also pick up your drawing instrument, move it, and start another line whenever you feel like it.

4. Do not allow your hand to move while you are looking at the paper.

5. Draw slowly and stop often. If your line is out of place, pick the pen up and move it to the right spot. Do not waste time erasing.

6. Aim for quality in the line. The best outcome for this exercise would be a single line that articulately describes the entire figure; the next best would be a single line that describes part of the figure.

7. Do this exercise immediately after doing the blind contour exercise.

8. In your first two drawing sessions, do the exercise several times for fifteen minutes, and use a pen. You may want to spend your time working on an area of detail. Later, increase the time to twenty or twenty-five minutes, and use the charcoal stick.

Use this technique whenever you make contour lines. If at any point your line fails to obey you, you will be able to bring it back under your jurisdiction by reverting to the original, slow version of this exercise.

Do the exercise four or five times in pen and charcoal; after you have the hang of it, you may be interested in trying it in other media. Experiment with pens, pencils, soft and hard charcoal, and brushes. Vary the thickness of your lines (Visual 2–19), your hand position, and your grip on the drawing instrument. As before, study your drawings, save them, and take note of the effects you like. When you consistently feel that you need more time,

visual | 2–19 |

A contour line of varying thickness. H. Stone, *Untitled (portrait),* steel nib and India ink, 10" × 8", 2002.

increase the time to forty-five minutes. After you have acquired some drawing skill, it can be rewarding to do longer versions of this exercise. Use good paper, experiment with different media, and add drawing time in forty-five-minute sets.

Demonstration 2-2: The Semiblind Contour Exercise

In this exercise, there are few drawing problems that cannot be alleviated by slowing down and stopping to look more often. The only thing you have to think about while you are drawing is the line you are working on, so do not worry about how the drawing will look when it is finished. Stay focused, and the product will take care of itself.

I did this demonstration drawing in thirty minutes, on an easel, using a medium-point fiber-tip pen. As in the blind contour exercise, I started by simply thinking. I placed my pen point on the paper, looked at the model, and imagined that the pen was touching a spot on the edge of her body. I tuned out the rest of the world and waited until I could clearly visualize that the pen was on her, instead of the paper, and then I allowed my hand to start moving, very slowly. I drew until I had the line in Visual 2–20.

In this exercise, it doesn't matter where you start and stop. You can make long lines or short ones. If you vary your routine, you will figure out more quickly what works best for you. In Visual 2–21, you can see that instead of continuing the line around the edge of the figure, I chose to draw a few small forms near the first line. I did this so I could more easily get the proportions right. It is usually easier to accurately draw small forms than big ones, and from this point of view I saw the figure as composed of many small forms instead of one large, uninterrupted one.

H. Stone,
*Semiblind contour
exercise demo,
Step 1.*

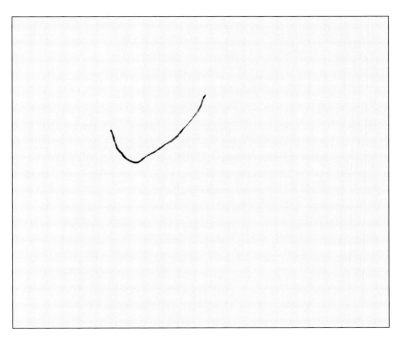

I continued to draw new shapes adjacent to the old ones. If you look closely, you can see that the line is not perfectly consistent. The darker spots show where I stopped to check my pen position. I would estimate that the drawing as shown in Visual 2–22 has between thirty and fifty of these spots. At this stage, I have a few recognizable forms and no egregious errors.

Before I began work on the outer contour of the model's back, hip, and leg, I drew her right ear. This gave me a place to start drawing the contour line (Visual 2–23). In fact, I drew it twice. I quit drawing the first line as soon as I could see that it was in error. It did serve a purpose in the drawing by helping me find the correct line. This technique of subdividing the figure into smaller forms to

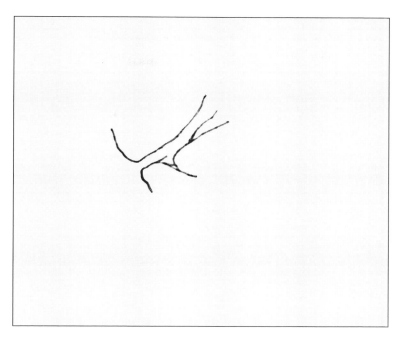

visual | 2–21 |

H. Stone,
*Semiblind contour
exercise demo,
Step 2.*

better see the proportions is described in detail in Chapter 7.

Step 5 (Visual 2–24) shows how I extended the model's lower-right leg and used it to locate the sole of the left foot. The wavy line coming out of her right shin was the top edge of the padding on the model stand. Part of the left leg was behind it, and I drew it, in the wrong place it turned out, to give myself a landmark I could come back to later. I subdivided some

of the forms on her upper torso into smaller shapes and corrected the upper arm and abdomen. It is true that few people would be able to tell that those lines were wrong, and leaving them as they were would keep the drawing uncluttered, but correcting them is a good mental discipline. I believe that the habit pays off later in better drawings.

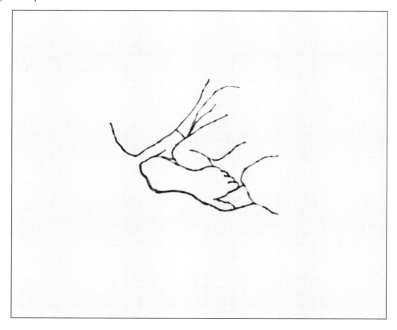

visual | 2–22 |

H. Stone,
*Semiblind contour
exercise demo,
Step 3.*

visual | 2–23 |

H. Stone,
*Semiblind contour
exercise demo,
Step 4.*

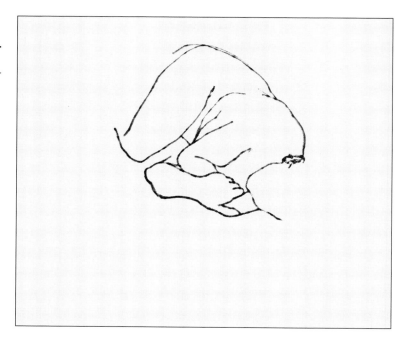

Step 6 (Visual 2–25) shows the corrected lower-left leg and the features of the face. People often speed up when they get to the face because they believe that they know what one looks like. To be sure that you get the face right, slow down and refocus your attention on the exercise. Draw deliberately, and you will be able to demonstrate how it looks even at unusual angles. In this drawing, the model's right ear served as a good point of reference. The hairline, from this point of view, was centered under her ear, and when that was in place, the eyebrow and eye were not too hard to place in position.

Less of a good contour line is better than more of a mediocre one. This is the key to using contour lines to draw complex structures such as hair. If you draw a few lines to indicate the edges you can see most clearly in the mass of hair, those lines will show its overall shape and imply that

visual | 2–24 |

H. Stone,
*Semiblind contour
exercise demo,
Step 5.*

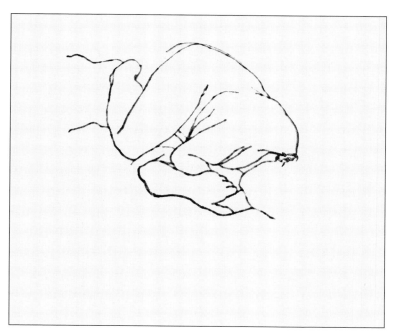

it is a collection of individual fibers. Just make sure that any mark you make corresponds to something you see, and it will look good almost every time.

Visual 2–26 shows the final version of this drawing, with the pillow, cushion, and model stand added. There is also a correction to the lower edge of the model's right thigh.

Look at the Drawing

Unlike the blind con-
tour exercise, whose
rewards are deferred,
we do the semiblind
contour exercise to
produce drawings that
make us happy. Look
at your drawing and,
grading on a curve, see
if there is anything
about it that you are
happy with. Were you
able to maintain the
quality of line that you
achieved in the blind
exercise? Does the figure look humanoid? Does it seem too big or too small?

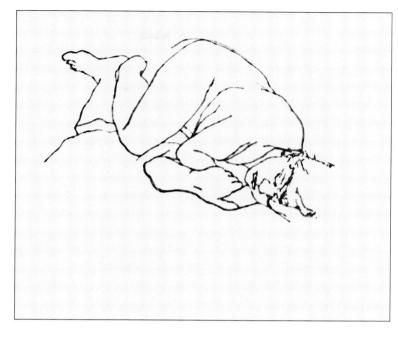

visual | 2–25 |

H. Stone,
*Semiblind contour
exercise demo,
Step 6.*

Because you were allowed to look at the paper, the proportions are probably improved over
those in the blind exercise. They are unlikely to be perfect. Although a few people seem to be
born with the ability to correctly see and draw proportions, for the rest of us proficiency takes
some time. For now, make better lines as you see the need for them, and don't worry about proportions beyond that.
In Chapter 7 you learn
several methods of fig-
uring out proportions.

Your first semiblind
drawings may show
only partial figures.
This isn't a problem.
If you would like
to produce drawings
that seem more com-
pleted, draw an area
of detail such as the
head and face, the
hands, or the feet. As
your skills improve,

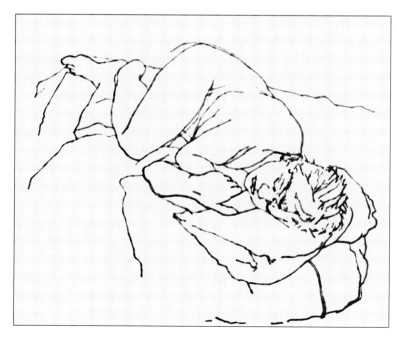

visual | 2–26 |

H. Stone,
*Semiblind contour
exercise demo,
final version,*
fiber-point
marker on paper,
30" × 22", 2006.

you will be able to draw faster and for a longer time, and your drawings will look more finished.

In this drawing, we are looking for:

- Active concentration present in all parts of the line. In other words, every part of the line is clear, confident, and truthful.
- Proportions improved over those in the blind contour drawing.
- False starts and inaccurate lines are acceptable if better versions are also present.
- Both angular and rounded forms present.

We are not looking for:

- Any lines that are not the product of direct, attentive observation. You don't have to draw everything you see, but don't draw anything you don't see.
- A slack or hurried line.
- Any shading techniques.
- Consistently omitted areas of detail, such as hands, feet, or the face.

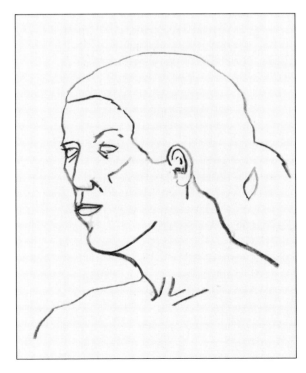

visual | 2–27 |

Bryan Hudson,
*Student Semiblind
Contour Exercise*,
charcoal on
paper, 14" × 11",
2004.

Some Student Semiblind Contour Exercises

These drawings were done in the same class sessions as the blind contour exercises in this chapter. Visual 2–27 shows a good, patient contour line drawn in vine charcoal. The drawing differentiates well between round and angular forms. You can see this in the contour line that defines the model's face and in the drawing of the eyes and mouth.

Visual 2–28 was drawn with a fine pen. The likeness is good, and the line is closely observed. This can be seen in the face, the hairline, and the subtle forms of the shoulder and back. Corrections were made to the ear, the arm, and the back of the head, which lets us know that the artist's sense of proportion is working.

Visual 2–29 also has a few visible corrections. My favorite part of this drawing is the life present in the face. The convexity of the forehead and the angularity of the chin are both exaggerated, creating a caricature that shows us not only the model's likeness but also her facial expression.

CHAPTER SUMMARY

A contour is an edge, and a contour line is a line that describes an edge. Contour lines do not exist in nature; they are constructed by artists to describe the human body's three-dimensional forms and to subjectively communicate personal content. The blind contour exercise is a visualization exercise whose purpose is to develop the ability to see the details of a contour and to create a line that expresses them. The quality of the process is the most important part of this exercise: keeping the hand and eye moving in synchronization without looking at the paper and not worrying about how the drawing is turning out. The semiblind contour exercise is used to create great line drawings. It is performed like the blind contour exercise, except the artist may stop drawing, look at the paper, and change the position of the drawing instrument at will. In time, practice with the semiblind contour exercise will evolve into an orderly and efficient technique for drawing contour lines.

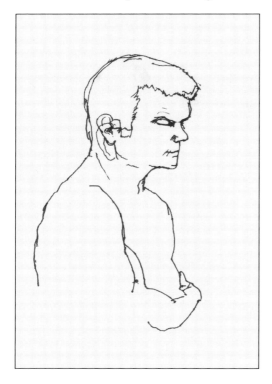

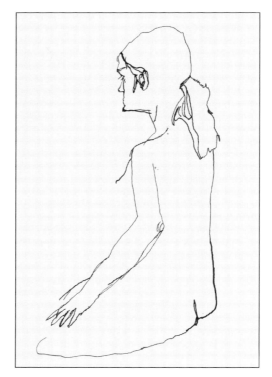

visual | 2–28 |

visual | 2–29 |

Alberta Mirais, *Student Semiblind Contour Exercise*, ink on paper, 30" × 22", 2004.

Eleanor L. Harris, *Student Semiblind Contour Exercise*, ink on paper, 30" × 22", 2004.

▶ *chapter questions*

True/False

1. A value drawing has contours.

2. The human eye naturally sees values.

3. The human eye naturally sees contour lines.

4. Value is the same as tone.

5. The basic objective of a life drawing is defining three-dimensional forms.

6. Value drawing is more accurate than contour drawing.

7. Value drawing is more subjective than contour drawing.

8. Basic life-drawing skill is largely an ability to see another person without preconceptions.

9. The blind contour drawing is the most useful drawing exercise.

10. When doing the semiblind contour exercise, it is important to work quickly.

Multiple Choice

11. Which statement about a contour line is not true?
    a. A contour line is an analogy, rather than a literal representation of visual reality.
    b. A contour line can be perfectly objective.
    c. A contour line is a graph of the artist's attentive process.
    d. A contour line can add meaning to a drawing apart from its descriptive function.

12. The blind contour drawing:
    a. Is intended to produce exhibitable drawings.
    b. Is done with the eyes closed.
    c. Develops new software for your brain.
    d. Is not helpful to experienced artists.

13. The most important part of the blind contour drawing is:
   a. In the first minute.

   b. When the artist's hand is moving.

   c. In the last minute.

   d. While reviewing the drawing after the exercise is finished.

14. The goal of the blind contour exercise is:
   a. A great drawing.

   b. To learn to draw faster.

   c. To spend the duration of the exercise in intense concentration.

   d. To get in touch with your inner artist.

15. Evaluate a blind contour drawing on:
   a. The accuracy of its proportions.

   b. How precisely the line defines the edges of the forms.

   c. The clarity of its organization.

   d. All of the above.

16. The semiblind contour exercise:
   a. Is very similar to the blind contour exercise.

   b. Is done to create a great drawing.

   c. Can be done with a variety of media.

   d. All of the above.

17. Most drawing problems that arise in the semiblind contour exercise:
   a. Can be remediated by starting the drawing over.

   b. Are problems in proportion.

   c. Can be easily addressed by erasing.

   d. Can be alleviated by slowing down and stopping more often to check position.

18. The semiblind contour demonstration established the figure's proportions:
   a. By measuring.

   b. By subdividing the figure into smaller forms.

   c. By viewing the figure through a rectangle made with the fingers.

   d. By roughing in the larger forms of the body before starting.

19. The best technique for drawing hair is:

    a. To use the semiblind contour technique to draw the edges most visible in the hair.

    b. To patiently draw a contour line for every hair you can see.

    c. To draw a line around the outside edge of the hair.

    d. To make hundreds of tiny dots with the point of the pen.

20. When doing the semiblind contour exercise, if you make an error:

    a. Forget about it because no one will know the difference.

    b. Erase the erroneous line and draw it correctly.

    c. Draw the line correctly without erasing the erroneous line.

    d. Start the drawing over.

Pierre-Paul Prud'hon, *Study of a Man*, black
and white chalk on blue paper, 22¾" × 13¼",
circa 1810–1820. *Los Angeles County Museum
of Art, Graphic Arts Council Fund and Museum
Acquisition Fund. Photograph © 2006
Museum Associates / LACMA*

CHAPTER

3

objectives

- Understand the function of value in describing the human form.
- Differentiate between chiaroscuro and modeling as techniques of value drawing.
- Define local color and understand how it can affect the use of value in drawing.
- Define mass tone and practice using mass tones to make a three-value drawing.
- Experiment with different ways of applying drawing media.
- Use hatching lines to create a four-value drawing.

introduction

Think of the things you can do with the side of a stick of charcoal. You can easily use it to lay down masses of gray or black, or apply a tone to the whole sheet of paper if you feel like it. You can create a smooth, refined surface, or a jagged, torn improvisation. How dark can you make that shape? How many ways can you find to blend the charcoal dust from light to dark? Wipe it, blend it, erase it, smudge it: It's like having a whole artist's palette in one compact package.

Creating an image by drawing masses and gradients of white, gray, and black is called **value drawing. Value,** sometimes called **tone**, is the level of lightness or darkness in a drawing. Using value well is the key to drawing a human figure with the appearance of reality.

VALUE IN LIFE DRAWING

Here is the short version of how to make a value drawing: study the pose carefully, and identify one shape of shadow. Duplicate the shape by drawing a gray mass on your paper. Identify an adjacent shape. Is it lighter or darker than the first one? Draw that shape with another mass of gray. Repeat until the paper is covered.

Pierre-Paul Prud'hon used this procedure, with some adjustments, when he created the drawing shown at the beginning of the chapter. This drawing was done in an academic style, characterized by accurate anatomical detail and sensitive use of black and white chalk on an off-white or middle-toned paper. Academic drawing is traditional drawing as it was taught in the French Royal Academy of Painting and Sculpture from its founding in 1648 through the nineteenth century. The style is still being practiced today, and it is considered by many to be the benchmark for objective realism in drawing.

In drawing, line is a fiction, but value is reality. An artist must invent a contour line, but a scene's values exist as objective visual facts, present for the artist to transcribe. When you look at a scene, your eye apprehends a continuous surface composed of a patchwork of colored forms. When you draw the scene, you compare the forms you see and make judgments as to which ones are darker. As you balance the relationships of light and dark, the image begins to appear. The more closely you are able to observe and duplicate these relative levels of light and dark, and the transitions between them, the more recognizable your drawing will be.

One of the exciting things about working with value is that even though the same shapes are visible to everyone, each artist will have her own way of reproducing them. David Rich's drawing (Visual 3–1) is, like Prud'hon's, a value drawing done from a live model. Rather than focusing on describing the model's body in detail, Rich uses masses of dark and light to create a context for the figure. He gives us a description of the space the model inhabits, a sense of

visual | 3–1 |

David Rich,
Isabelle, charcoal
on paper,
23" × 30", 2002.

visual | 3–2 |

Thomas P. Anshutz, *Standing Male Nude*, charcoal on cream laid paper, 24½" × 18⅛", 1851–1912. *Minneapolis Institute of Arts, Gift of David M. Daniels.*

where the light is coming from, and places us, the viewer, in the same room as he is—close by and at his level. Rich uses value **abstractly**, creating forms whose color, shape, and place in the composition are interesting for their own sake, as well as for their role in describing the figure.

Visual 3–2, by Thomas Anshutz, is an unfinished value drawing that uses lights and darks to create a sense of atmosphere. The shoulders and head are well lit; they have hard edges and well-defined anatomical features. The parts of the body farther from the light are a little darker. The edges of the lower body are soft, with the forms dissolving in shadow. The impression is that the air is visibly present and absorbing light.

These three artists each used value drawing to express their own interests. Prud'hon created a highly accomplished drawing within established conventions; Rich worked with the structure of the picture and the psychology of drawing another person; and Anshutz established the character of the light in the studio. Value drawing allows each of us to build a unique, personal drawing on a common foundation of visual truthfulness.

Because a line does not occur in nature, to draw a contour line is to create a useful, descriptive abstraction. When you draw values, you are duplicating in the most literal way the levels of brightness that your eye is able to see. Values do exist. Two artists can agree where the lightest and darkest areas of a scene are, and differences of opinion can be arbitrated by a camera.

The most common impediment to accurately drawing another person is not a lack of coordination in the hand, it is the habit of drawing one's idea of what the person looks like, rather than what the eye is actually seeing. Value drawing is an effective way to address this problem.

In our day-to-day life, we do not have a balanced view of other people. For example, we tend to pay more attention to facial expressions than we do to the exact proportions of the head. Likewise, we usually spend little time studying our colleagues' feet. The value drawing in Visual 3–3 is Pablo Picasso's entrance exam to the art academy in Barcelona. He was a skilled artist as a teenager, but in this drawing, the feet are too small. If you look at them closely, their structure is accurate, but they are simply the wrong parts for that model. This error is not

visual | 3–3 |

Pablo Picasso,
*Naked Man
(entrance
examination),*
pencil on
cardboard
19¹³⁄₁₆" × 12¹³⁄₁₆",
1895 © 2007
*Estate of Pablo
Picasso / Artists
Rights Society
(ARS), New York.
Image courtesy
Dr. Enrique
Mallen, On-Line
Picasso Project.*

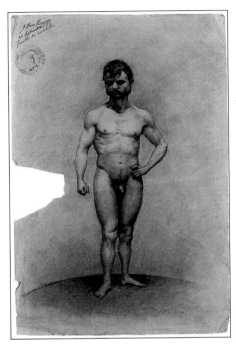

uncommon. It comes from drawing the idea of the feet, rather than the feet as they present themselves to the eye. Our idea of what a person looks like is a kind of summary, colored by our experience with the person, or with people who remind us of them. This interpersonal shorthand helps us get along in the world, but it interferes with our ability to see and draw people objectively. Value drawing helps us to disregard the summary process and reproduce the forms as we see them.

Value Drawing Terms

In value drawing, the artist makes judgments about how light or dark the various parts of the drawing need to be. This is a straightforward process when the subject is a human body because a given person's skin is usually fairly uniform in value. The bare paper represents the lightest areas of the figure, and the rest is darkened as necessary to represent receding forms or the effects of shadow. Complications set in when the model is shown in a multicolored environment, or when the model is literally a colorful person. How do you balance the values when drawing forms of different colors? Understanding what **local color** is can help.

Local color is color as it is before shadows, adjacent colors, or the color of the light falling on it are considered. Think of local color as the starting color of something, before it is placed in an environment. If someone has red hair, then red is its local color, even if it looks orange when seen at sunset or black when viewed by moonlight. Visual 3–4 shows three examples of local color in life drawing. On the left, a red-haired model rests her head on a printed fabric throw pillow. The hair shines where the light hits it most directly and gets a little darker in the shadows. A question of interest to me as I drew this picture was whether the darkest places in the hair were lighter than the darkest spots on the pillow. The man in the middle has black hair, and his hair, like the hair on the left, is lit from overhead. In this drawing, the challenge was getting the light area on top of his head to look as though it was his scalp peeking through thinning hair, instead of the hair's highlights. The model on the right has black hair, but I didn't feel that it was necessary to give you that information in the drawing. How much local color do you need to show when you draw? It's your choice.

Chiaroscuro is use of light and shadow to define form. The word is actually two Italian words grafted together: *chiaro,* meaning light, and *oscuro,* meaning dark. A chiaroscuro drawing shows how the figure looks when it is illuminated by a single light source. The shapes of the light areas and shadows describe the body's forms and help clarify the space surrounding it.

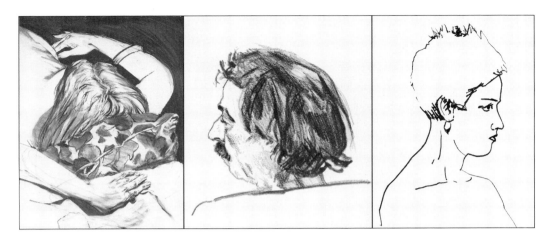

Three approaches to local color.

Chiaroscuro drawing was invented during the Italian Renaissance, 500 years ago. Raphael Sanzio was one of its first practitioners. We can immediately tell that his drawing in Visual 3–5 is a chiaroscuro drawing because the the light falling on the figure comes from a single direction. The model's face and upper torso are in shadow, and his head casts a shadow onto his right arm and shoulder that helps establish the relative positions of all three structures.

Raphael Sanzio, *Nude Man with Raised Arms*, black chalk, 11.45" × 12.79", circa 1511–1512. © *The Trustees of the British Museum. All rights reserved.*

Chiaroscuro drawings usually emphasize the structure of the body at the expense of local color. For example, Visual 3–6 is a simple chiaroscuro drawing of a woman's head. The light is coming from above and behind her, so most of what we see is in shadow. We can get a sense of the head's shape from this drawing, but it does not tell us the color of the model's skin or hair.

Modeling, like chiaroscuro, uses value to describe form, but it disregards light and shadow. Modeling gets right to the primary job of life drawing, mapping the three-dimensional

H. Stone, *Head in Profile*, sumi ink, 18" × 18", 2000.

Michelangelo
Buonarroti
(1475–1564), *A
Male Nude Seen
From Behind,*
black chalk on
paper,
11.5" × 9.17",
circa 1539–1541.
© *The Trustees of
the British
Museum. All
rights reserved.*

form of the human figure onto the two-dimensional surface of the paper. Modeling drawing takes its name from its similarity to making sculpture. When you are modeling a figure in clay, you push on the clay to change its shape. The more you want the form to curve away from you, the more pressure you need to apply. In modeling drawing, you press on a stick of charcoal instead of a mass of clay. Any surface of the figure that presents a flat face to you is left blank. As the form curves away from you, it is drawn progressively darker. Surfaces that are nearly perpendicular to the **picture plane** are made black. Complex forms drawn with a modeling technique will therefore continuously vary in value according to their shape.

Michelangelo's drawing in Visual 3–7 the model's arms are rendered in chiaroscuro. A light falls on them from above, illuminating their upper surfaces and creating shadows that express their structure. We might expect the upper surface of the left shoulder to be similarly lit from overhead, but this region of the drawing gives us a detailed description of the musculature of the back without implying that the light is coming from a particular direction. This area is drawn using modeling. Unlike chiaroscuro, modeling drawing is a direct analysis of the figure's anatomy; it has nothing to say about the environment external to the figure. You will have the opportunity to practice modeling drawing in Chapter 6.

Three hundred years after Michelangelo, Edgar Degas created the modeling drawing in Visual 3–8. The surface of the body is light where it faces us, getting darker as it tilts away from the picture plane. We can see a rib and shoulder blade in the transition from the model's side to her back, and the torso gets darker to show us its slight concavity along the spine. On the other side of the backbone, it lightens again, and then darkens to black at the soft edge of the model's back.

Although limiting yourself to one set of drawing skills at a time is an excellent way to learn, it is worth remembering that your larger mission as a figurative artist is to define the body's forms as specifically as possible, while making art that is your own. Explore different ways of achieving this, and develop a set of techniques that feels right for you.

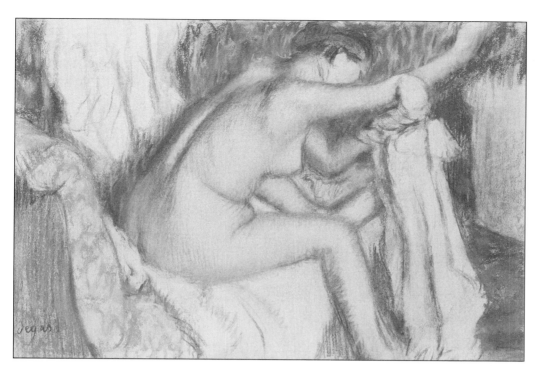

visual 3–8

Edgar Degas
(1834–1917),
*Woman Drying
Her Arm*, pastel
and charcoal on
off-white wove
paper, 12" × 17.5",
late 1880s to
early 1890s. *The
Metropolitan
Museum of Art,
H. O. Havemeyer
Collection,
Bequest of Mrs.
H. O. Havemeyer,
1929
(29.100.553)
Image © The
Metropolitan
Museum of Art*

In the exercises in this chapter, we experiment with various ways of using drawing media. Some artists prefer to apply the media spontaneously, and others want to patiently create a controlled, blended surface. This level of smoothness or refinement of the drawing's surface is called the **finish**. Kay Ruane's drawing (Visual 3–9) has a high level of finish. She applies graphite with great care to create an understated chiaroscuro and an unusual, silvery light. The level of detail, closely observed textures, and fine surface invest the drawing with a preternatural clarity, so that our vision seems particularly keen while we look at it.

visual 3–9

Kay Ruane,
Midnight,
graphite,
11" × 17", 2002.
*Courtesy of Kay
Ruane.*

Loren Klein's drawing (Visual 3–10) is similar to Ruane's in subject, but with a finish that would be called **painterly**, instead of refined. A painterly finish is one in which the movements of the artist's hand are visible in the medium. In Klein's drawing, charcoal is applied both as masses and lines. It is rubbed into the paper and removed with an eraser, and the artist's

Loren Klein,
Sketchy Nude,
charcoal on
newsprint,
24" × 18".
Courtesy of Loren Klein

personal **calligraphy** is visible throughout. As in Ruane's drawing, this surface is carefully crafted to create a unique sense of light; the air seems to glow wherever the eraser scrubs out the charcoal. Is a drawing with a high level of finish a better drawing than one assembled more loosely? Not necessarily. The decisions made by the artist have to do with what the larger message of the piece is. Is it possible to look at Ruane's drawing without visualizing its construction as a quiet, meditative process? What does it mean to spend a long time creating a drawing in which little is left to chance? On the other hand, why would someone consider it important to draw the human figure quickly and loosely?

H. Stone, *Three-Value Study*,
charcoal on
paper, 24" × 30",
2004.

Exercise 3–1: Three-Value Drawing

A **three-value drawing** is a chiaroscuro drawing composed of shapes of black, white, and one shade of gray (Visual 3–11). It is a useful exercise for learning how to see values, but it has many other applications as well. Because it generates flat masses of interesting shape, artists often use this technique for making quick studies in preparation for larger paintings or drawings. The three-value technique is a way of boiling a scene down to simple forms, but it can also be adapted to make more detailed drawings (Visual 3–12).

Because we limit our formal vocabulary when we do a three-value drawing, we must make the most of the tools we are allowed to use. Take your time, and follow the instructions without worrying how the picture will turn out. Like all new skills, it will be a little stiff and unfamiliar at first, but persevere, and you will have a drawing method that will be a helpful sidekick in your life as an artist.

Materials

- Compressed charcoal. Get several sticks of various sizes (see Visual 3–13).

- Erasers. Get several cheap pink rubber erasers, a couple of more expensive white polymer ones, and a kneaded eraser. Use a pocketknife to cut some wedges for erasing small areas.

- An 18" × 24" pad of your everyday drawing paper. Work larger if you want to.

- Washrag or equivalent.

Procedures

1. Place the model under a window, a spotlight, or other directional lighting.

2. Before you start, study the figure and identify the lightest shapes you can see. As you work, keep in mind that these will be areas of blank, white paper.

3. Identify a darker form adjacent to one of the white areas. Using the side of your drawing stick, reproduce this shape on your paper as a **mass tone**, or solid, flat gray shape.

4. Study another shape adjacent to the one you just drew. Is the new one lighter or darker than the old one? If it is darker, make it black; if it is lighter, make it white.

5. Working from the general to the specific, develop the drawing in three values.

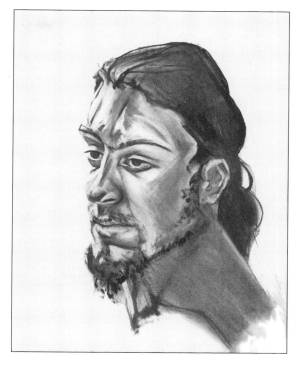

visual | 3–12 |

This is a variation of the three-value exercise with a couple of changes. I used a few gradients here and there, such as the blend from gray to white on the model's cheek. If you look carefully, you may be able to find more than strictly three values. There are not any contour lines in the drawing. H. Stone, *Head of a Beatnik*, charcoal on paper, 18" × 24", 2003.

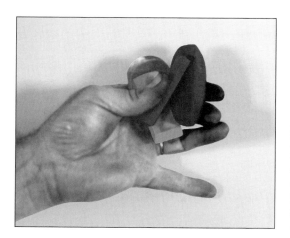

visual | 3–13 |

Suggested materials for three-value drawing, left to right: white polymer eraser, pink rubber eraser, stick of compressed charcoal, large piece of compressed charcoal.

Draw the forms loosely at first, and then bring the image into focus by adding detail and using your eraser to make corrections. Develop the background as well as the figure.

6. Do not use any contour lines or construction lines in this exercise.

7. If you lose track of where you are, you can always clarify your drawing by locating a familiar place on the drawing, and starting the three-value exercise again. If you have performance anxiety, starting the drawing with a few quick strokes to locate the figure on the page can shift your thoughts from what the drawing might be to what it is.

8. Do the exercise a few times for twenty minutes, and then increase the time.

Demonstration 3-1: Three-Value Drawing

I started this drawing with a light gray form (Visual 3–14), leaving out the shapes on the torso that I anticipated would be white. Even though these initial marks would probably be revised some before the drawing was finished, I took care to make the shape as close as possible to what I was seeing. I started in the middle of the drawing so I could get an idea where the figure would be positioned on the page.

This drawing took an hour or so to finish. Compare it with the drawing I did in Visual 3–11, which took twenty minutes to do. The difference between the two is in the level of detail. Start by positioning the large forms, and subdivide them into smaller and smaller forms as long as you have time. If you start by drawing an area in detail, you may run out of time before you are able to get much of the figure onto the page.

visual | 3–14 |

H. Stone, *Three-Value Drawing Demonstration, Step 1.*

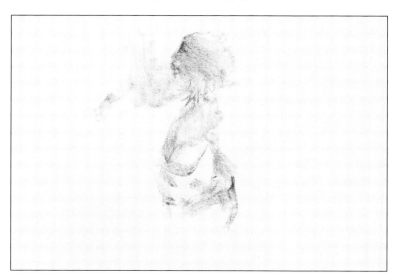

In this exercise, edges are defined by placing a dark form next to a lighter one. I studied the profile of the face, and noted that the background was darker than the figure in that area. Because the head was gray, the background needed to be black (Visual 3–15). Making the edge of the form the correct shape is fairly difficult, and you may not be able to do it well at first. Use your eraser to make corrections, and keep practicing.

visual | 3–15 |

H. Stone, *Three-Value Drawing Demonstration, Step 2.*

Visual 3–16 shows the drawing only a little later. I have drawn the eye, developed the background more, and darkened the cast shadow on the neck. It is a common error when drawing eyes to depart from the exercise and draw them without really studying them. This can result in eyes that are football-shaped, have strange irises, or look flat rather than spherical. Eyes are the most intricate form on the face, and reducing them to three values may mean slowing down, studying them, and making many corrections. It is natural to not want to lose the momentum of the drawing, but don't allow yourself to get lazy and skip over important parts.

Remember that in this exercise you don't have to draw every detail, as long as whatever marks you make are determined by something your eye is seeing. In this drawing I just tried to duplicate the few darkest areas of detail in the region around the eye (Visual 3–16).

In Visual 3–17, you can see that some of the major unknowns of the drawing have been addressed: how the figure will fit on the page, what the finish of the drawing will be, and the overall balance of light and dark. This is also the point where the figure begins to really emerge. The arm was defined by drawing the gray background and the black space between the elbow and the torso. If you stay focused on making perfect gray shapes, you may be surprised at how quickly and clearly you can

visual | 3–16 |

H. Stone, *Three-Value Drawing Demonstration, Step 3.*

H. Stone, *Three-Value Drawing Demonstration, Step 4.*

cause the body's structures to emerge.

Hair is always a knotty problem. When drawing hair, it can be hard to not get distracted by those thousands of individual strands; but to get it to look right, you need to forget about them. Use values to clarify the relationship between the big, helmet-shaped mass and the subsidiary masses. Do this by duplicating the darkest shapes in the hair, paying particular attention to which of their edges are hard, and which ones are soft.

In this drawing the light comes from above, so the highlight is on the top of the head. The bottom edge of the hair makes a hard edge against the lighter neck, so I drew the detail I was able to see there in sharp focus. I also added some irregular black shapes that I could see near the highlights at the top of the head. These added some structure to the upper half of the hair and made the small highlights stand out more than they did on the gray.

Visual 3–18 shows the final drawing. Some areas, such as the model's legs, were drawn in quickly because I was running out of time. Areas of detail, such as the hands, went more

H. Stone, *Three-Value Drawing Demonstration, final version,* charcoal on paper, 24" × 18", 2003.

slowly. If you look closely at the hands, you will see that they are drawn using the same three-value exercise as the larger forms. I tried to make sure the hands were in the right place before I started working on their details.

I didn't care about achieving a fine finish on this drawing, so I didn't smooth out the charcoal, beyond erasing to make corrections in some areas. If you want to, experiment with using your washrag and erasers to create different surface treatments.

Look at the Drawing

Always look your drawing over as soon as you finish it. It isn't necessary to analyze every drawing you do in depth, but it will speed up your learning if you make a few mental notes about what looks right and what could have been done better. First, step away from the drawing and look for an overall legibility in it—is there a figure there? Can you tell by looking at the drawing where the light was coming from? Did you slip and use contour lines instead of masses of value? Were the edges clean and articulate, or did you tend to overlook detail and simplify them?

At this stage, don't worry if the proportions are not exactly right. Just do your best with them, and we will work specifically on them in Chapter 7.

In exercises such as this, where your primary interest is in building drawing skill, it is not too important how you feel about the final product. If you are not happy with your drawing, take note of what you do not like about it, and concentrate on staying on task during the next drawing. It is in the nature of this art form that most of the drawings you do will fall short of your hopes for them. It is not constructive to feel embarrassed or overly frustrated about your work; just keep practicing, and in time you will produce good drawings.

In this exercise we want to see:

- A recognizable human figure.
- Flat masses of gray, white, and black.
- Crisp edges on most forms.
- Which direction the light is coming from.
- The drawing continuing beyond the figure into the background.
- Areas of detail drawn with the three-value technique.

We do not want to see:

- Areas that are not clearly identifiable as figure or background.
- Any use of contour lines.
- Soft edges on most forms.
- Ambiguous or contradictory indicators of light direction.

Visual 3–19 shows a good example of a student three-value drawing.

Megan Garner,
Student Three-Value Exercise,
charcoal on
paper, 22" × 30",
2004.

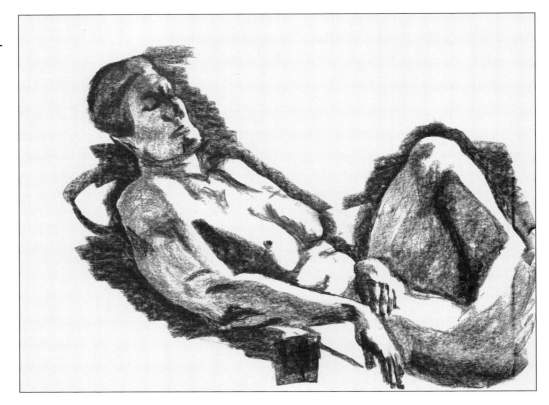

Exercise 3-2: Three-Value Drawing on a Middle Tone

In this variation of the three-value exercise, you will cover the entire surface of the paper with a middle tone, add darks with your charcoal, and pull the lights out with an eraser. This kind of drawing is often made as a study for a portrait painting because the process can be translated to oil paint with the image-making strategy unchanged. A gray or brown turpentine wash, called an **imprimatura**, is applied to the canvas; the lights are blotted out with a rag, darks are added, and values are balanced as detail is developed.

A variation of this exercise is to work on toned paper using white and black crayons, as Pierre-Paul Prud'hon did in the drawing shown at the beginning of the chapter.

Procedures

1. Cover the entire surface of the paper with an even middle tone. A good way to do this is to drag the side of a piece of charcoal lightly over the entire sheet. If you want a smooth finish, use a washrag to smooth out the surface.

2. Study the model to decide what areas on the figure are the lightest. Use an eraser to pull these shapes out of the gray surface of the paper.

3. Study the model again, and decide where on the edge of the figure the background is darker. Without using contour lines, apply areas of black to define these edges.

4. Review the drawing for errors in proportion. If you see any, correct them with the eraser and charcoal.

5. After you have drawn the larger forms, and if you approve of the figure's placement on the page, start developing the details. Do several of these drawings for thirty to forty-five minutes each.

Demonstration 3-2: A Three-Value Drawing on a Middle Tone

Visual 3–20 shows how I prepared the surface. I started by applying a rough layer of charcoal using the side of a stick of compressed charcoal. After that, I used a small square of cotton diaper, soft from dozens of washings, and saturated with carbon from blending other drawings, to smooth the charcoal out. Work on the surface until you get one you can live with, but don't waste time trying to make it perfectly smooth.

Study the model before you start drawing. Look for the lightest areas, and think about where you are going to put them on the page. Aim for making the figure large enough to fill the composition, with little of it extending off of the edges. When you have an idea of where the first light areas will go, use an eraser to remove these forms from the gray background. After you have installed this first white shape, study it and compare it to what you see on the model. If you can see any differences between the two forms, use your eraser and your dirty rag to make corrections.

Get into the habit of always fixing an error when you see it. It's true that sometimes a drawing won't survive the repair attempt, but over the longer term, the discipline of correcting mistakes will speed the improvement of your eye and drawing ability. Do not get too attached to the success of a particular drawing. At this point, a drawing is only successful if producing it has helped you gain skill.

In Visual 3–21, I have pulled out enough white that it is clear where the body is going to be on the paper and what its positioning will be. Notice that some edges are crisp and clear, and others are softer. We are working in a traditional chiaroscuro format in this exercise, and one of the conventions is that the

visual | 3–20 |

H. Stone, *Three-Value Drawing on a Middle Tone Demonstration, Step 1.*

visual | 3–21 |

H. Stone, *Three-Value Drawing on a Middle Tone Demonstration, Step 2.*

harder edges are in regions that are lit well, and softer edges are in the darker areas. Thomas Anshutz' drawing (Visual 3–2) is an example.

Starting by organizing the larger forms, instead of drawing a detailed area, allows you to make major corrections before you commit much time to the drawing. If I had been dismayed by my work to this point, I could have overhauled the composition without much trouble.

Visual 3–22 shows the figure after the first set of blacks was added. I started the foot by applying black around it to create a **reverse silhouette**, and then developed it by adding a few small black marks as details. The trick here is to apply as little black as possible, letting the image emerge out of the gray middle tone. The right arm was drawn by creating more white areas and a few black details. At this stage, the right shoulder and the lower edge of the torso look like I was cheating by using contour lines. Although they look like lines, they are long, thin black forms where the body touched the padding on the model stand. These were forms I saw, so I was allowed to draw them.

visual | 3–22 |

H. Stone, *Three-Value Drawing on a Middle Tone Demonstration, Step 3.*

The picture looks pretty close to its final self in Visual 3–23. The eraser has given the model's right foot a crisp white upper surface. Her left leg was drawn in the same fashion as the right, with a reverse silhouette and some erasing. The drawing at this point demonstrates just how little actual work you have to do to get an image. Most of what you see was created with a little erasing and a little smudging; and the structure is implied, rather than explicitly drawn. This magic trick of getting an image with minimal means is useful in a life drawing, where your drawing time is limited, and it is always interesting to look at.

visual | 3–23 |

H. Stone, *Three-Value Drawing on a Middle Tone Demonstration, Step 4.*

The drawing is finished in Visual 3–24. The main changes were in the background under the model and on the lower edge of the torso. I softened that edge because I thought it would help the figure to nestle more naturally into the cushions she is resting on, as well anchoring the figure better onto the surface of the paper. The background of the arm was darkened to clarify the hollow area behind it. Compare the finished drawing to the previous version. Do you see a difference in mood? Which version do you prefer?

Look at the Drawing

A toned background can give a drawing a sense of unity and good taste that many people mistake for quality. When you evaluate a drawing done on a toned background, it is important not to be distracted by the beauty of the technique. Be especially rigorous in looking at how clearly the forms are expressed. This is a

visual | 3–24 |

H. Stone, *Three-Value Drawing on a Middle Tone Demonstration, final version,* charcoal on paper, 24" × 18", 2003.

chiaroscuro exercise, so the drawing should imply the location of the light source. The light raking across the figure should create shadows that define the body's shapes. If the figure's shapes are clear and accurate, you have succeeded in the most important task.

Think about how your use of the surface contributes to the overall emotional tone of the drawing. Using a toned background, an artist can cause a human body to emerge as if by accident from a loose, chaotic background, similar to the way in which a sculptor roughs out a form from a block of marble. Alternatively, the figure can be sensitively articulated, on a smooth, controlled surface. One kind of finish is not better than the other. The surface of the drawing is successful according to how well it communicates your intentions.

In this exercise we want to see:

- The figure emerge from a gray background.
- Light areas made by erasing.
- Some blending and softening of edges.
- The implied location of a single light source.

We do not want to see:

- Any use of contour lines.
- Ambiguous areas that do not declare whether they are part of the figure or the background.
- Any forms that are not drawn from observation.

Michelangelo Buonarroti (1475–1564), *Head of a Satyr*, pen and brown ink on paper, 11.02" × 8.26", circa sixteenth century. *Louvre, Paris, France/ Giraudon/ The Bridgeman Art Library*

HATCHING

In the first two exercises in this chapter you worked with **mass tones**, which are solid shapes of a single value. You produced these by controlling the density of the charcoal on the paper. **Hatching,** or crosshatching, produces variations in value by creating networks of parallel lines, as Michelangelo did in Visual 3–25. Hatching lines are used to create an interesting, active surface, to contribute to the drawing's sense of mood, and as a medium for showing the artist's personal **calligraphy**.

Using hatching lines, you can create an active surface and accurately describe the model at the same time. Because hatching produces grays optically, by using arrays of solid lines that the eye will average into levels of gray, it is a good technique for making drawings that will be reproduced. If you are interested in fine art printmaking or drawing comics, you will want to make friends with this technique.

Visual 3–26 is a very loose hatching drawing

visual | 3–26 |

H. Stone, *Three-Value Drawing with Hatching*, charcoal on paper, 24" × 18", 2003.

made at the same drawing session as the first three-value demonstration, shown in Visual 3–18. Both pieces are three-value drawings, but they have different moods because of the way their surfaces look.

Hatching is a versatile technique that is naturally compatible with contour line drawings (Visual 3–27). Hatching lines can be used to make gradients as well as flat areas of tone; the lines can be thin or thick, long or short, and you can use them in layers to show subtleties of lighting or nuances of form in shadow areas.

Four-Value Drawing

Four-value drawing, also called four tone-drawing, is a way of enhancing the definition of three-dimensional forms in a chiaroscuro drawing by showing the effects of reflected light. Four values is not a limit on the number of tones that can be used in the drawing; it is a way of classifying the different kinds of light and shadow. The four values, from lightest to darkest, are highlight, reflected light, deep shadow, and cast shadow. This technique can be

visual | 3–27 |

H. Stone, *Contour Line Drawing with Hatching*, steel nib and India ink on paper, 17" × 14" (sheet size), 2003.

visual | 3–28 |

H. Stone, *Four-Value Drawing*, compressed charcoal on Rives BFK paper, 30" × 22" 1998.

applied rigidly, with every bulging form subject to its analysis, but more often it is manifested in a lightening of shadow areas so that details of form don't get lost there. Visual 3–27 shows reflected light effects in the figure's back and arms, and Visual 3–28 shows all four values used in a compressed charcoal drawing.

The close-up of the head and shoulders in Visual 3–29 shows how the four values are used in this drawing. The light is coming from the model's left and creates highlight areas on the left side of her face. As the form curves away from the light, it darkens into the deep shadow areas, which we see in the center of the forehead, down the bridge of the nose, and near the center of the chin. The side of the model's face

visual | 3–29 |

H. Stone, *Four-Value Drawing (Detail)*, compressed charcoal on Rives BFK paper, 30" × 22", 1998.

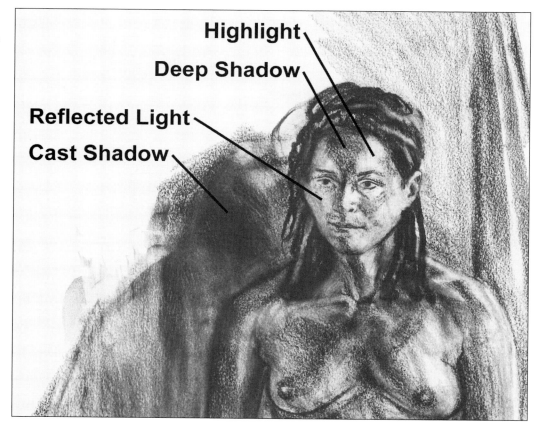

closer to the wall is a little lighter where the light reflecting back from the wall illuminates it. The darkest shadow is the one the head casts onto the wall.

Using the four-tone drawing system creates a **figure-ground relationship**, which is a dialog between the figure and the background that helps the figure fit into the composition. The line drawing with four-tone hatching in Visual 3–30 shows how this can work. The portion of the drawing above the sleeping woman reads as space behind her, and the shadows she is casting onto the model stand give us a sense of the depth and shape of the space in front of her. Compare this drawing with Visual 3–31, which is the same drawing with the figure's cast shadows removed. The space behind the model still works, but it is not clear whether the place in front of her is supposed to be a continuation of the surface she is resting on or a bare area of paper. This ambiguity creates instability in the drawing that contradicts the sense of repose coming from the model. The drawing is no longer balanced and consistent.

Four-value drawing has been so useful in art that filmmakers have swiped it to use in creepy movies and police procedurals. Next time you watch a thriller, take note of how often you see a face with a highlight, a darker shadow, and a lighter shadow. Sometimes they will light the two sides of the face in different colors to emphasize the effect. If you see a lighting scheme you like, make a quick drawing of it, and try it when you get in front of a model.

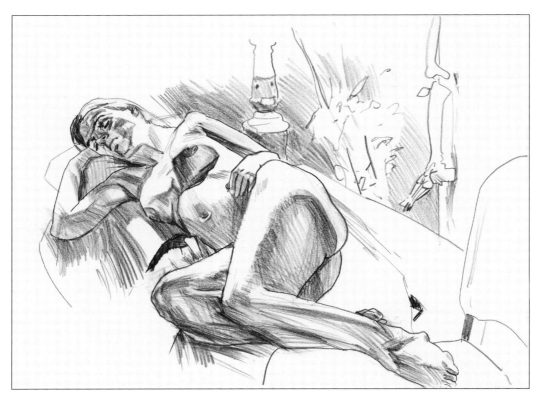

visual | 3–30 |

H. Stone, *Four-Value Drawing*, pencil on Rives BFK paper, 30" × 22", 1998.

A four-value drawing with the most of the cast shadows removed.

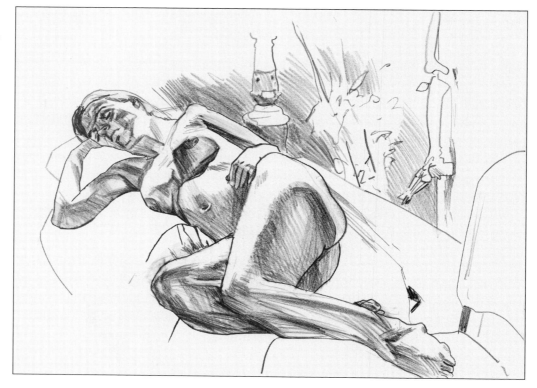

Exercise 3-3: Four-Value Drawing with Hatching

This exercise gives you practice applying hatching lines in layers to create a four-tone drawing.

Materials

- Several sharp 6B pencils.
- Pink, polymer, and kneaded erasers, preferably fairly clean.
- A pad of everyday paper, 18" × 24" or larger.

Procedures

1. Do not use contour lines for this exercise.

2. Do not use **smooth shading**. Use hatching lines to create all grays.

3. Keep your hatching loose, and apply it at the speed that feels right for you.

4. Feel free to use your eraser.

5. The first few times you try this, work for twenty minutes. It may be helpful to draw parts of the body at first, rather than the entire figure. Extend the time when you feel ready.

6. If you want to, try some hatching drawings using a pen. A ballpoint pen is an invaluable tool for drawing people in the park, in coffee shops, and in business meetings.

Demonstration 3-3: A Four-Value Drawing Created with Hatching

As in first two exercises in this chapter, we will develop larger forms first and then make successive corrections until we are happy with the drawing, or we run out of time. Visual 3–32 shows my beginning, a set of hatching lines on what will become the model's face. I chose to

visual | 3–32 |

H. Stone, *Four-Value Drawing with Hatching Demonstration, Step 1.*

draw a portrait in profile for this picture, but you may want to draw something else. I did this drawing for forty minutes.

Visual 3–33 shows the drawing three or four minutes after starting. The reverse silhouette of the face is working out well, but the squiggly dark form along the jaw looks more like a beard than a deep shadow area. The deep shadows in a four-tone drawing usually require some balancing before they look right, and this one is no exception. It has to go.

Step 3 (Visual 3–34) shows the completed face, hairline, and ear. The eye is very simply drawn. The ear is a little more complex. When you draw small, detailed areas, use the three-value technique and you won't go wrong. This stage of the drawing shows where I went wrong, in my second attempt to draw the chin. My friend still

visual | 3–33 |

H. Stone, *Four-Value Drawing with Hatching Demonstration, Step 2.*

visual | 3–34 |

H. Stone, *Four-Value Drawing with Hatching Demonstration, Step 3.*

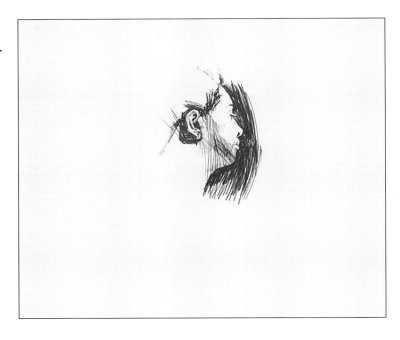

needs a shave. I'm going in again....

Visual 3–35 is more like it. I dug out all of the previous hatching with a pink eraser and took it easy when I redrew it, and this time it seemed to work. The four tones are all present now: the deep shadow and reflected light on the chin and neck, and the cast shadow on the breastbone. I drew the hair by quickly scratching in the darkest shapes on the figure and background. The drawing isn't bad now, and I could declare it done, but that dark cast shadow behind the ear didn't exactly fit in.

To balance the ear, I developed the shadow behind it, which the hair was casting onto the neck (Visual 3–36). This inspired me to build out the forms of the hair nearest the face and neck. I also worked a little more on the darkest parts of the neck to make the line of deep shadow along the jaw look a little less conspicuous. It would be fair to call the drawing done now

visual | 3–35 |

H. Stone, *Four-Value Drawing with Hatching Demonstration, Step 4.*

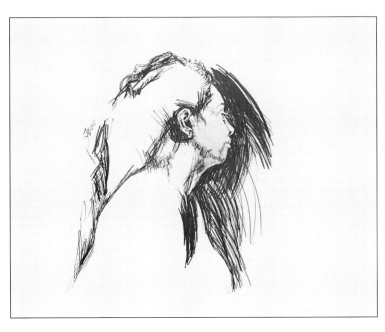

because the forms of the face are adequately defined, but I didn't feel the drawing well enough represented the subject as an African American woman. To do this better would mean balancing her black hair and brown skin with the conditions of light as they exist in this state of the drawing. In other words, I got interested in incorporating local color effects into the picture.

Visual 3–37 shows the finished drawing. Correcting her skin color meant deepening the shadow on her jaw line; filling out the shadows around her eyes, nose and mouth; and softening the transition of her face from shadows to highlights. I did this by using a fresh, sharp pencil to add a few layers of fine lines. These lines had to be added selectively; there isn't a formula for making someone's skin tone darker. To place the hatching, I responded to the values as I saw them at that time and place.

visual | 3–36 |

H. Stone, *Four-Value Drawing with Hatching Demonstration, Step 5.*

Look at the Drawing

Part of the appeal of a hatching drawing is the visual conflict that occurs when a clear image is visible in an agitated, accidental-looking environment. In evaluating a hatching drawing, look for all three of these things: a likeness of some sort, a level of authority in the stroke, and how the drawing reconciles the two.

How do you know if your stroke has authority? If you were able to loosely draw your hatching lines without inhibitions, you probably made some interesting marks that you recognize as belonging to you in the same way that your signature does. Do your marks look confident, or tentative? Hatching lines that are personal and drawn with assurance can be said to have authority.

visual | 3–37 |

H. Stone, *Four-Value Drawing with Hatching Demonstration, final version,* pencil on paper, 18" × 24", 2006.

The relationship the drawing establishes between the recognizable image and the **calligraphy** of the strokes is, like many qualities in art, subjective and impossible to evaluate using a set of policies. Does it diminish a drawing if the image is barely visible? It is common for artists to hide a figure in a field of hatching, and seeing it emerge is part of the experience of the work. On the other hand, what if the figure is well articulated, but the hatching lines are so restrained as to be almost invisible? The history of art is full of such drawings. It is your sense of visual balance that will make this relationship work, and you develop this sense by practicing.

In this exercise, we are looking for:

- A recognizable structure. Your drawing does not have to be perfect, but a viewer should be able to identify what you were drawing.
- Identifiable areas of light, deep shadow, reflected light, and cast shadow.
- All values created by hatching lines instead of smooth shading.
- Hatching lines applied with confidence.

We are not looking for:

- Any use of contour lines.
- Any use of smooth shading.
- An absence of reflected light areas.
- Areas that are not identifiable as either figure or background.

CHAPTER SUMMARY

Value is the level of light or dark in a region of a drawing. Value drawing is creating an image with masses and gradients of black, white, and gray. When you draw the values in a scene, you are reproducing something that your eye literally sees, unlike contour lines, which are abstract constructions. Value affects the sense of realism in a drawing, and it also can be used to establish structure and mood.

Value is used in drawing in two ways. Chiaroscuro drawing is rendering form by drawing the effects of light on the form. Modeling is using value to describe the body's three-dimensional shapes sculpturally, without regard to the sources of illumination in the scene. The three-value exercise is a chiaroscuro drawing that reduces all of the visible values to black, middle gray, and white. This exercise is used for developing drawing skill and as a way of creating studies for other works of art. Four-value drawing is a type of chiaroscuro drawing that emphasizes the kinds of light and shadow striking the form, instead of the absolute levels of brightness.

Value drawings are made by using the side of the drawing instrument to create a smooth finish or by building up a network of lines that optically blend to form masses of gray. Lines used in this way to create values are called hatching lines.

▶ *chapter questions*

Multiple Choice

1. The picture in Visual 3–38 is a:

   a. Chiaroscuro drawing.

   b. Modeling drawing.

2. Imagine that two horizontal lines divides Visual 3–38 into three equal parts. Which section contains violations of the drawing procedures in this chapter?

   a. Top third.

   b. Middle third.

   c. Bottom third.

3. Four-value drawing:

   a. Is a form of hatching drawing.

   b. Is a form of chiaroscuro drawing.

   c. Is a form of modeling drawing.

   d. Is a form of contour drawing.

4. Your hatching lines have authority:

   a. If they have been applied very aggressively.

   b. If they look like Michelangelo's.

   c. If they are recognizable as yours.

   d. If they all look the same.

5. To draw various colors of skin:

   a. Make the highlight colors proportionally lighter or darker.

   b. Draw the forms in the usual way, and then darken the entire figure until it matches the subject.

   c. Leave the lightest and darkest areas alone and work only with the middle tones.

   d. Draw the values as you see them at the time.

visual | 3–38 |

H. Stone, *Drawing for Chapter Three Questions,* compressed charcoal on paper, 24" × 18", 2005.

6. Hatching:

   a. Can be done with a pen.

   b. Should not be tried with compressed charcoal.

   c. Must be done according to a strict set of procedures.

   d. All of the above.

7. Local color:

   a. Can change the contour of a form.

   b. Is present in every value drawing.

   c. Is present in every modeling drawing.

   d. Can affect the value of the form.

8. Traditional life drawing:

   a. Was invented by a single artist.

   b. Was invented approximately 500 years ago.

   c. Does not use contour lines.

   d. Is not being practiced today.

9. Academic life drawing:

   a. Is a style of traditional drawing that started in the middle 1800s.

   b. Is a style of traditional drawing that started in England.

   c. Is a style of traditional drawing that gets its name from a French organization.

   d. Is a nontraditional style of drawing.

10. Chiaroscuro drawing:

   a. Was invented long before modeling drawing.

   b. Was invented at about the same time as modeling drawing.

   c. Was invented long after modeling drawing.

   d. Is not used in modern life drawing.

H. Stone, *Gesture Drawing*, sumi ink on paper,
14" × 24", 2005.

CHAPTER 4

objectives

- Understand the use of gesture in life drawing.
- Explore the metaphor of balance in the standing human figure.
- Learn and practice gesture exercises.
- Practice drawing with a sumi brush.
- Integrate gesture with other drawing skills by creating a palimpsest drawing.

introduction

Gesture is implied movement in a pose. Tensed and relaxed muscles cooperate to make standing, moving, and balancing possible, and gesture drawing creates an abstract representation of this dynamic process. Each artist must invent a personal set of techniques for gesture drawing; it is part seeing and part feeling, and a little like dancing.

We do gesture drawings to learn to give our figures a convincing sense of weight, but another benefit of mastering gesture is the connection it makes between the artist's emotions and drawing skill. Gesture is the process by which the artist identifies with the model. It brings structure, authority, and truthfulness to the artist's personal drawing style.

GESTURE IS EMPATHY

How does it make you feel to look at someone? Tell me with your charcoal. Place its point on the paper, and use your hand to create a movement whose topic is the model. Just look, and move. This drawing that you made, the record of your connection to the model, is called a gesture drawing.

Gesture is the sense of movement of a pose. Considering that in life drawing, we almost always draw people who are doing their best to remain still, what could the "movement" of a static body position refer to? The movement of a pose is the interaction of stressed and unstressed areas of the body to achieve balance.

The human body moves by operating muscles in pairs. For example, for an arm to move, a muscle must flex, and another one must relax. You can feel this cooperation at work by placing one of your hands on the front of your other upper arm. Use that arm to pick up a fairly heavy book, and you will feel that muscle, the *biceps brachii*, tighten. While you are holding the book, feel the back of your upper arm. The muscle there, the *triceps brachii*, will be relaxed. Bring your arm up and push the book toward the ceiling, and the working relationship will reverse, with the biceps relaxed and the triceps taut.

Think about the complex interactions that occur when a movement requires many muscles. Twisting the torso to the left or right requires a group of muscles to shorten, to tug the shoulders and upper back around, while other muscles must relax and lengthen, to release these structures and allow them to turn. In addition, when muscles tighten, they place joints under stress, which causes them to subtly change shape. For a person to stand, the body must manage a complex interaction of structures and musculature. Gesture drawing is making a statement of the way that muscles cooperate to keep the body at equilibrium.

Gesture drawing expresses the artist's concise experience of the model. Instead of patiently creating an objective record of the model's musculature and features, the artist rapidly summarizes the body's attitude. Gesture drawing can be exhilarating. You move with freedom and generosity, and your marks are charged with meaning. You seek the true poetry of drawing, and you will find it in yourself, as you develop the capacity to see with empathy.

Because it creates its own means of expressing a subjective impression, gesture drawing is a type of **abstract** art. Visual 4–1 demonstrates this. In this two-minute gesture drawing, there are a few straight lines in the legs and torso, and these lines seem to be repeated in a few places, as if they did not get positioned right the first time. Some places on the figure have contour lines, and some do not, and the lines that do exist don't show much detail. The gray mass in the torso does not give a sense of where the light is coming from. How can we evaluate such a drawing?

Start by studying what the drawing tells you about the position of the model's body. What side of the standing figure are we looking at? Is there a twist in the torso? Which leg is holding up most of the weight? Using the drawing as a guide, could you stand in the same position? If you can answer any of these questions, the drawing must be communicating something, but it is not easy to describe how it works.

When we draw contour and value, we are trying to precisely draw shapes as we see them. To make a descriptive drawing with either of these techniques, we must respond as directly as possible to the visual information our eye relays to us. The basic skill we have to develop in order to draw this way is seeing objectively, without judgments or preconceptions. If we have the skill of seeing, training the hand to obey is simply a matter of practice.

With gesture drawing, the information we are looking for is interpreted by our minds and bodies as we make our marks. We briefly study the pose, try to feel it in our own bodies, and try to express empathy for it on the paper. We look for areas of stress and heighten them with marks on paper. We work furiously on some areas of the body at the expense of others. Gesture drawing is a stream-of-consciousness activity whose goal is to create an abstract equivalent to the model's stance. Like life itself, a gesture drawing has to be improvised, with no means of slowing the process down or creating a fixed reference.

H. Stone, *Gesture Drawing*, charcoal on paper, 8" × 10", 2005.

Communicating Gesture

You have made a gesture drawing, and it was good. You covered a piece of paper with lyrical marks, and it felt right. Now let's send this drawing to a focus group. Would the group be able to agree on what these marks mean, or would each person in the group have a different interpretation? Would they consider the drawing a masterpiece of nonverbal communication, or an exercise in existential self-indulgence? Making yourself understood is one of the fundamental problems you will face as an artist. You get to choose how you will define this problem for yourself, but each work of art you create will hold you accountable for your choices. Will the work say what you want it to say? Is the work as smart as you are?

Unless it was your intention to mystify your audience, you probably would prefer that people agree on what this drawing represents. If they don't, your descriptive powers have fallen short.

visual | 4–2 |

Francisco José de Goya y Lucientes (1746–1828), *Love and Death (Caprichos no. 10: El Amor y la Muerte)*, Etching with Aquatint, 8.46" × 5.9", 1799. *Private Collection / The Bridgeman Art Library*

El amor y la muerte.

One traditional way to place content in art is to use the human figure in a kind of pantomime. Francisco Goya does this in Visual 4–2, in an etching called *Love and Death.* We see a man in some distress, a woman cradling him, and a sword on the ground in a deserted setting. We don't need to be able to read the Spanish title to understand that a duel has ended badly.

The dying person at stage center gives us a clue that the piece has a serious theme, but a weighty topic does not by itself make a great work of art. The meaning of the piece is conveyed in the way it is executed. The area of emphasis is the man's torso and the embrace that supports it. As we study his stance, we can see that the stiffness in his legs is the only life visible in his body: his arm hangs limply, and he slumps over onto his date. His right knee is stressed in a last attempt to keep him upright as his strength ebbs away. With a little imagination, we can feel the coldness and hardness of the stone as his lower back presses into it. Goya connects the duelist's death with physical sensations we all can share.

A narrative picture about dueling could have several messages: it could celebrate a triumph over the bad guy, or it could be an encouragement to practice one's swordsmanship. Narrative art can be, like a military march, intended for a literal-minded audience, but Goya's mastery of the movement in the central figure makes his meaning clear: this is a tragic event that did not need to happen.

Goya's piece uses both narrative and drawing technique to communicate a focused message about a social problem. In Visual 4–3, Rembrandt reduces the story to a minimum and relies entirely on his drawing skill to carry the meaning of the picture. The subject of the drawing is most likely Rembrandt's common-law wife, Hendrickje Stoffels. She isn't on a stage, or being used to tell a story; she is taking a nap in her own house. By choosing to draw a portrait of real person in her usual setting, Rembrandt commits himself to truthfulness as he observes it.

The image was drawn with a brush in an ink called bistre, made from water and soot. The drawing uses chiaroscuro, with the light source from above left. The face and hair are rendered in a straightforward three-tone technique. The drawing constructs the torso, arms, and ankle with solid, confident brush strokes that are not exactly contour lines, and not exactly mass tones. They define the body's position very specifically, yet we are also aware of them as abstract, spontaneously applied marks. This drawing holds our attention with the clarity of the image and the beauty of the strokes used to make it.

It is always interesting to see the human figure drawn with great economy, and in this picture Rembrandt did pull a rabbit out of a hat. Is the drawing more than a technical trick? Rembrandt is drawing a scene familiar to anyone who has been married, but in spite of the informality of the setting, Rembrandt is not taking the moment for granted. His attentiveness is visible in every part of the drawing: in her headband, her hairline, the values in her face, and the gathering of her clothes. The drawing is not a study of intimacy; it is an expression of intimacy, and the care he takes in drawing it allows us, in a sense, to participate.

Exercise 4-1: Drawing Gesture with a Sumi Brush

Learning to draw gesture is partly connecting your own body to the movement you see in the pose, and partly developing a vocabulary of marks that express movement convincingly. In other words, it is learning how to render gesture with empathy and authority. These are your personal qualities, rather than the model's, so you will have to construct your own way of drawing them.

The purpose of this first gesture exercise is to help you develop authority in your stroke. In Chapter 3, your hatching lines were said to have authority if you could recognize them as your own. In this exercise you will continue to practice making marks with intention and confidence, using an instrument created for the purpose, the sumi brush. The sumi brush is used for Asian calligraphy, an art form in which an artist's use of the brush is considered to demonstrate the individual's character, lyricism, and power.

visual | 4–4 |

Judy Stone Nunneley, *Detail of Gesture Drawing* (see Visual 4–9), sumi ink on paper, 2006.

A sumi pen and
brush.

Materials

- Sumi brush. A sumi brush is made of various types of animal hair glued into a bamboo tube. Get a fairly large one, with a tube as big around as your finger. You don't need an expensive one for this exercise.

- Sumi ink. Sumi ink is composed of carbon black, water, and water-soluble glue. It is very black when used undiluted, and it is a beautiful gray when used in washes. Use it black in this exercise. Don't use India inks or other types of ink for this exercise because they are likely to contain a varnish that will stiffen the brush and make it hard to clean.

- Drawing paper. Traditionally, this exercise is done with newsprint, but it will look better on white paper. You can use your everyday pad, but the insider's choice is commercial printing paper, which is just as cheap as newsprint, much whiter, and more stable. It isn't archival, but the sheets are larger, which is preferable for this exercise. Often a large commercial printing company will have leftovers that they will let you have. Go to the back door and ask. To use them, clip a ¼-inch stack of sheets onto a drawing board and replenish them as necessary.

- Yogurt cup or other small cup for ink. Glue or tape its base to a square of cardboard so it won't easily tip over.

- Paper towels.

- A coffee can or large plastic cup for water.

Procedures

1. Inspect the brush. Feel the hair. If you have used a bristle brush or watercolor brush, you may notice that the sumi brush is less springy than they are.

2. Put a little more than an inch of ink into the small cup you have taped to the cardboard. You won't pour leftover ink back into the bottle, so keep adding to the little cup as you need it.

3. Prime the brush by dipping it in clean water.

4. Shake the excess water off of the brush and dip the brush into the ink. Spend five minutes experimenting with the kind of marks you can make with this brush. Keeping the brush filled with ink, make thin marks and thick marks, and fast marks and slow marks. Make some strokes that go from thin to thick and vice versa. Pay attention to how the marks change as the brush uses up its ink. Make the marks large, extending over most of the paper, and using your entire arm, rather than just your hand or wrist. If you can practice making strokes with your hand, arm, and upper torso, it will help you draw the model's proportions more accurately.

5. The first series of poses will be for thirty seconds each. When the model takes a pose, spend ten seconds or so studying it. Look for areas that are stiff or flexed and areas that are relaxed. Rotate your drawing board to best fit the pose from your point of view.

6. When you are ready, make one quick, spontaneous mark that summarizes the movement of the pose. Look at your drawing and the pose, and make another quick mark or two to complete your summary.

7. This is an abstract exercise, so forget about how the drawing will look and concentrate on feeling the movement in the pose and making one mark that summarizes it. Don't make contour lines—think of this as more of a poetic stick figure. Use the entire sheet, one sheet per pose, and as you get done with each drawing, throw it on the floor, preferably ink side up.

8. Do ten of these thirty-second drawings, and then take five minutes or so looking at everyone else's. Don't dig through their piles of drawings, just take a quick look over what they have been doing and then get back to work.

9. Do twenty more thirty-second drawings. Pick out two or three that you consider to be the best ones. In an abstract exercise such as this, how can you tell which ones are best? The best drawings will feel right—they will affirm that they directly and honestly communicate the essence of the pose.

10. Never leave a sumi brush, or any kind of brush for that matter, sitting in water. When you aren't using it, rinse it, shake it, and lay it on its side on the paper towel.

Look at the Drawings

When the drawings are dry, post the ones you selected so that everyone can see them. If you are shy about having everyone look at your drawing, remember that these sessions are for practice and that this exercise is a means to an end. Turn off your internal critic, tell your performance anxiety to shove off, and think of this session as a time of helpful, positive teamwork.

There isn't one single correct way to do this exercise. Because of the very short drawing time, there will be no details or sense of the lighting. One of the purposes of the exercise is to help you develop an honest, personal drawing style, so it is normal to struggle to find the stroke you are looking for, and if the struggle is visible in the drawing, so much the better.

In this exercise, we are looking for:

- Authority in the stroke. Would you define the stroke as confident, or tentative? Was it executed quickly and smoothly? Does it suggest that it looks the way the artist wanted it to?

- A sense of what the pose was. It is interesting how a few strokes can communicate the model's position. Could you take the pose yourself, using the drawing as a guide?

- A figure that fits comfortably on the page. Does it fill the sheet, or is it small, floating on the page? If the marks are made primarily with the wrist and hand, they will probably have neither the size nor the urgency we are looking for.

Matthew Rivard,
*Student Gesture
Drawing,* sumi
ink on paper.

Let's use our three criteria to analyze drawings that four students made at the same time, from the same pose. Starting on the right side of the room, with Visual 4–6, Matthew Rivard has made a solid, dark stroke, which shows the entire figure in profile from head to foot. He shows the body's balance and weight with some subtlety, drawing a sharp right angle for one knee, a softer one for the other, and a slight torsion in the body. Although the positioning of the arms is not entirely clear, it would not be difficult to assume the rest of this pose using the drawing as a guide. The drawing does nicely fill the page.

The next drawing around the circle is Megan Garner's, in Visual 4–7. Her stroke is also good and solid, and it has a distinctive, flowing curviness. By showing how the model must lean back to maintain balance, her drawing communicates a sense of the weight pressing the model's knees into the padding on the floor. Garner's drawing defines the pose quite clearly, including the elbows, the flex in the calves, and the slight hyperextension of the left ankle.

The next drawing, in Visual 4–8, is a front view by Bryan Hudson. The first stroke started at the model's neck, moved down the body in a gentle S-curve to the left knee, and continued

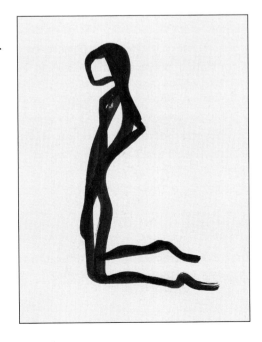

Megan Garner,
*Student Gesture
Drawing,* sumi
ink on paper.

back to the ankle and foot. Hudson's drawing also gives a convincing sense of how the body's weight is held up by the legs, but it does so by placing a convex bend in the thighs, so that they contain a tension almost like that of a flexed leaf spring.

Visual 4–9, by Judy Stone Nunneley, uses angular strokes, applied with confidence, to summarize the pose. Like the others' drawings, hers is complete and demonstrates how the pose achieves stability by leaning the torso and shoulders back to balance the forward thrust of the hips and by tilting the head forward.

All of these drawings meet the objectives of the assignment, and yet each of them is drawn in a distinctive way. Each of these artists tells a personal story from a common set of facts. The drawings have in common the theme of balance.

THE METAPHOR OF BALANCE

The Metaphor of Balance is Western culture's great contribution to the world's visual art.

Although many cultures create balanced compositions in their art, the idea of balance as an active process, requiring attention and vigilance, originated at the beginning of the Western humanist tradition, in Classical-era Greece, 450–323 B.C.E. This period was the first time in history that the position assumed by a relaxed, standing person had been accurately observed and rendered in art.

visual | 4–8 |

Bryan Hudson, *Student Gesture Drawing,* sumi ink on paper.

Doryphoros (Visual 4–10) is an exact Roman copy of a Greek bronze created by Polykleitos during the Classical period. It is the product of close study of human anatomy, proportion, and body mechanics. One leg is straight and carries most of the body's weight. The other is bent, causing the pelvis to laterally tilt, while the shoulders tilt in the opposite direction. The torso's balance is a dynamic process, maintained by the cooperation of flexed and relaxed muscles.

For the ancient Greeks, balance was a concept vital to civilized art, architecture, literature, music, politics, and personal conduct. A standing, unclothed human figure was for them a concise statement of the interconnectedness of all intellectual effort.

visual | 4–9 |

Judy Stone Nunneley, *Student Gesture Drawing,* sumi ink on paper.

Contrapposto

The standing position of the Doryphoros is called **contrapposto**, or weight-shift. Balance as an active relationship between the body's structures is clearly visible in the contrapposto stance. The body in contrapposto is not in a state of repose; it is held in position by forces balancing each other and by tensed muscles cooperating with relaxed ones. Drawing this state of muscular

give and take in a convincing way is one of the more interesting challenges in life drawing.

Visual 4–10 and Visual 4–11 are contrapposto images made 2400 years apart. If you would like to immediately become part of the Classical tradition, you can do so by adopting a contrapposto stance yourself. Stand up without leaning on anything, imagine that you are waiting in a long line, and observe your position. Look down: if one of your feet is positioned directly below your head, you are in a contrapposto stance. One leg is straight, and holding up most of your weight. The other leg will either be bent, or a little in front of or behind your body, or both. As you settle into the pose, your hips will tilt a little to one side, and your shoulders will tilt the other way to keep you in balance.

People get into contrapposto positions so that they can rest one leg while standing on the other. As you stand in this pose, notice where your body feels the most stress. As you maintain the pose for a longer time, you feel these stressed areas more clearly. Can you tell the difference between stresses occurring in muscles and those that occur in joints? When you get tired, shift the pose so that your weight is predominantly on the other leg. Do the stressed areas in your second pose mirror those in the first?

Exercise 4-2: Stress–Gesture Drawing

There are many ways to demonstrate a sense of balance in a life drawing, such as balancing line and value, or figure and background, but the most important one is showing the literal balance of the figure. This balance is the visible effect of the forces coming from the figure and acting on the figure. A solid, stable figure depends on how well the artist was able to observe and render the way the particular pose achieves its balance.

Visual 4–13 shows two drawings of a standing figure, drawn by David Park. The picture on the right is a contour line drawing, and the one on the left emphasizes gesture. In this drawing, which has little detail or refinement of surface, the standing figure demonstrates an extraordinary sense of solidity. A look at the forces affecting the pose can give us a clue how it does this. The primary force, of course, is gravity. We can see its effect on the figure's straight leg: in contrast to the rounder forms used to draw the rest of the figure, the leg's inner contour is angular. The effect of rigidity this creates is reinforced by the emphatic, repeated vertical strokes of gray and black along that edge. The foot widens and flattens, yielding to the downward force communicated by the leg.

The upper body is held in a state of contained tension by the tilting of the head and shoulders, as they lean to the right, against the rigidity of the leg. It is easy to visualize the spine as an archers' bow at maximum pull. The backbone pushes the pelvis down onto the hip, and the pelvis tilts in response. The pose settles into a somewhat impatient-looking contrapposto stance. The subtlety and power of this drawing come from Park's sensitivity to the way that the masses and forces of the model's body interact to achieve equilibrium.

The best artists will figure out their own way of drawing balance. It is a skill that is part thinking and part feeling, and it is developed by looking and practicing. Drawing the movement of the pose, as you did in Exercise 4-1, is a great start, and the stress-gesture exercise builds on that foundation.

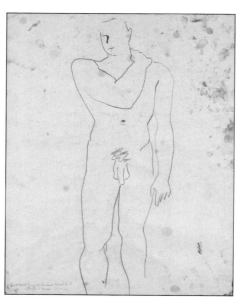

visual | 4–12 |

H. Stone, *Summary and Example of the Elements of Gesture,* compressed charcoal on paper, 18" × 36", 2004.

visual | 4–13 |

David Park, *Male Nudes: a Double-Sided Drawing,* oil and black ink on paper, 16.5" × 13.25", 1966. © *The Estate of David Park. Photography by PHOCASSO / J.W. White.*

Materials

- Paper as in Exercise 4-1.
- Compressed charcoal.

Procedures

1. This exercise has two parts, both performed at top speed. If possible, work while standing at an easel. Draw with your entire arm, and resist the temptation to draw contour lines.

2. The first part of the exercise is a very quick (no more than fifteen seconds) summary of the movement of the pose, in the same way you did with the sumi brush. In other words, make one or two quick marks to express the essence of the pose. Don't be afraid to exaggerate the movement: make angular forms more angular, and rounded forms more round.

3. The second part is very quickly drawing the regions of stress. Study the pose, looking for areas that are twisted, flexed, or holding up weight. Express these stresses by drawing on top of the couple of marks you made in Step 1.

4. You will be inventing your own drawing vocabulary, so don't allow yourself to become inhibited. Experiment with scribbling, pressing hard, moving your hand fast, and moving it slow. When something feels right and natural, repeat and practice it.

5. Do a series of ten drawings of two minutes apiece.

Look at the Drawings

Because the point of this exercise is to communicate a sense of the body's mechanics through an abstract set of marks, there are many correct ways of doing it. Evaluating a stress gesture drawing is kind of like evaluating music. It can be hard to describe how one performance is deeper or more authentic than another, but knowledgeable people will tend to agree on which one is better.

In a stress-gesture drawing, we are looking for:

- A generally clear drawing. Are all of the important structures present? Are there areas of ambiguity that don't seem to contribute to the sense of the whole? Are the marks confident? A good gesture drawing will be satisfying even though it lacks detail.

- A sense of how the model's weight was distributed in the pose. Which leg is supporting more weight? Does the figure seem to settle into its setting?

- An immediate sense of which areas are tense and which ones are relaxed. If the drawing communicates this well, you won't have to wonder which is supposed to be which.

We are not looking for:

- A contour drawing.
- A chiaroscuro drawing.
- Areas of detail.

I am leading off by discussing one of my own stress-gesture drawings because I can say with confidence what I was thinking as I drew it. The first part of the exercise, summarizing the pose, is shown in Visual 4–14. Starting off, I gave the pose a quick look, taking note of the tilt and positioning of the hips, shoulders, and legs. I made my summary, still keeping an eye on the model.

The summary drawing balances the abstract marks, which are interesting for their own sake, with the recognizable description of the pose. Making this first set of marks interesting is a matter of making an empathetic connection to the pose. When you try this for the first time, you may be at a loss for how to make this connection. I did it by imagining what it would feel like to take that pose myself and then trying to actually feel those sensations in my drawing arm. This is a skill that develops with practice, so don't feel inhibited. Keep your hand moving, and be sensitive to when the drawing starts to feel right.

In this case, the first part of the drawing came out as a fairly deliberate, careful-looking set of lines. On another day, it could be an aggressive set of lines appearing almost instantly and looking much like lightning bolts, a cloud with arms and legs, or an explosion in the neoclassical style.

Visual 4–15 is the finished drawing. I used the side of the charcoal stick to create some middle grays to fill out the figure and provide some smoother marks to indicate some of the more relaxed areas. My strategy for drawing the stressed areas was to make dark, abrupt marks, which you can see in the pelvis and lower back. The jagged line across the chest was intended to indicate the torsion in the shoulders. In this drawing I was paying particular attention to keeping the blacks clearly differentiated from the grays, to help prevent the forms from getting diluted or ambiguous.

visual | 4–14 |

H. Stone, *Stress-Gesture Drawing, Part 1*, compressed charcoal on paper, 22" × 30", 2005.

visual | 4–15 |

H. Stone, *Stress-Gesture Drawing, Part 2*, compressed charcoal on paper, 22" × 30", 2005.

Is this drawing generally clear? I would say so. It wouldn't be too hard to assume the same pose as the figure from the information the drawing gives us. Does the drawing give a sense of how the weight is distributed? It does, but it could be better. I think it would be more successful if I had properly drawn in the model's left foot. As it is, the leg does not quite connect itself to the floor; therefore, the figure's masses do not plausibly find an anchor, and the drawing is not as solid overall as I would like for it to be. Does the drawing immediately communicate tension in some areas and relaxation in others? I think so because the tense, or stressed, areas are consistently black, and they are drawn with more urgency than the gray areas.

If a drawing makes a good first impression, and I can continue to look at it without picking out problems, I consider it to be fairly well balanced. According to these criteria, this drawing is successful.

Nunneley's drawing (Visual 4–16) uses angular and round forms to express the stressed and relaxed regions of the pose. The biggest curve in the drawing is the exaggerated bend of the spine, and the upper body is assembled on this bow in much the same way as in David Park drawing (Visual 4–14). The two legs meet at a sharp, uncompromising point, which is the visual center of the drawing. The straight leg is composed of a subtle S-curve with a bulge at the top, where the thigh is. The pelvis and its tilt are indicated by a quickly drawn circle with a line cutting across it.

Is the drawing generally clear? Yes, it is. The figure is complete, and all visible parts are drawn with confidence. There are not any marks that do not seem to have a purpose or contribute to the sense of the whole. Does the drawing give a sense of the weight distribution? Again, yes. The drawing has one rigid leg and one relaxed one, with the shoulders and spine doing their part to counterbalance them. From this drawing's point of view, it is impossible to name which leg is the straight one, but you could adopt this pose, or its mirror image, using this drawing as a plan. Does the drawing immediately communicate tension in some areas and relaxation in others? You could touch the various parts of the drawing and say instantly whether they are tense or relaxed, so the answer is yes.

Rivard created this somewhat understated drawing (Visual 4–17) working from the same pose in the same session as Nunneley's, in Visual 4–16. The darkest part of the drawing is the large X composed by the crossed legs. He emphasizes the stress here with repeated, focused strokes. Although the model's right foot is shown very minimally, with one line, its positioning is the key to the torsion, or twist, of

visual | 4–16 |

Judy Stone Nunneley, *Student Stress-Gesture Drawing*, charcoal on paper, 22" × 30", 2004.

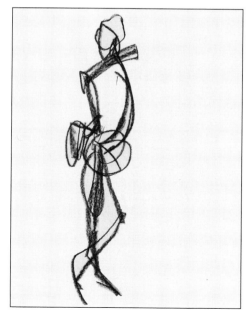

the leg. In contrast, the upper body is described by a very few well-placed lines.

In completing Rivard's scorecard, we would conclude that yes, the drawing is generally clear. It is satisfying to look at. The structures are mostly complete, and the use of the medium is confident, without any lines that seem to lack purpose. The drawing plausibly carries most of the weight on the straighter leg, but as in my drawing, its expression of the model's weight would be improved by the inclusion of both feet. This drawing excels in its statement of the tension and relaxation in the pose. The lower half of the body is dark and as strained as a pair of pliers pulling a tooth. The upper half is light and casually drawn. Rivard's drawing expresses the figure's dynamics by a change of mood between the stressed and relaxed areas.

visual | 4–17 |

Matthew Rivard, *Student Stress-Gesture Drawing*, charcoal on paper, 22" × 30", 2004.

If you do this exercise correctly, you will create some drawings that are recognizably yours at the same time that they provide a good general description of the model's pose.

Exercise 4-3 Palimpsest Drawing

A thousand years ago, scribes wrote on vellum, a fine paper-like substance made from calf skin. Vellum was made by hand, and it was expensive. When a manuscript was no longer wanted, the

visual | 4–18 |

H. Stone, *Palimpsest Drawing*, compressed charcoal on Rives BFK paper, 44" × 30", 2004.

page was scraped clean and the vellum used again. A document that has been recycled in this way is called a palimpsest.

Sometimes the earlier content of a palimpsest is faintly visible, along with the scrapings and erasures from the attempts to remove it (Visual 4–19).

This layering effect can be quite beautiful. The paler writing, more remote in time, does not conflict with the current material; it creates a home for it. A palimpsest's ancient surface, worked by many hands, is the biography of the document itself: the people who made it, the places it has been, and your role as its most recent viewer. Palimpsests record the passage of time.

When we draw another person, our time is always limited. We may or may not see our subjects again, and even if we do, they will be a little different, and so will we. We can express some of the uniqueness and ephemerality of our drawing time by creating a palimpsest. This palimpsest will not be made so that we can reuse the substrate, and we won't erase the entire drawing before we start another one. We will build the drawing in layers, erasing only as much as we need to in order to make room for new images. Earlier images will show through the layers here and there; such an image is called a pentimento.

In addition to creating a meditation on the nature of time, creating a drawing palimpsest is an opportunity to struggle in the most direct way with issues of composition, proportion, and integrating the drawing skills you have been practicing. In the palimpsest that you will make in this assignment, you will start with short poses, drawing several gesture drawings on one page. Then the poses will last a little longer, and you will place these somewhat more developed drawings on top of the gesture drawings, erasing when you need to. The last couple of

visual **4–19**

Artists unknown, *The Archimedes Palimpsest*, ink and paint on parchment, third century and twelfth century B.C.E. The original work was a mathematical text, which was erased and converted to a prayer book. *Courtesy Christie's Images, Inc.*

poses will be the longest, and you will use them to create drawings that are as finished as you can make them, also on top of the drawings you have been working on.

Materials

- A set of erasers, including at least one white polymer eraser and two or three cheap pink rubber erasers.

- Several sticks of compressed charcoal, some small, some large (see Visual 3-13).

- Paper: you can use the inexpensive paper that you have been using for your other exercises, but this exercise works best if you get a piece of decent art paper, 22" × 30" or so. It does cost more, but it stands up better to erasing. Clamp or tape the paper securely to a drawing board, with a pad of a few pieces of cheaper paper under it. The type of paper you use will affect the way the final product looks, so it is a good idea to experiment with different kinds of paper until you find a look that you like.

Procedures

1. Draw standing up if you can.

2. Create a time budget for the drawing session. For example, for a three-hour session, you might do ten two-minute gesture drawings, three five-minute gesture drawings, one ten-minute gesture drawing, and then break. Then three ten-minute drawings and one fifteen-minute drawing, and then another break. Then, one twenty-minute drawing and one twenty-five-minute drawing.

3. Use only one piece of paper during the entire drawing session. Place it on your easel horizontally.

4. Start with stress-gesture drawings as in Exercise 4-2. Draw the figures as large as you can make them and still fit them on the page. Feel free to overlap and layer them.

5. As the poses get longer, develop each drawing more. For example, in the five-minute drawings, you may choose to develop the large masses of value using more charcoal and an eraser. For longer poses, add contour lines as they seem necessary, and develop the values in more detail.

6. At some point, you will need to start dismantling one drawing in order to create a new one. A good general rule is to add the new drawing where the overall composition seems most ambiguous. Don't agonize too long about where the new one will go; just keep your hand moving and drop the new drawing in wherever it feels best.

Demonstration 4-1: A Palimpsest Drawing

I am drawing on 22" × 30" Rives BFK. Visual 4–20 shows my first two-minute drawing. This first drawing will almost certainly be hidden when the piece is finished, so this is a good opportunity to put your performance anxiety aside and let fly. I was pretty happy with this one because it does show the body's structure and balance, and the lines I drew are nice and emphatic. It sometimes occurs to me that in a better world, this purely spontaneous kind of drawing is the only art we would ever need.

My second drawing, shown in Visual 4–21, is a little lighter than the first because I used the point of the drawing stick to grab the gesture, and I didn't use mass tones. I was trying to suggest the basic forms of the model in a way that felt right at each moment. The second drawing is clearer than the first, and it could be used as a study for a sculpture in clay or wire, or for a painting.

Drawing number three (Visual 4–22) overlaps the second drawing, and that drawing will never be the same. This is the first time in this project that I had to face the choice between one drawing and another. If number two was really a masterpiece, I could have overwritten the first one instead, but, knowing that these drawings are doomed to serve as the imprimatura for the later drawings, I dropped the new one in where it felt most natural. The image is around for a couple of minutes, and then is gone. This is life drawing, and that's life, isn't it?

visual | 4–20 |

H. Stone,
*Palimpsest
Drawing
Demonstration,
Step 1.*

visual | 4–21 |

H. Stone,
*Palimpsest
Drawing
Demonstration,*
Step 2.

visual | 4–22 |

H. Stone,
*Palimpsest
Drawing
Demonstration,*
Step 3.

The fourth drawing (Visual 4–23) went on top of the first drawing. As I recall, this was a five-minute pose. I made a few large marks to locate the pose on the paper and then concentrated on what was most interesting to me at the time, the model's head. I used the white polymer eraser to pull out the background and then used line and value techniques to draw the model's head and shoulders. I used one of my modified, wedge-cut cheap pink erasers to scrub out the towel that was hanging over the model's shoulders. For the media I was using, the white polymer eraser seemed to be better at creating a white erased surface, and the cheap pink one was better at creating painterly, expressive marks.

Visual 4–24 shows the palimpsest a few drawings later. The torso took fifteen minutes to draw. There were at least two drawings underneath that one, but I wasn't happy with them. A failed drawing is not a problem in this project: just call in the wrecking crew, and then build another one. I wasn't happy, either, with the large head. It wasn't too bad by itself, but it was too big for the torso. I rubbed the side of the face out to make sure that it did not end up in the final picture.

This composition took a total of four forty-five-minute drawing sessions, and Visual 4–25 shows the progress at the beginning of the last session. The substandard head at top center in Visual 4–24 has been replaced by a better one drawn in a straightforward three-value technique, with a contour line describing the edge of the jaw and cheek. The torso was sacrificed to another drawing, of which only traces can be seen. The head on the right, seen in profile, also covers another drawing.

At this point in my drawing, there are several recognizable pieces of a human figure, but there is also a surface covered with some aggressive black marks, some white spaces, and some rubbed-out areas. We have a work of art that is telling us that it is not complete.

visual | 4–23 |

H. Stone,
*Palimpsest
Drawing
Demonstration,
Step 4.*

H. Stone,
*Palimpsest
Drawing
Demonstration,
Step 5.*

H. Stone,
*Palimpsest
Drawing
Demonstration,
Step 6.*

The later, longer poses in a drawing session are usually seated or reclining positions because the model is tired. My plan for the last forty-five minutes is to have a finished reclining figure covering most of the lower half of the picture. I want for this figure to lighten up the composition and to be clear and specific enough to counterbalance some of the unrecognizable forms now occupying the center of the paper. The preliminary gesture drawing for that figure is visible in tilted set of parallel lines in the lower-left quarter of the paper.

One of the things to take away from this exercise is the idea that the individual parts of a work of art must yield to the interests of the whole. There were several pretty good drawings that I chose to cover up because they did not fit into the larger composition. Practicing the palimpsest exercise will help you to become more confident in making that judgment about your own work.

Visual 4–26 shows the drawing halfway through the last forty-five-minute session. I was scrubbing pretty hard with both erasers to get the model's right thigh as light as I wanted it to be. The right hand and arm are drawn using the three-value exercise. It would not be a disaster if the composition had to be ended here, but I could not declare it finished because the model had no feet.

It is not uncommon for people to leave the hands or feet off of their life drawings because they are hard to draw. The problem is that if you habitually fail to draw the extremities, you will never learn to draw them. If you can see a hand or foot, don't procrastinate. When you draw the leg, draw the foot; when you draw the arm, draw the hand.

The final version of my palimpsest is shown in Visual 4–27. The last figure worked out pretty well. The likeness isn't bad, and having a fairly detailed light area in position does give more structure to the piece. I find it remarkable how well an erased and rubbed surface is able to suggest human skin. I think it is because human skin is composed of layers in the same way the surface of the drawing is. Getting the model's skin to lighten up was quite a bit of physical work, but it was necessary to the success of the drawing, and the struggle visible in the surface gives the drawing more presence.

Feet can be daunting, and these were as hard to draw as ever. I reverted to the three-value exercise, concentrating particularly on the shapes of the darkest areas. This was successful, in part because the soles of the model's feet were black from walking around in the soot that had been distributed all over the floor from everyone's frantic drawing and erasing. That gave me a crisp local color form to work from.

Look at the Drawings

The palimpsest exercise is an experiment whose purpose is to develop concentration, drawing technique, and artistic judgment. Because it is an activity in which many personal decisions are made spontaneously and intuitively, it is not always helpful to publicly analyze the final product in detail.

visual | 4–27 |

H. Stone,
*Palimpsest
Drawing
Demonstration,
Step 8.*

Spend a few minutes honestly evaluating your drawing according to the criteria below.

In this drawing we want to see:

* Confident marks. This does not mean that every mark should be heavy, only that your marks should be intentional, rather than random.

* Evidence of constructive attention in every part of the picture. You did some parts of the drawing fast, and some slower, but every part should demonstrate that you were thinking while you were drawing. This drawing is not a brainstorming session, so we do not want to see evidence of noodling around and using up the **picture plane** with purposeless marks.

* Quality in the use of line and tone. This exercise is intended to build onto your existing skills in contour and value, so your edges should be clean, and your lines should be confident and accurately descriptive.

It is good to look at several palimpsest drawings at a time, whether they are produced by many artists in one class session or by yourself over a period of time. If you do this, you will find that some are more interesting or attractive than others, and that people will generally agree which pictures these are. In this exercise, you are learning how to use images in your own way, so give your work a fair chance to persuade you that it is good. As your style develops, you will learn to give a name to the elements that make one of these pictures better than another, but for now, just take the ones you like best and pin them up where you can see them every day. When you get tired of looking at a drawing, replace it with a more recent one.

CHAPTER SUMMARY

Gesture drawing is physically identifying with the model's pose and drawing that relationship. This empathy and the ability to draw it are both skills that will develop with practice.

Drawing the active balance of a standing human figure is an enduring problem in art and an activity that can connect our current work with deep traditions of visual art. This active balance is called contrapposto, and an understanding of it is necessary to draw a standing human figure that plausibly has weight. Practicing gesture drawing is the key to understanding contrapposto well enough to apply it in art.

Gesture drawing is also useful as a way of planning and developing a finished work of art. The palimpsest exercise is one way to use gesture drawing as an armature, or substrate, for a finished drawing.

▶ *chapter questions*

Multiple Choice

1. Gesture is:
  a. The movement of the artist's arm in drawing the pose.
  b. Any movement of the human body.
  c. The literal movement of the model.
  d. The sense of movement of a pose.

2. Movement in life drawing is:
  a. Building the drawing up in layers.
  b. The overall sweep of the composition.
  c. The interaction of stressed and unstressed areas of the body to achieve balance.
  d. The interaction of a single muscle pair.

3. Gesture drawing:
  a. Involves patiently studying the pose.
  b. Requires making an empathetic connection to the model's stance.
  c. Is drawing a model who is moving.
  d. Seldom produces any recognizable structures.

4. Gesture drawing:
  a. Is performed according to a strict set of rules.
  b. Cannot be evaluated.
  c. Is a type of abstract art.
  d. Is drawn from the feelings alone.

5. Gesture drawing:
  a. Is a way of learning how to draw a figure with weight.
  b. Gives a sense of where the light is coming from.
  c. Is a high-speed version of contour drawing.
  d. Focuses on the individual structures of the body.

6. A contrapposto stance:

    a. Is a special stance used only by art models.

    b. Divides the model's weight evenly between the legs.

    c. Is a weight shift stance.

    d. Traditionally requires a discus or javelin.

7. The Metaphor of Balance:

    a. Was first used by the ancient Egyptians.

    b. Was first used by the ancient Romans.

    c. Was first used in the French Academy in 1648.

    d. Was first used by the ancient Greeks.

8. To summarize the Metaphor of Balance:

    a. A standing human figure represents all people.

    b. A standing human figure represents truth.

    c. A standing human figure represents the interconnectedness of all intellectual effort.

    d. A standing human figure is a famous political or military character.

9. A palimpsest:

    a. Is a recycled document.

    b. Is always a drawing.

    c. Is never a drawing.

    d. Is a recent invention.

10. In a gesture drawing:

    a. It is impossible to tell what the pose was.

    b. We quickly summarize the pose.

    c. We quickly draw the light and dark areas.

    d. We quickly draw the figure's background.

George Bellows (1882–1925), *Study for Young Man Standing*, conté crayon, 11³⁄₁₆" × 7⅜", Twentieth century. *Minneapolis Institute of Arts, Gift of Dr. and Mrs. John E. Larkin, Jr.*

CHAPTER 5

objectives

- Place quick studies in context in a personal practice of life drawing.
- Practice quick-contour drawings.
- Practice shaded quick-contour drawings.
- Practice creating a balance between line and value in drawing a quick study.
- Practice using a gesture drawing to plan and compose a quick study.

introduction

A quick study is a drawing created in a single session. Drawing quick studies is an intense form of practice that challenges skills in line, value, and composition. Whether the subject is only available for a short time, or the artist wants to capture life as it happens, a quick study is a direct method of creating a balanced descriptive or documentary drawing.

WHAT'S THE HURRY?

"If a man throws himself out of the fourth floor window, and you can't make a sketch of him before he gets to the ground, you will never do anything big."

Eugène Delacroix (1798–1863)

You have twenty minutes to draw another person. Can there be a more clearly defined problem in art than this? Twenty minutes, and you can't paint over your mistakes. It does not matter how well you can tell the story afterward because every mark on the paper is either right or it's wrong. The project is not impossible. The question is always, is it possible, right now, for *you*? The clock is ticking.

A quick life drawing has traditionally been used to depict subjects that can't stay still long enough for a comprehensive treatment. Artists must move fast to make pictures of children, animals, and people in motion, or of unwitting subjects such as patrons of bars and coffee shops. Like gesture drawing, the quick study is a spontaneous art form in which it is more important to be true to the moment than to produce a polished product. A quick study differs from a gesture drawing in that it is meant to be a complete descriptive drawing, rather than an exercise. It is created to show what the subject looks like, document the subject's activity, or describe the setting the subject inhabits.

For an example of this, we can take Delacroix at his word by looking at a set of his quick studies in Visual 5–1. On the left is an upside-down guy who could actually be falling out of a window.

On the right are three drawings of men in various positions. This picture does have some of the free-association quality of a gesture drawing, but the goal is different. Instead of being an abstract study of movement, this is a set of straight-forward contour drawings. There is visible evidence that the drawing was done quickly: the figures have parts missing, and some of the forms are **open**, in other words, there is no clear boundary between the **figure** and the **ground** in some areas. Delacroix probably would not have wanted this picture to be his only message to posterity, but it does not misrepresent what the rest of his work is about. The drawing demonstrates the same action, movement, and exoticism found in his paintings, but in a set of short, matter-of-fact statements.

Visual 5–2, a quick study drawn by Paul Visscher, is a contour drawing with chiaroscuro. The contour lines are all confident and descriptive, and the values are cleanly applied. The pose is a difficult one, involving a **foreshortened** head. The drawing gives us a good description of the face, neck, and hands, and the forms are defined well enough to be used as a study for a painting or sculpture. Like Delacroix, Visscher leaves some forms open.

visual | 5–2 |

Paul Visscher, *Untitled*, vine charcoal and charcoal pencil on newsprint, 24" × 18", 2000.

Lisa Colwell's drawing (Visual 5–3) is a quick line drawing with some light hatching. This drawing shares some of the concerns of gesture drawing in that it emphasizes how the model's weight is suspended, and it demonstrates how her body slightly twists and her head tilts. The torsion that stresses the left leg is indicated by repeated contour lines. The loose hatching contributes a sense of urgency to the image at the same time it provides mass tone and gives an interesting texture to the surface.

Why is it important to draw fast? To learn to see more and to express it more honestly. These three drawings do not look the same, but each one is a succinct statement of its maker's talent, temperament, and artistic interests. Whatever you are able to best accomplish in drawing will be visible in a quick study. The exercise is always personal, and for better or worse, truthful.

visual | 5–3 |

Lisa Colwell, *Twenty-minute drawing*, pencil on Stonehenge paper, 22" × 30", 2002.

A quick study is completed in one sitting, and although it can take up to forty-five minutes to draw one, it is usually done much faster. It often will have areas that are incompletely drawn, and sometimes some structures will be suggested rather than drawn in detail. The finish may be rough, and there may be visible false starts or extra contour lines (Visual 5–4). Like unfinished areas and open forms, these are not considered serious flaws in a quick study.

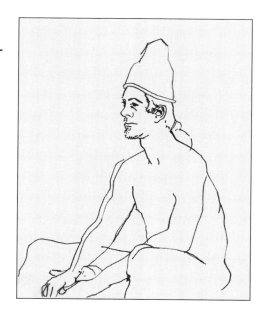

This man has an extra contour line. H. Stone, *Five-Minute Study*, sumi pen on paper, 11" × 14", 2005.

A quick study is not usually a contemplative activity. The idea is to draw the other person as directly as you can, without giving yourself time to try to outsmart the process. In other words, the short drawing time forces you to respond only to what you are seeing, and not to thoughts or ambitions related to the drawing. If you can avoid the temptation to be inattentive while you are working, you will find that quick drawing will speed the development of your **visual memory** and drawing skill.

THE DIALOG BETWEEN LINE AND VALUE

In Chapter 2 and Chapter 3, you practiced using line and value. In this chapter, you will use them both in the same drawing in a kind of tag-team, or dialog. This is a flexible, cooperative relationship between the contour lines and the mass tones, in which they take turns doing the work of describing the figure, while staying out of each other's way.

At some point in your career in life drawing, you have probably asked yourself the question, "What if I had all the time that I needed?" The answer might look like this:

- Every part of the drawing would be developed completely, with nothing vague or absent.
- Contour lines would be complete, sensitive, and consistent.
- Values would be used to describe in detail the forms inside the contours.
- Proportions would be accurate.
- The level of finish would demonstrate craftsmanship and consistency.

In other words, you would have time to make the drawing could look exactly the way you wanted it to. On the other hand, such a drawing would make it pretty obvious where you needed to brush up on your ability to see and render forms.

Revolution-era American artist John Trumbull's drawing (Visual 5–5) has been completed to this level. The drawing gives an immediate impression of refinement and gracefulness. A very thin contour line follows and articulates every edge, and values are applied in controlled, subtle gradients. It is clear where the bulges and hollows of the body are, and whether the transition from one form to its neighbor is abrupt or smooth. Within the figure, there are no large expanses of flat, bare paper, and no awkward, undifferentiated regions of black. This is a drawing without compromises.

A quick study is a different kind of drawing problem. The ideal of completeness must yield to that of improvisation. The line may express lyricism or urgency at the same time as it describes the contour. Values may hold the figure in its place on the paper as well as articulating the shape of the body. The drawing can be unified, and the forms expressed with economy, through the interaction of the values and the contour lines.

Edgar Degas provides an example of this in his quick study of a dancer at rest (Visual 5–6). This is a contour drawing with visibly repeated lines, augmented with areas of mass tone.

The drawing does not present an immediate impression of calm. The model's face is drawn in profile using a contour line, and the back of her head is a dark form on a light background. This darkness continues down the model's torso and back until it reaches her right elbow. The elbow is defined with a small amount of shading, but the rest of the arm is drawn with contour lines. Mass tones and values take over again in the right hand, with the highlights on the fingers erased out of the gray mass that starts on the back of the hand and spills onto the model's knee. The right leg below the knee continues as a shape of bare paper thrown into relief by the hatching darkening the background. The model's left leg is almost entirely created with contour line, with some pale grays articulating the shape of the foot, and some darkening of the background behind the foot to anchor it to the floor.

visual | 5–5 |

John Trumbull (1756-1843), *Study from Life: Nude Male*, black and white chalk drawing on blue laid paper, 19½" × 12", 1795–1796. *The Metropolitan Museum of Art, Morris K. Jesup Fund, 1998 (1998.309) Image © The Metropolitan Museum of Art.*

There isn't an area in this drawing in which the forms are completely described using both value and contour line. The story gets told by line in one area and by value in another, and the transitions between the two are subtle and unstudied. This dialog demands attentiveness on the part of the viewer, who must mentally complete forms suggested by the drawing. The artist had to struggle to accurately render the scene before it disappeared, and, in order to understand it, the viewer must think the drawing through in a similar way. Through this metaphor, in which the process of seeing the drawing parallels the process of making it, the viewer makes a connection to the artist.

visual | 5–6 |

Edgar Degas
(1834–1917),
*Ballet Girl in
Repose*, charcoal
on light tan wove
paper, 11" × 9",
1880–1882.
*Minneapolis
Institute of Arts,
Gift of Julius
Boehler.*

Visual 5–5 and Visual 5–6 were created in different situations, for different purposes. Practicing with both long and short poses will develop your overall drawing skill and help you to identify what kind of drawings you are most interested in making.

Exercise 5-1: Quick-Contour Drawing

During the gesture exercise, you were probably tempted at times to make a contour drawing at high speed. In this exercise, you will do just that. The quick contour exercise is simply a race to draw the best line drawing you can in a limited time, without making corrections or thinking about the final product. When you do this exercise, concentrate only on making the line the right shape, and keep it moving.

In this exercise and the ones to follow, experiment with starting your drawings at different places. It may seem logical to start at the model's head and move down the body, but you will get better control of the proportions and placement of your figure if you make a practice of varying your starting point.

Quick-contour drawing is a great general drawing technique, so you may want to use it to draw your friends, animals, or people you see in public.

Materials

- Several 6B pencils. Keep enough on hand that you won't have to interrupt the exercise to sharpen them.
- 11" × 17" or 18" × 24" drawing pads as needed.

Procedures

1. Before starting this exercise, do a fifteen-minute blind contour exercise as described in Chapter 2.

2. Start your series of quick-contour drawings immediately after the blind contour exercise. To make the contour line, use the same semiblind contour technique you practiced in Chapter 2. This is the technique of drawing the line while looking at the model and then stopping your hand to look at the paper and check position. At first this will seem like a clumsy and inefficient way to make a quick drawing, but in time, with practice, your attention will flicker between the model and the paper, and you will keep track of both of them at once.

3. Try to keep your speed up without omitting details or simplifying the line.

4. Make the figure as big as you can, still trying to fit all of it on the page. This part of the exercise is to help you begin to get control of the proportions of the figure and of its placement on the paper.

5. Do not erase. If you make a line that you don't like, keep drawing and don't worry about fixing it. Do your best on each drawing, and when it is done, forget about it, turn the page, and start another.

6. Do a series of six five-minute drawings.

visual | 5–7 |

Susan McDonald, *Suite of Four Life Drawings*, pencil on paper, figures approximately 12" tall *Courtesy of Susan McDonald.*

Look at the Drawing

A reasonable goal for this exercise is to produce one drawing you are happy with out of every set of six. It is useful to keep them in a pad so you can monitor your progress.

In this exercise, we are looking for:

- A single, confident, accurate line.
- All or most of a recognizable figure.

We are not looking for:

- Any mass tones or other shading.
- Conspicuous errors in proportion. It isn't unusual to make the bottom half of the body too big or small in an unconscious attempt to fit the whole thing on the paper. If the figure needs to spill off the edge of picture in order to keep its proportions accurate, let it. Proportion will be discussed in detail in Chapter 7.
- A wispy, tentative line (Visual 5–8). This is a scratchy, nervous line made with a reciprocating motion of the hand. Make your line a solid line, drawn with a firm, confident motion.
- A labored line, in which the line is repeated a number of times. The goal is to use no more than one good line to describe an edge.

Visual 5–9 shows a successful quick-contour drawing by Edgar Degas. This drawing, of a singer performing a song about a dog, was made in a café, and he later used it as a study for a painting. Even though the mood of the drawing is relaxed, there isn't any laziness in it. Degas shows us everything he wants us to see and nothing extra. The two faces in profile are drawn with a single, articulate line. Details such as the lace at the bodice and the loose hair at the back of the neck are suggested, rather than being drawn in detail or omitted, and each arm has a hand at the end of it. The drawing has three faces and four noses. For some reason, Degas was not happy with the disembodied nose, so he didn't waste time continuing the drawing; he

visual | 5–8 |

Mannerisms that can dilute the quality of the line: (Left) A wispy, tentative contour line. (Right) A labored contour line. Both of these techniques in the hands of accomplished artists can be used to make good, descriptive contour lines. When you are learning, they can interfere with your confident expression of the form.

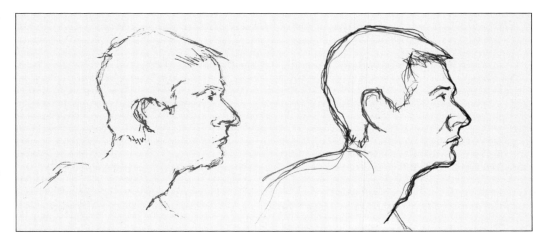

Edgar Degas,
*Sketches of Café
Singers*, 9¾" × 13",
1877.

moved a little to the right and started again. The only erasing is in the rather uncharitable drawing of the head in the upper right. It's interesting that Degas chose to create his painting from the other two images, in which the face is drawn in less detail.

Wouldn't it be great to be able to draw like this? It is possible if you practice. This is a skill that you work at for a while without visible progress, and then suddenly you can do it. The best part is that when it starts working for you, you won't draw like Degas, you will draw like yourself.

Exercise 5-2: Shaded Quick-Contour Drawing

The shaded quick-contour drawing is probably the most useful and frequently used variety of figure drawing. Contour drawing by itself can produce very beautiful work, but at times it can seem like playing a guitar with only three strings. Adding some regions of value can give the drawing atmosphere and solidity, assuming that you apply the new mass tones so that they make the drawing better, rather than worse.

How can you be sure that your values will do this? Remember that line and value are both means of defining form, and in a limited time span you will want to use them parsimoniously. To use both line and value successfully, stay focused on the task of describing the forms. If it is not clear in your drawing what the shapes of the model's body are, the drawing needs either more line, or more values. On the other hand, if a contour line or mass tone does not contribute to a description of shape, it does not really need to be there.

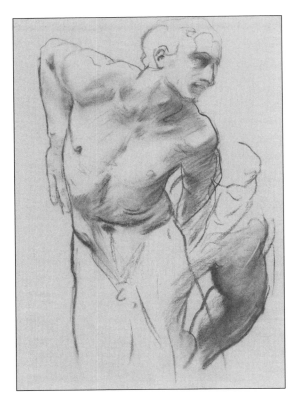

After working with the quick-contour exercise, it may seem logical to do this exercise by making a line drawing of the entire figure and then shading it in as if it were a coloring book. This is not necessarily the best way to use a limited drawing time. In this exercise, we practice creating the dialog between line and value by drawing line for a while, then drawing mass tones for a while. If the line is telling the story, we won't need to add values, and vice versa.

Materials

- Compressed charcoal and vine charcoal.
- A full complement of erasers.
- Everyday paper, at least 11" × 14".

Procedures

1. Before you do this exercise, spend forty-five minutes doing the blind contour exercise and the quick-contour exercise sequence.

2. Place the model under a directional light so that the shadows will help you see the body's forms more clearly.

3. Start the drawing by placing a mass tone to indicate one of the larger regions of shadow.

4. Augment the dark area you just drew with one or more contour lines.

5. Draw the rest of the figure by alternating drawing lines and values.

6. Do one drawing for twenty minutes and another for twenty-five minutes.

7. Start the second drawing in a different place on the figure from the previous one.

8. Experiment with different ways of applying the mass tones. On one drawing, use the side of your charcoal to lay the masses down flat, and on another build up the masses with hatching lines. Vary the mood of your marks, as well. For example, sometimes you may want to make cool, controlled marks, and other times hard, aggressive ones.

9. Experiment with compressed charcoal and vine charcoal, and notice the difference between them.

Demonstration 5–1: Shaded Quick-Contour Drawing

I drew this drawing on 22" × 30" paper, using a small stick of compressed charcoal that I broke into short lengths. After looking the model over, I decided to start with the solid area of shadow on the bottom half of the face and the neck. I

H. Stone, *Shaded Quick-Contour Drawing Demonstration, Step 1.*

placed it in the upper half of the picture, a little left of center, estimating that this would allow me to fit the entire figure on the paper. After I made a gray mass there with the side of the charcoal, I installed the hair in black. I then made a few black marks for the darkest areas of the face and added some contour lines (Visual 5–11).

When I do a shaded quick-contour drawing, I usually start with the two goals of keeping the drawing light and not erasing. I try to keep the drawing light as a means of ensuring that each mark I make contributes to the sense of form of the drawing. I try not to erase so that I can spend the limited available time making the image, and not redoing one I have already made. My educated guess is that I meet both of these goals in one drawing out of every four.

In Visual 5–12, I have drawn a contour to define the left edge of the model's body and added some shading in the forearm and torso. I am using the contour line to extend the figure into its position on the **picture plane** and as a way of creating some **negative space** to use to check proportions. At this stage, the negative space is the shape of the background between the hand and the shin. If this shape is correct, it will confirm that the arm, the torso, and the model's right leg were drawn at the right size. If the shape is wrong, I can make the correction while the drawing is still young.

In Visual 5–13, I continued to alternate line and value. I studied the relative positions of the shoulders to help me draw the contour line for the model's right side. I made a false start on the line from the forearm to right wrist, which I dealt with by leaving it alone and drawing a better line, continuing it into the hand.

H. Stone, *Shaded Quick-Contour Drawing Demonstration, Step 2.*

H. Stone, *Shaded Quick-Contour Drawing Demonstration, Step 3.*

From your work with gesture, you probably have an appreciation of just how complicated human legs are. Muscles and joints are elastic, and they change shape as they interact. Convex and concave contours reverse themselves as point of view changes. Thinking of these structures as spheres, cones, cubes, and so on does not do justice to the complexity of their structure or of the relationships between them. Fortunately, you do not have to run a complete mechanical simulation in your head to be able to draw legs accurately.

H. Stone, *Shaded Quick-Contour Drawing Demonstration, Step 4.*

Compare Visual 5–13 and Visual 5–14. In Visual 5–13, you can see the line that defines the top edge of the model's right leg. I drew this with some care, and with careful reference to the left hand above it, because I planned to use this line to help me construct the legs.

The key to this construction is the shape shown in Visual 5–15. This is the shape of the negative space between the two lower legs. I drew this shape into place adjacent to the existing contour line on the right shin, shown in Visual 5–13. If this single, small shape is correct, I have properly positioned the left knee, calf, and foot.

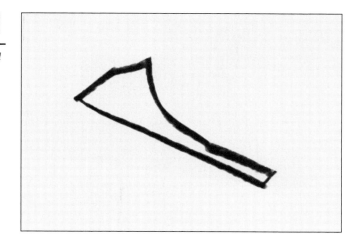

H. Stone, *Shaded Quick-Contour Drawing Demonstration, negative form.*

With my negative space defined, it isn't too difficult to get the left foot, and then the right foot, into position. I used the position of the left hand as a reference to get the big toes in the right place. I used the semiblind contour exercise to draw the line for the lower edge of the right leg.

In Visual 5–16, I have drawn the line that defines the top edge of the model's left leg, and I sparingly placed some mass tones in the legs and background. I am happy with the

visual | 5–16 |

H. Stone, *Shaded Quick-Contour Drawing Demonstration, Step 5.*

figure at this point. I could declare the drawing finished, but that would leave the model's arm hanging in the void. Expanses of bare paper such as this offer the opportunity to wreck the drawing by quickly adding some ill-considered, generic strokes in the background. To avoid this, maintain a policy of only making marks that correspond to something that you see. You don't need to develop the background to the same level of detail that you did the figure; you only need to provide enough context that the figure's positioning makes sense.

The completed drawing is shown in Visual 5–17. Although I added a little more shading to the figure, most of the new work took place in the background. My interest was in getting the figure to nestle comfortably into its environment, so I darkened the background in a few places around the edge of the figure to match the value relationships as I saw them.

Look at the Drawing

The shaded quick-contour drawing is the best benchmark of your drawing skill. You should save all of these drawings and review them from time to time to get a sense of how you are progressing.

Although it is great to produce the occasional masterpiece, what is better is to develop a level of consistency in your day-to-day drawings. This means that you will refine your skill, eliminating shortcuts, mannerisms, and other bad habits, and increase your ability to see honestly and draw articulately. If you practice this way, you won't have to work at developing a personal style; your style will find you.

visual | 5–17 |

H. Stone, *Shaded Quick-Contour Drawing Demonstration, final version,* compressed charcoal on paper, 22" × 30", 2006.

In this exercise we are looking for:

- A single line of good quality. The line should describe the contour, with round forms round and angular forms angular. It should be solid and confident, and free of distracting mannerisms.

- Mass tones that contribute to the sense of form of the figure, and that work in cooperation with the line.

- A drawing that is not too dark overall. If you try to keep the drawing as light as possible, you will have fewer structures that lose their definition from being overworked, and you will spend less time trying to correct errors. Working light helps you stay out of your own way.

We are not looking for:

- A line with distracting mannerisms as shown in Visual 5–8.

- Murky values that fail to define forms.

- Clumsy or artificial-looking areas of the figure.

- A figure that is significantly incomplete.

ON WORKING TOGETHER

visual | 5–18 |

H. Stone, *Twenty-Minute Drawing*, vine charcoal on Rives BFK, 30" × 22", 1993.

How can you tell when the contour lines are cooperating with the values to create a sense of form? First, if the drawing seems too dark, the team isn't working together. Second, look at the drawing for a minute or so, pick out a light region on the model's skin, and compare it to any light place on the background. Does one area seem lighter than the other? If the figure looks a little lighter, or seems to glow a little bit, it means that your eye is being persuaded to see the model's body as a three-dimensional form. If the forms are there, the white space in the figure will tell the story. Try this test on the twenty-minute drawing in Visual 5–18.

The contour line in this drawing did its part by being rounded and angular in the right places, as shown in area *A* in Visual 5–19. The values here are small marks of light gray. When you encounter a complex area such as the interaction of arms, shoulders, elbow, and chin in Visual 5–19, it is easy to feel that you are not quite up to the challenge. The solution is to mentally relabel the structure. Instead of thinking of it as concentrated area of anatomical detail, think of it as a set of flat, adjacent forms, such as a map, or a puzzle. Understate the values, so that they do not hide the contour line.

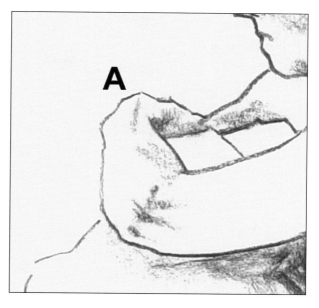

H. Stone, *Detail, Twenty-Minute Drawing*, vine charcoal on Rives BFK, 30" × 22", 1993.

To make the lines and values work together, remember that you only want one to speak at a time. The hair in this drawing (Visual 5–20) is an example of quieting the values so that the line can have its say. I used the three-value exercise as before, but reduced the darkest areas to small lines or wedges—punctuation, in a sense, for the white and middle-toned forms. If this were just a value drawing, abbreviating the blacks this way would not provide enough structure, but now that we can coordinate line and value, it will work well as part of the ensemble. With the values restrained so that they cannot overwhelm the contour lines, we can incorporate subtleties in the line such as variations in thickness to make an edge seem to soften in light (Visual 5–20, *B*).

Exercise 5-3: Developed Gesture Drawing

The last quick-study exercise builds on existing skills like the others, but its focus is a little different. It is similar to the palimpsest exercise in Chapter 4, except that you will attempt to produce a presentable drawing of a single figure instead of working with the whole **picture plane**. In this exercise, you will do a

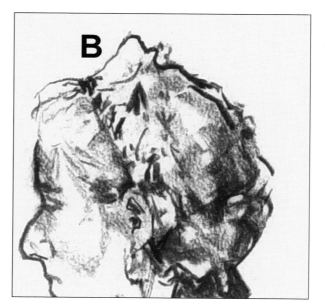

H. Stone, *Detail, Twenty-Minute Drawing*, vine charcoal on Rives BFK, 30" × 22", 1993.

H. Stone,
*Developed
Gesture Drawing*,
pressed charcoal
on Rives BFK,
30" × 22", 2000.

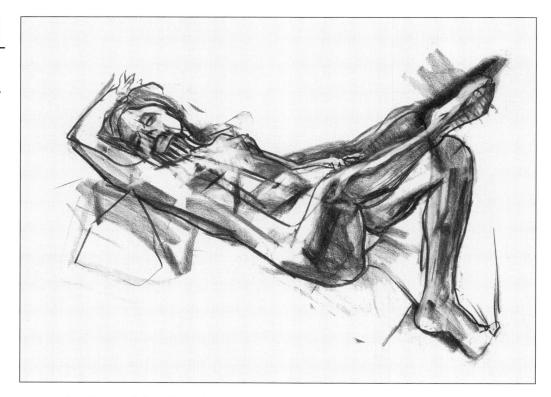

gesture drawing, and then draw the figure on top of it (Visual 5–22). The purpose of the exercise is to refine your control over the placement of the figure and help you calibrate your sense of proportion.

Materials

- Compressed charcoal.
- A set of erasers.
- An old washrag or equivalent for blending.
- 11" × 14" paper or 18" × 24" paper. An everyday grade of paper is fine for this exercise.

Procedures

1. Place a spotlight or other directional light on the model.

2. Using compressed charcoal, do a gesture drawing. Start with a quick summary of the pose, and then work on the stressed areas. Draw with confidence; do not be tempted to make light, tentative marks. Keep your hand moving, and use your charcoal to connect all parts of the figure.

3. Still working very quickly, use your eraser to make adjustments in proportions and in the placement of the figure on the paper. When the figure is placed the way you want

visual | 5–22 |

H. Stone, *Two-minute Gesture Drawing with Shadow Masses*, compressed charcoal on paper, 8" × 10", 2005.

it, start adding the darkest shadow masses.

4. Develop the image by adding and erasing mass tones and contour lines. This is a chiaroscuro drawing, so find the best-lit areas and develop their shapes with your eraser.

5. To warm up and help you do a good job on the longer drawing, start by drawing five two-minute versions of this exercise (Visual 5–22 and Visual 5–23). You won't have time to be a perfectionist. Emphasize the gesture and shadow masses, and don't worry about making corrections.

6. After the short warm-ups, do the exercise for thirty-five minutes.

visual | 5–23 |

H. Stone, *Two-minute Gesture Drawing with Shadow Masses*, compressed charcoal on paper, 8" × 10", 2005.

visual | 5–24 |

H. Stone,
*Developed
Gesture Drawing
Demonstration,
Step 1.*

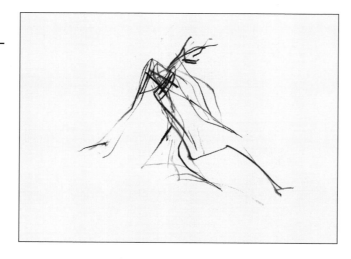

Demonstration 5-2: Developed Gesture Drawing

After the series of two-minute drawings (Visual 5–22 and Visual 5–23), I started the thirty-five-minute study on 30" × 22" paper. I started by drawing some very quick marks to locate the most stressed joint in the model's body, her left shoulder (Visual 5–24). After that, I established the angle of the shoulders, the positioning of the arms, and the forward tilt of the head. At this point in the drawing it isn't too important that the drawing be comprehensible to anyone else. The marks I am making are notes to myself about where I want the figure to be and where the stresses in the figure are.

Soon after making the preliminary marks, I realized that the figure was too small and placed too high in the composition. I fixed that by adding some more scribbled lines in the new position of the lower back (Visual 5–25). Because the body is held up by the inverted V-shaped structure made by the leaning torso and the left arm, I wanted to make sure that the size and positioning of that arm was acceptable before continuing. An error there would cause the pose to look implausible. I placed a contour line down the left side of the torso, added some shadows, and then drew the arm with the semiblind contour technique. I used the left buttock as a reference point for the location of the hand, and the shape of the white negative space between the arm and the torso to check the length of the arm and the tilt of the torso. I also placed a bent black line where the spine is, to indicate its forward bend.

visual | 5–25 |

H. Stone,
*Developed
Gesture Drawing
Demonstration,
Step 2.*

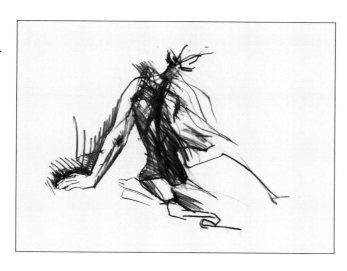

Visual 5–26 shows the drawing with the head in place. The head has a complex geometry in this pose, tilted forward and to the right, and also rotated slightly to the right. Fortunately I did not have to draw this entire structure at once; I only had to know what to draw next. For example, I knew that the neck is centered on top of the shoulders, so it could be installed there with

confidence. Then, using the top of the spine as a landmark, I estimated the position of the chin and nose and then drew them, concentrating on getting the profile at the correct tilt and the nose in the right place.

The challenge at this point in the drawing is to add the remaining large structures of the figure in proper proportion to the existing drawing. Visual 5–27 illustrates the process I used to get the model's right hand in the right place. First, I found an approximate location for the right wrist with respect to the left wrist and the tip of the nose. I drew the lower edge of the arm, wrist, and hand, and checked the wrist's position by visualizing a triangle connecting it to the nose and the other wrist. To verify the accuracy of my triangle, I took note of how far to the right of center the upper corner was shifted. After making corrections, I added the upper contour line and then some mass tones.

In Visual 5–28, I added the leg and the cloth the model was sitting on, and I developed some forms in the background. In addition, I used my washrag and eraser to soften the forms in the right shoulder and clarify the light areas on the right hip and the top surface of the shoulders.

visual | 5–26 |

H. Stone, *Developed Gesture Drawing Demonstration, Step 3.*

visual | 5–27 |

H. Stone, *Developed Gesture Drawing Demonstration, Step 4.*

visual | 5–28 |

H. Stone, *Developed Gesture Drawing Demonstration, Step 5.*

visual | 5–29 |

H. Stone,
*Developed
Gesture Drawing
Demonstration,*
Step 6.

I noticed a couple of errors in the drawing at this point. The first is that the neck is cone-shaped, and the second is that the head is too small. I worked on the neck by lightening its back contour and darkening the background there (Visual 5–29). I determined that the error in the size of the head was above the eyebrows, and I corrected it by adjusting the thickness of the hair.

At this point, the darkest masses on the back struck me as too harsh, and not representing any known structures particularly well, so I made a few more adjustments. I clarified the edges at the back of the neck (Visual 5–30) and at the left knee. I found that the high contrast and active surface on the model's back was preventing it from being read as a single surface that was in shadow, so I softened the lights and darks there by rubbing them with a rag. The plan was that this would consolidate the torso into a single solid form.

Look at the Drawing

This kind of exercise, in which you are immersing yourself in the medium, is helpful for discovering what kind of drawing fits you best. If you are in a class, where you can see the other students' drawings, spend a few minutes walking around and studying them. Because differences in style and personal temperament will be visible in these drawings, evaluating one of them is first a matter of finding sound drawing in a piece that may not look like anyone else's. After that comes appreciating the artist's unique take on the project.

visual | 5–30 |

H. Stone,
*Developed
Gesture Drawing,*
pressed charcoal
on paper,
30" × 22", 2006.

In this exercise, we are looking for:

- A good first impression. Can you clearly see a human figure in the drawing? Is the figure relatively complete? Is it interesting and pleasurable to look at?

- Agreeable placement of the figure on the page. Is it clear that the figure is intended to be the subject of the drawing?

Is the figure tiny, and floating on a white background? Would the drawing be better if the figure had been moved a couple of inches?

- Clearly constructed forms. This is the same criterion we have emphasized in other drawings. Could this drawing be used as a plan for a piece of sculpture? If not, then the drawing cannot be considered fully successful. Because this is a chiaroscuro drawing, well-described forms will also give a sense of the direction the light is coming from.

- A balance between line and value. Are forms described by line in some areas and value in others? Are there places where the form isn't clear because the line and mass tones are interfering with each other?

- The artist's personal contribution to the piece. What makes the drawing different from someone else's? With practice, each artist will develop a distinctive way of using the charcoal, literally a "personal touch." This will be as recognizable as handwriting. When you look at this drawing, can you see the hand that made it?

We are not looking for:

- Lines and values that do not work together for the good of the drawing. They may obscure each other, define forms redundantly, or they may simply not fit comfortably together.

- Ambiguously shaped body structures.

- A figure that is significantly incomplete.

- Extraneous marks that do not contribute to defining the figure or integrating it into the composition.

CHAPTER SUMMARY

A quick study seizes the opportunity to draw a subject in the time that is available. Drawing quickly is a direct way to build and demonstrate drawing skill.

Because drawing time may be very short, a quick study may lack the refinements of a finished drawing.

Unlike a gesture drawing, a quick study is intended to describe the figure with descriptive drawing techniques such as contour line and value. Drawing quick studies has an element of improvisation in composing the picture and creating a balance between line and value. Each artist will handle these processes in a distinctive way, which will be visible in her personal drawing style.

▶ *chapter questions*

Multiple Choice

1. In a shaded quick-contour drawing:

   a. The body's forms are fully defined by both line and value.

   b. The body's forms are defined mainly by line.

   c. The body's forms are defined mainly by value.

   d. The body's forms are sometimes defined by line and sometimes by value.

2. In a shaded quick-contour drawing:

   a. Some contour lines do not need to contribute to a description of shape.

   b. To use line and value successfully, stay focused on the task of describing forms.

   c. There is almost never a need to think about negative space.

   d. Hatching is not a productive technique.

3. A developed gesture drawing:

   a. Is a type of modeling drawing.

   b. Is a type of chiaroscuro drawing.

   c. Uses neither modeling nor chiaroscuro.

   d. Is a hatching drawing.

4. One technique for helping the line and values to work together is:

   a. Make sure that every part of the drawing is fully shaded.

   b. Shade only the background.

   c. Create a smooth finish on the drawing by blending the drawing medium.

   d. Use the darkest values sparingly.

5. Why is it important to draw fast?

   a. To produce more drawings in a given time.

   b. To get your first thousand mistakes out of the way faster.

   c. To learn to see more, and to express it more honestly.

   d. To build strength in your hand and arm.

6. A quick study:
   a. Can take as long as three hours to draw.
   b. Will demonstrate whatever you are able to best accomplish in drawing.
   c. Is a drawing that focuses on speed, rather than accuracy.
   d. Can never be considered complete.

7. Which of these is not acceptable in a quick study?
   a. An incompletely drawn figure.
   b. A rough finish.
   c. Conspicuous errors in proportion.
   d. Visible false starts.

8. Drawing quick studies:
   a. Often is a kind of improvisation.
   b. Will help your drawing style become more like everyone else's.
   c. Is out of place in a coffee shop.
   d. Is a skill that is seldom used in the art world.

9. If you draw a line you don't like in a quick-contour drawing:
   a. Immediately start the drawing over.
   b. Keep drawing and don't worry about fixing it.
   c. Erase the line and draw a better one.
   d. Stop working on the inaccurate line and make a better line on the same drawing.

10. If you draw a line you don't like in a shaded quick-contour drawing:
   a. Immediately start the drawing over.
   b. Keep drawing and don't worry about fixing it.
   c. Erase the line and draw a better one.
   d. Stop working on the inaccurate line and make a better line on the same drawing.

Bonus Question: Was Edgar Degas right-handed or left-handed? The answer is in Visual 5–6.

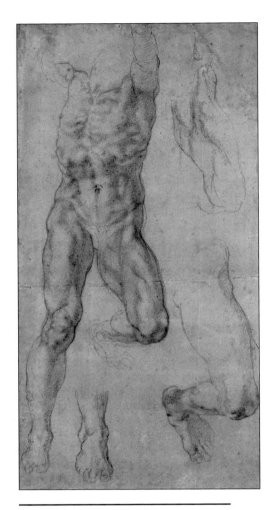

Michelangelo Buonarroti, *Four Studies for Haman*, red chalk, 8.11" × 15.9", 1511–1512. © *The Trustees of the British Museum. All rights reserved.*

CHAPTER

6

objectives

- Define structure as a part of the mechanics of drawing.
- Understand how modeling drawing defines three-dimensional form.
- Compare modeling and chiaroscuro as techniques for rendering form.
- Practice traditional modeling drawing.
- Work with some contemporary approaches to modeling drawing.
- Experiment with figurative abstraction using modeling as a point of departure.

introduction

Modeling is a drawing technique that defines form sculpturally, disregarding local color and the effects of light falling on the form. To make a traditional modeling drawing, an artist analyzes in detail the protrusions and hollows of the model's body and renders them using gradients of gray. Unlike chiaroscuro, which uses light to connect the figure to the space outside of it, modeling drawing emphasizes rendering the structure of the figure independent of its surroundings. Modeling drawing's analytical discipline and emphasis on structure make it a natural starting point for personal inquiries into methods of describing form in life drawing.

MODELING

MODELING AND THE MECHANICS OF DRAWING

The mechanics of a drawing is the set of proficiencies visible in its use of the drawing media. The mechanics of a piece have nothing to do with its message or meaning; the term refers to the drawing's structure, value, and likeness. Structure is the way the drawing's forms are organized, value is the way that levels of gray are used in the piece, and likeness is the degree to which the drawing recognizably depicts its subject. If a drawing is visually boring, or poorly constructed, the problem is probably in one of these three areas: the structure is ambiguous, oversimplified, or contrived; the values are insensitive or lacking in drama; or the drawing does not sufficiently resemble its subject. Compared to other art forms, life drawing takes a narrow approach to the issue of structure. Because life drawing uses a limited range of subject matter, decisions about how to draw the subject take on a heightened significance. The body's forms, and the way they are defined in the drawing, are central to the drawing's meaning.

Visual 6–1 is a chiaroscuro drawing similar to those you practiced in Chapter 3. The space, and the location of the objects that inhabit it, are unambiguous because of the directional light that fills the picture. We can easily imagine ourselves walking around the bed or sitting on the window sill. This unified picture space is part of the picture's structure, and it was created by careful attention to the consistency of the light in the room.

You may recognize the image in Visual 6–2. This is a study by Michelangelo for the figure of Adam as it was painted on the Sistine Chapel ceiling. The drawing is a detailed study of the musculature of a reclining man's body. Structure is communicated by an emphasis on the solidity of the body's forms, as described by modeling and contour line. The figure's anatomy is described with great precision using gradients of tone. The likeness is accurate both in the placement of the

figure's muscles and in the balance between tension and relaxation that determines the body's position. Do you have an idea of how big the room is, or where the model is located in it? No, you can't find that information in this drawing. There is no directional lighting and no extra space. The drawing's space is only as deep as it needs to be to contain the figure, and it is defined by the solidity of the body that occupies it.

Michelangelo thought of himself primarily as a sculptor rather than a painter, so it is not surprising that his paintings and drawings describe the human body's forms very specifically. He used modeling drawing as a way of creating studies for sculpture, sometimes drawing a frontal view, turning the paper over, and drawing the same figure from the back, exactly superimposed.

How He Did It

Michelangelo used a straightforward application of modeling in both his drawing and his painting. Look at the torso in Visual 6–2 and study where the lights and darks are. Imagine that you have a brick of soft clay in your hands, and you want use the drawing to create a clay model of the torso.

A pretty good place to start would be at the relatively flat center of the chest, over the breastbone. You will leave the white areas of the drawing alone, but you will gently push down into the clay wherever the value gets a little darker. If it gets darker still, push down a little harder, so the surface of the clay curves away from you a little more steeply. If it gets lighter again, lighten the pressure you are applying to the clay. Using this formula of curving the surface of the clay away from you in proportion to how dark the drawing is, you could make an accurate model of Adam from this drawing.

In modeling drawing you are still applying pressure to make the surface curve away, but you are pushing down on a piece of charcoal, rather than on a clay surface. When you push harder, the charcoal makes a darker mark, which indicates that the surface tilts a little more. Modeling drawing is mapping the body's three-dimensional forms to the paper by drawing them darker in proportion to how much they tilted away from the **picture plane**.

The picture plane is another name for the surface of the picture. In conventional modeling drawing, any surface that is parallel to the picture plane will be white on the drawing (see Visual 6–3). Where the surface of the form tilts away from the picture plane, it will be represented with a slightly darker value. The steeper the tilt of the surface, the darker it will be drawn, until a surface that is just short of being perpendicular to the picture plane will be drawn as black.

We can call a surface parallel to the picture plane a **reference plane**, a term that comes from 3D modeling software. We will begin a modeling drawing by locating the reference planes.

Visual 6–4 is an illustration of how a convex form is rendered using conventional modeling drawing. In the top image, the reference plane is white, and each adjacent plane is a little darker, according to how steep an angle it makes with the picture plane. The bottom picture shows the same method of developing form, but using a continuous gradient rather than discrete mass tones.

Whether you do your modeling with **planar modeling** or continuous gradients will depend on your temperament, your preferences, and the emotional tone you are trying to create. In Visual 6–5, Käthe Kollwitz constructs the head of a sleeping woman using planar modeling made with hatching lines. The smaller, simpler drawing at the upper left gives us a clue to her process of organizing the head's forms. She has established the part of the hair, the forehead, the top of the

visual | 6–3 |

Any surface that is parallel to the picture plane will be white on a conventional modeling drawing. These white surfaces are called *reference planes*.

nose, and the cheekbone as the planes to be left white. She quickly defined the basic shape of the head by dropping in a few flat areas of pale gray. The larger head takes this process further, developing the rough shape of the head into a more detailed model.

Think about how you would make a wood sculpture of this head. You might start by using a large chisel and a mallet to cut a few large planes out of a block of wood to establish the head's general shape. After that, you could use a smaller chisel to refine each large form into a set of smaller ones. You could continue this process of subdividing forms until you reached the level of detail you wanted. This is how Kollwitz developed this drawing, creating the first set of planes with large areas of hatching and refining the forms by layering in smaller sets of planes. The result is a portrait head with no ambiguous or tentative areas.

Is there more to this drawing than technical accomplishment? What can you learn about the subject from the way the artist chose to draw her? Any well-made modeling drawing will convey the solidity of the forms, but, in addition, this one uses careful, deliberate hatching to suggest age through a connotation that the drawing's surface is abraded or weather-beaten. The sympathetic study of a tired person is a staple in art, but most artists tell the story by covering the subject's face with dirt, wrinkles, or a dazed, pathetic expression. By understating the point, Kollwitz respects the person she is drawing and shows us with compassion and a

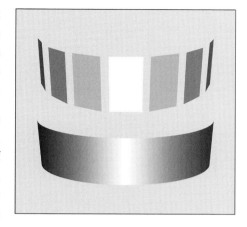

visual | 6–4 |

How modeling drawing describes form: the darkness of a surface is proportional to how far the surface tilts back from the reference plane. The form can be described as a series of planes, using mass tones (top) or with a continuous gradient (bottom).

visual | 6–5 |

Käthe Kollwitz, *Two Studies of a Woman's Head,* black chalk on tan wove paper, 19" × 24¾", circa 1903. *Minneapolis Institute of Arts, Gift of David M. Daniels. © 2007 Artists Rights Society (ARS), New York / VG Bild-Kunst, Bonn.*

William Bailey,
Woman's Head,
N.D., pencil on
paper, 15" × 11 ⅛".
© William Bailey,
Courtesy Betty
Cuningham
Gallery, New York.

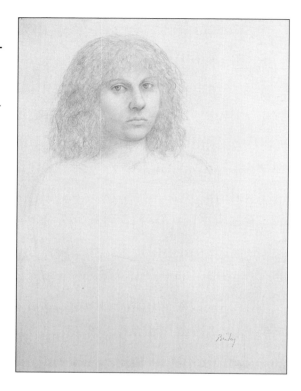

certain tough-mindedness that this woman really needs her rest.

A great drawing will communicate subjective feelings that may be hard to put into words. If we were to describe William Bailey's drawing in Visual 6–6, it would sound in some ways like Kollwitz's: They are both portraits of women, using modeling techniques. Bailey often uses very fine hatching to build very smooth gradients of value. The sitter is looking us right in the eye: what could it mean to draw this with such a highly refined finish? Would you say that this picture presents a different emotional tone from the previous one? Which sitter do you feel that you know better?

Each of these drawings was produced with simple tools by an accomplished artist. These drawings are the product of long-term intellectual explorations that use modeling drawing as the method.

VARIATIONS OF TRADITIONAL MODELING DRAWING

Traditional modeling drawing uses the technique described earlier in this chapter, in which the reference planes, parallel to the picture plane, are left white, and other surfaces are darkened according to how much they angle away into the picture. This standard application of modeling is versatile and powerful, and some artists have made it a life's work to master it. However, most modeling drawings do not use a pure traditional modeling technique without modifying it or augmenting it with other uses of value.

Théodore Géricault's drawing in Visual 6–7 is surely one of the more dramatic life drawings ever created. After recruiting his friends as models, he drew it as a study for a 16' × 23½' painting of a maritime disaster that took place in 1816. It is so well made that it is possible to see it, live with it, remember it, and be moved by it without really understanding how he did it. At first glance, it seems like a chiaroscuro drawing illuminated from above, but a light in this location would wash out many of the details of the sufferer's torso. The body must be defined by modeling, then, but if we look for the reference planes in the usual place, on the surfaces of the body parallel to the picture plane, they are not there. Those areas that we would expect to be white contain complex descriptions of musculature. The whites have moved to a new location at the ridges of the lower ribs and the upper surface of the left arm, the legs, and the lower torso. Géricault has rotated the modeling frame of reference so that the reference plane is on the top of the figure, rather than the front.

When you are learning how to draw, it is good to focus on one skill at a time, but few accomplished artists work that way once they have been successful with the basic techniques. No technique is perfect; for example, chiaroscuro alone cannot always adequately define the forms in the dark areas, and modeling sometimes creates a sense of **classicism** and emotional distance that can be at odds with effective portraiture. Accordingly, skilled figurative artists do not allow the requirements of a particular technique to interfere with a clear definition of forms. They will modify techniques as necessary—often using modeling in a personal, nonstandard way, or combining modeling and chiaroscuro. For example, Peter Paul Rubens used both modeling and four-value chiaroscuro in *Abel Slain by Cain*, in Visual 6–8. Although this drawing has some similarities to Géricault's, its reference plane is in the customary orientation parallel to the picture plane, as shown by the modeling on Abel's shoulders and the front of his abdomen. Light coming from above generates the four values that provide a transition from the figure to the surface he is lying on. Using two different techniques in this way is contradictory by modern standards, but Rubens did describe

visual | 6–7 |

Théodore Géricault, *Study for one of the Figures in "The Raft of Medusa,"* charcoal, 11.38" × 8", 1818. *Musee des Beaux-Arts et d'Archeologie. Image © Copyright Musee des Beaux-Arts et d'Archeologie de Besancon (cliché Charles CHOFFET).*

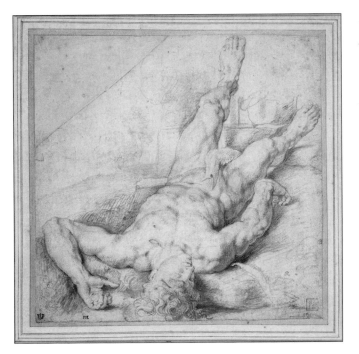

visual | 6–8 |

Peter Paul Rubens (1577–1640), *Abel Slain by Cain*; red chalk, touched with white partly oxidized, reinforced with the point of the brush dipped in red, on paper, 8.42" × 8.26". *Fitzwilliam Museum, University of Cambridge, UK / The Bridgeman Art Library*

that body comprehensively. Whatever you want to accomplish in life drawing, defining the body's form is the first goal. If you lose track of this, and become preoccupied instead with perfectly executing one particular technique, you may create competent life drawings without any life in them.

Exercise 6-1: A Traditional Modeling Drawing

This exercise is your opportunity to make a modeling drawing in the genuine old-master manner. This will be a drawing in which the forms are defined by gradient modeling and a compatible contour line. You goal for the modeling is to make a smooth blend of value from something pretty close to a solid black, through the grays, to the white of the paper.

Work at building the blend as you apply the charcoal, rather than by smudging and rubbing the charcoal after has been applied. The hardest new skill here is likely to be maintaining a light hand as you draw. As a teacher, I have often watched in fascination as a drawing in progress, possessing all of the dignity and privilege of a work of art, is transformed into a dirty sheet of paper. It's like witnessing a miracle in reverse. Modeling is easy to overwork, making the drawing so dark that it gets gloomy and unclear. Using vine charcoal rather than pressed charcoal helps keep it light.

Materials

- Vine charcoal. It usually comes in hard, medium, and soft. Although the softest version is still pretty hard, get a few sticks of soft and a few of medium, and see which grade likes you best.
- A small piece of clean terrycloth, or a washrag or other cotton cloth. This will be your big eraser.
- Two or three cheap pink rubber erasers and a pocketknife to cut them into slices as necessary. You will use these to erase details. A kneaded eraser will also work for this purpose.
- 18" × 24" or larger drawing pad, or individual 22" × 30" sheets of 100% rag drawing paper. Modeling drawing doesn't burn through a lot of paper, so you can probably afford to use a decent grade for this exercise.

Procedures

1. Budget three hours for this project. Plan on drawing for forty-five minutes at a stretch and taking a fifteen-minute break.
2. It is best if you warm up before you do the modeling exercise. Before starting, do a fifteen-minute blind contour exercise as described in Chapter 2.
3. Illuminate the model with soft, nondirectional lighting if you can. The best lighting will mitigate hard shadows that might tempt you to do a chiaroscuro drawing.

4. Study the pose and figure out how you will fit it on the paper. Do you want to show the entire model, or zoom in on an area of detail? Do you want to start drawing the middle of the model on the middle of the paper, or begin somewhere else?

5. Find an interesting area of detail and draw its outside edge using the semiblind contour technique.

6. Define the forms of the area you are working on with some modeling. As you do this exercise a few times, experiment with different ways of using the charcoal: smooth modeling using the side of the stick, and hatching lines using the point.

7. If you see that you have made an error, wipe the problem away and draw it again. It's OK to draw a structure as often as necessary to get it right.

8. Develop the figure by leading with a contour line, and articulating the interior forms with modeling. Try not to draw the entire form with a line and then fill it in with modeling.

9. When the third forty-five-minute drawing session starts, and you have a substantial portion of the figure drawn, study the lightest and darkest values. Are there any spots that are so dark that they don't seem to fit into the rest of the drawing? Are there large, flat regions of white in which no shape is defined? Do different parts of the drawing look like they were drawn by two different people? Spend the last session balancing values and making the modeling consistent.

Demonstration 6-1: A Traditional Modeling Drawing

After I studied the pose, I planned to compose the drawing so that the model's torso would extend from one side of the paper to the other, substantially filling the picture. The paper was 30" wide, so this plan would produce a large enough figure that I could comfortably use modeling to draw the detailed forms. You can see many small examples of modeling drawing in the history of art, such as Michelangelo's study of Adam in Visual 6–2 and Géricault's shipwreck drawing in Visual 6–7. Either of those drawings would fit on a sheet of notebook paper. Paper was scarcer and more expensive in the old days, and the artists had to make do with what they could get. I have to believe that if Michelangelo could have chosen from the variety of papers available to us, he would have worked bigger.

I started the drawing with some quick planar modeling of the head (Visual 6–9) and a couple of contour lines to extend the drawing a little bit onto the picture plane. With these lines, I anticipated where I would want to continue the drawing and gave myself a logical place to work. By using **open forms** at this stage, I avoided the problem of integrating a complete, floating, disembodied head into a blank sheet of white paper.

Compare Step 1 (Visual 6–9) with Step 2 (Visual 6–10), and you will see that I made an immediate error in drawing the left breast too small. Visual 6–10 shows a trace of the first contour

H. Stone,
*Traditional
Modeling
Demonstration,
Step 1.*

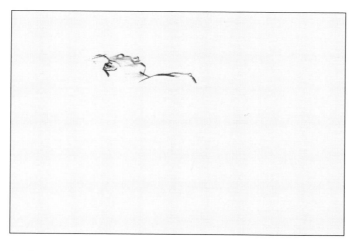

under the corrected one. I extended the upper contour line both left and right from the center, and then started adding light modeling. I worked slowly and carefully, thinking about where the modeling would go before I placed it. I left liberal expanses of white at the reference plane, so I would have room to refine the modeling later. I was concentrating on getting the forms in the right places, so I could see if the elements of the torso plausibly worked together before I spent a lot of time on details. This would allow me to make any major corrections early in the drawing.

H. Stone,
*Traditional
Modeling
Demonstration,
Step 2.*

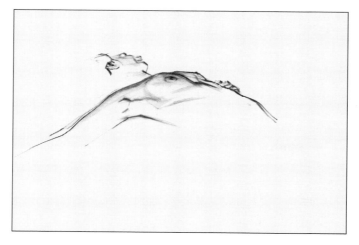

Hands can be a problem in modeling drawing because their complexity can tempt an artist to stray from the modeling path and draw them in a less demanding technique, or leave them out completely. The traditional solution is to practice. Most artists who work with the figure have a supply of hand studies, such as Lawrence Alma-Tadema's chiaroscuro drawing in Visual 6–11, documenting their process of learning how hands work.

Sir Lawrence
Alma-Tadema
(1836–1912),
*Study of Hands—
Miss Gould,*
graphite on white
wove paper,
6" × 10⅜", 1903.
*Minneapolis
Institute of Arts,
The Tess
Armstrong Fund.*

You can see another correction in Step 3 (Visual 6–12). When I developed the lower abdomen, I erased the first contour lines and drew a better one, covering the traces of the old ones with modeling. Then I modeled the abdomen below and to the right of the hand and added a light contour line that would help me construct the model's right leg.

visual | 6–12 |

H. Stone, *Traditional Modeling Demonstration, Step 3.*

In Step 4 (Visual 6–13), I added some modeling to the ribcage, softened the previous modeling in the lower abdomen, and further developed the form there. The most important addition at this stage was the contour line that defines the lower edge of the torso. This was, in a sense, the turning point of the drawing because I could now see how the figure would fit on the page, and I could verify that the structure was acceptable and would not require any major overhauls.

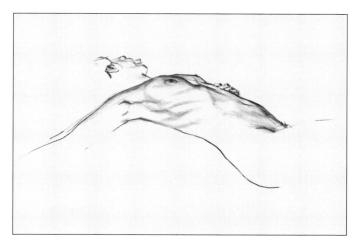

visual | 6–13 |

H. Stone, *Traditional Modeling Demonstration, Step 4.*

Now, after the big decisions have been made, is the time to critically evaluate the drawing and see if its basic assumptions are valid. For example, does the body seem to be one structure, or a bunch of disconnected elements? Does it fit on the page the way you wanted it to? Are there inaccuracies in the visible anatomy, or areas in which the technique is substandard?

This is no time for a failure of nerve. If you see an opportunity to improve the drawing, make the change even if it means dismantling some presentable work. If you get complacent at this stage, when you are discovering what a drawing can grow into, you will never find out just how good you can be.

Step 1 through Step 4 were done during the first of the three forty-five-minute drawing sessions. Step 5 (Visual 6–14) shows the drawing at the end of the second session. I spent this session bringing the face, neck, and torso to a consistent level of definition. I made a correction to the model's right arm and added some mass tones to the background to provide a soft transition from figure to ground. I borrowed this trick from Rubens to help connect the figure to the rest of the composition.

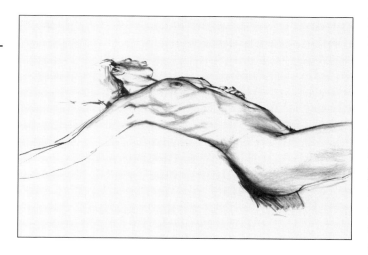

I started the work on the head by creating the hairline. I drew the hair by applying the modeling technique to its masses. On the face, I softened the existing planes, lightened it in places, and added a dark area above the jaw line to indicate the slight hollowness between the jaw and the cheekbone. From the standpoint of textbook modeling, it isn't perfect, but the forms are fairly well defined, and I have something I can develop further. The same can be said for the neck, to which I added some preliminary modeling.

Visual 6–15 shows the completed drawing. This is the result of spending the last forty-five minutes balancing tones, drawing hair, and tweaking the figure–ground relationship. One of the more significant changes is the reduced white space in the figure. I had initially left the reference plane oversized, so I would have room to create softer transitions from the first set of grays to white. Creating a soft edge between bare paper and a medium value is not always easy, but it is necessary in order to define the reference plane with any degree of sensitivity.

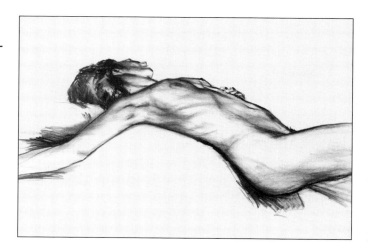

I used a rubber eraser to firm up the forms in the hair, and I darkened the junction of the hair and the neck as a means of softening the edge and making them seem more like parts of the same structure.

Look at the Drawing

Traditional modeling is a sophisticated skill that seldom looks good the first time it is applied. The goal is to see improvement over the course of several drawings. The most common problems when learning modeling are failure to understand the drawing system and lack of control over the medium. If you don't know what you are trying to accomplish here, read the chapter again, talk to others, look at some great drawings from the past, and give it another try. If you know what you want to achieve, but your modeling looks shaky, make a note of one specific thing you would like to do better and work on it when you do the exercise again. Repeat as necessary.

In this exercise, we are looking for:

* Sensitive modeling that accurately describes the convex and concave forms of the person you drew.
* A single, accurate contour line that works well with the modeling to help describe the figure.
* Smooth gradients in the modeling, created either with the side of the charcoal or with fine hatching.

We are not looking for:

* Awkward, clumsy, or inaccurate modeling.
* A contour line that is oversimplified or too dark, or which contains distracting mannerisms.
* A contour line that is not visible because too much charcoal was used in the modeling.
* Planar modeling.
* Chiaroscuro used to define large areas of the figure.

If the proportions have some problems, that is not a huge issue at this point. Chapter 7 deals with proportions in detail.

I am pretty much satisfied with my drawing, even though I wouldn't say that it is perfect. In some respects, I prefer the more relaxed look of the unfinished drawing in Visual 6–14, but that figure had several unarticulated areas. The final drawing is my response to a nagging artistic conscience telling me that the figure needed more definition.

The modeling of the body was generally successful with a couple of exceptions. It got a little too dark along the lower edge of the torso from the lower back to the upper leg, which compromised the contour line a little bit. Similarly, the edge between the hair and the neck is not entirely successful because it is too dark. I made a mental note to work on drawing this structure more clearly next time.

IMPROVISATIONS

As we have seen, the two standard techniques for using value to define form are modeling and chiaroscuro. In the twentieth century, electric lighting and photography trained people to believe that chiaroscuro is the most natural way for form to reveal itself to the eye. However, as an intellectual discipline, modeling is the bigger tent. Modeling is a direct struggle with form; like chiaroscuro, its practice goes back 500 years to the Italian Renaissance, when artists believed that profound secrets were to be found in the architecture of the human body: its shapes, its proportions, and the interaction of its parts.

visual | 6–16 |

Richard Diebenkorn, *Seated Nude*, charcoal on paper, 33" × 23½", 1966. *San Francisco Museum of Modern Art, Gift of the Diebenkorn family and purchased through a gift of Leanne B. Roberts, Thomas W. Weisel, and the Mnuchin Foundation.* © *Estate of Richard Diebenkorn*

Some contemporary artists, such as Richard Diebenkorn (Visual 6–16), have continued this exploration using nontraditional drawing techniques. This kind of work is sometimes given the name **figurative abstraction**.

When an artist departs from the conventions of figure drawing, judging the quality of the product becomes more difficult. When you create an abstract drawing of the human figure, you are constructing your own way of describing forms. How do you retain your urgency, truthfulness, and intensity of focus when you are inventing a new vocabulary? Will the integrity of the process be visible in the finished drawing?

We can gain some insight into the difference between abstract art and self-indulgent noodling around by starting with procedures we know about and moving them into new territory. Because we will be grappling directly with the forms, rather than the effects of light on the forms, we will start with a modeling exercise.

Exercise 6-2: Gesture Drawing with Modeling Drawing

Much of this project will be familiar to you. You will start with an abstract drawing exercise you know how to do, gesture drawing, and lay a modeling drawing on top of it. The drawing will be done under time pressure to induce you to keep the modeling simple.

Materials

- Compressed charcoal and vine charcoal.
- Cheap pink rubber erasers.
- Everyday paper, at least 11" × 14".

Procedures

1. Feel free to start your drawing day with this exercise. It's a good warm-up for other life-drawing projects.
2. The model should be well-lit with soft, nondirectional lighting.

3. Each drawing should last fifteen minutes. The first two or three minutes will be a gesture drawing, and the rest will be modeling.

4. Even though you have practiced gesture drawing, and it is familiar to you, don't let it become routine. Each time you do it, start it with the freshness and energy you would bring to it if were doing it for the first time. Summarize the pose in a few strokes, and then continue to express its movement with your own kinds of marks.

5. After two or three minutes, when the pose is visible in the drawing, start the modeling. A good way to begin is by using an eraser to pull out the reference planes. When these have been located, start adding dark masses. Refine the forms by alternating drawing and erasing.

6. Work quickly, and make corrections as you notice the need for them.

7. If you do not feel that you are being challenged enough, shorten the time span to ten minutes, or even five minutes.

Demonstration 6-2: Gesture and Modeling Drawing

I used a stick of compressed charcoal for this drawing because it is more difficult to erase than vine charcoal. I wanted some physical struggle to be visible in the final drawing. Visual 6–17 shows my first summary marks. When you make this set of marks, it is fine to exaggerate and scribble all over if you need to. You are learning to create a drawing that comes from your own sense of inner necessity; in other words, you are learning to draw it the way you feel it. It is not helpful to be self-conscious.

Step 2 (Visual 6–18) shows the drawing at the end of the gesture stage. My main interest during this time was keeping my hand moving and my eye on the model. It might be interesting some time to draw to this point, work on the

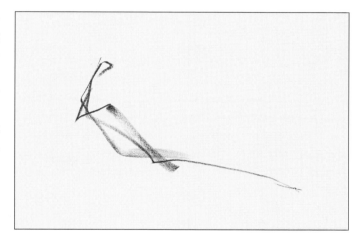

visual | 6–17 |

H. Stone, *Gesture and Modeling Drawing, Step 1.*

visual | 6–18 |

H. Stone, *Gesture and Modeling Drawing, Step 2.*

H. Stone, *Gesture and Modeling Drawing, Step 3.*

background, and see how well the result would work as a finished work of art. This drawing, however, had a different destiny….

I started the work shown in Step 3 (Visual 6–19) by using an eraser to create the reference planes for the top half of the body. While I was erasing, I removed the contour of the face and upper shoulder and redrew it more accurately with a better contour line. I also used contour lines to add the right arm, hand, and details to the upper torso. At this point, the head would make a good study for a chainsaw sculpture at the fairgrounds. Because it meets the requirements of the exercise, and looks presentable, it is done. The task now is bringing the rest of the body to a level of finish consistent with that of the head.

In Step 4 (Visual 6–20), I have established the reference planes for all of the body except the model's left leg. The left thumb and fingers are doing their part. The modeling of this drawing is pretty rude compared to that of the traditional drawing shown earlier in this chapter, but there is no reason it cannot be equally true to the artist's experience. This is where the integrity of the process becomes important. If you are using the looseness of the drawing as an excuse to omit structures that are hard to draw, then your process lacks integrity. If you are able to clearly define the body's difficult structures while sustaining the drawing's looseness and energy, then you are improvising with authority and *brio*.

The finished drawing in Visual 6–21 shows the completed left leg, some background forms, and some rubbing and scrubbing here and there to balance the values.

H. Stone, *Gesture and Modeling Drawing, Step 4.*

Look at the Drawing

This drawing will succeed or fail according to two criteria:

1. How well does the use of the medium reflect the artist's personality?

2. How well does the drawing describe the structure of the scene?

There is a relationship between the look of the marks you make when you draw and your temperament. When you look at the drawing you made, do you feel any affection for it? Does it seem somewhat generic, or do you feel that it is uniquely yours? Would others agree that the marks are recognizable as coming from your hand?

visual | 6–21 |

H. Stone, *Gesture and Modeling Drawing, final version*, compressed charcoal on paper, 22" × 30", 2006.

Structure in a drawing is the definition and positioning of its elements. If I wanted to make a painting of this pose, most of the problems of structure that I would face have been solved in this drawing. In other words, it is clear from the drawing how the body is shaped, how it is positioned, where it is in the room, and where it will go on the picture plane.

Exercise 6-3: Interconnectedness Drawing

This is an exercise in figurative abstraction. You will draw the figure, emphasizing how its parts connect together to create a single structural unit. The setting and media will be familiar to you, and the marks you make on the paper will probably come from the repertoire you have been building since you started life drawing. The object of this exercise is for you to maintain your focus on an idea and keep the idea connected to your hand while you are working. You are used to doing this with gesture drawing, when you concentrate on maintaining an empathetic participation in the figure's movement. Here the theme will be the interconnectedness of the figure's components, and you will work at staying on topic for a longer time.

This exercise is an exploration, so you won't necessarily end up at the same place as anyone else. Stay focused and trust your drawing skills, and you will make your thinking visible in your own way.

visual | 6–22 |

Alberto Giacometti (1901–1966), *Annette*, pencil on paper, 15⅜" × 11¾", 1954. *The Sidney and Harriet Janis Collection.* (602.1967). *Digital Image © The Museum of Modern Art, New York, NY/Licensed by SCALA/Art Resource, NY. © 2007 Artists Rights Society (ARS), New York/ADAGP, Paris.*

Materials

- Pressed charcoal and vine charcoal.
- Cheap pink rubber erasers.
- Everyday paper, 18" × 24".

Procedures

1. The model should be well lit with soft, nondirectional lighting.

2. The pose should last twenty to forty-five minutes. This is a great exercise to do with a "ship-wreck pose," such as the one in Visual 6–7.

3. Start the drawing with a few gesture marks to locate the figure on the paper.

4. Continue by quickly drawing lines that connect all of the parts of the figure as you see them. Don't be afraid to make new kinds of marks. Experiment and see what kinds of lines feel right for you. When you find a good mark, flag it so you can remember it (I use an arrow and an exclamation mark), and practice with it later.

5. Keeping your hand moving, inventory your drawing for missing parts. When you notice that you have left something out, add it to the drawing by connecting it to the network of lines you are building.

6. When you feel that the entire figure is present in some sense on the paper, use your charcoal and eraser to refine the edges of the figure. Look for marks that don't seem to be a part of the figure, or aren't compatible with the drawing in some way, and remove them. This is also a good time to correct errors in the proportions.

7. If you are happy with how this process is going, continue to develop the drawing this way for as long as you like. If the drawing really seems to need a contour line, go ahead and add one. If you want to physically engage the form, and wreak it out of the surface of the paper, grab your eraser, plant your feet, and go.

8. Probably the first few times you practice this exercise, you will want to use all of the available drawing time, so the drawing will be finished when the time is up. If you choose to pursue this line of work, you will need to decide when to declare a drawing finished. The conventional answer, which derives from classicism, is that the drawing is finished when anything you could add to it, or take away from it, would make it worse. Some who are not fans of classicism might say that this is a good reason to leave the paper blank. In practice, when you are creating your own way of working you will just have to figure it out for yourself.

Demonstration 6–3: Interconnectedness Drawing

Like the previous drawing, this one starts with a quick summary of the figure's positioning (Visual 6–23). It is not necessary or best to start every drawing this way, but it is helpful when the drawing will use layering, erasing, and palimpsest effects.

In Step 2 (Visual 6–24), I began connecting the parts of the figure together. I started out by adding interior lines and quick contours to fill the figure out. As I did this, I noticed parts of the figure that were missing and incomplete, and I worked on adding them. I find this inventory process to be the hardest part of this drawing because it is a reversal of the usual way to draw the figure. One of the enduring standards of life drawing is economy of means: getting the maximum definition of forms with the minimum amount of drawing. Spilling black all over the picture plane in order to graph the extent of the body is not business as usual, and it demands new thinking. This, of course, is the point of doing it.

Step 3 (Visual 6–25) shows the inventory continuing. I added some connection lines to the model's right shoulder and in a few other places. The preliminary eraser work was not intended to be correction; I was experimenting with using the smeared and erased forms to tie the figure together.

As you do this exercise, you may find that contour lines tend to appear along the edges of the figure even if you

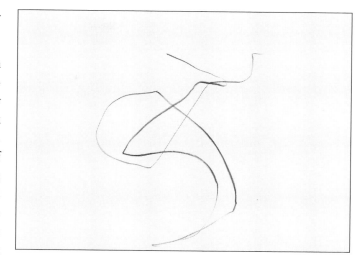

visual | 6–23 |

H. Stone,
*Interconnectedness
Drawing, Step 1.*

visual | 6–24 |

H. Stone,
*Interconnectedness
Drawing, Step 2.*

visual | 6–25 |

H. Stone,
*Interconnectedness
Drawing, Step 3.*

H. Stone,
*Interconnectedness
Drawing, Step 4.*

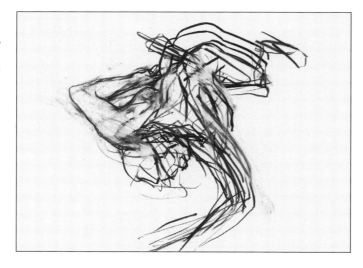

are not consciously trying to draw them. This is not a bad thing, but make sure that you work with interior lines as well. This is a time for you to experiment, so do not be conservative. Too much reliance on contour lines, especially early in the drawing, will limit the range of possibilities for the final drawing.

I was being fairly conservative myself at this point (Visual 6–26). I continued the idea of using an eraser to help hold the figure together, with erased additions in the model's right arm and some new drawing in the hand. The eraser creates linear forms and gives the surface a characteristic blurred look. My thinking was that both of these effects would help to visually merge the figure into a single object separate from the background. I did not intend to draw two contour lines to define the hip; I did one, and it wasn't big enough, so I did another one. A more adventurous way of doing this would be to rework the hip with connectivity lines in the interior of the form.

Step 5 (Visual 6–27) shows the point where I found the groove with this drawing. The body's structure became logical to me, and I no longer had to struggle to figure out where the next mark would go or what it would look like. From this point on, the task would be to add to an existing drawing, rather than create one from thin air. There are some new contour lines and an adjustment of the size of the torso, but the important changes from the standpoint of the premises behind the drawing are the addition of interior lines and erasures. There's a big area of black in the lower back which doesn't correspond to a structure I saw directly. I placed it there as a way of making the hips and lower back

H. Stone,
*Interconnectedness
Drawing, Step 5.*

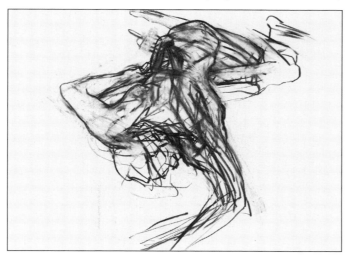

seem like a solid construction, rather than a network of lines on the surface of the paper. In the same way I added more connectivity lines across the model's back, stretching from the lower back to the model's left shoulder. On this shoulder, you can also see a form like a backwards "S," which I hoped would integrate the shoulder's structure and establish its position with respect to the head.

Visual 6–28 shows another dark, heavy structure on the back, connecting the lower back to the head. The shoulders adjacent to the head have received some new connections, and the model's right upper arm has been redrawn, with some minimal modeling added. A few solid, angular lines were added to the model's right shoulder to connect it to the rest of the torso. The size of the head was also modified to properly proportion it to the resized torso.

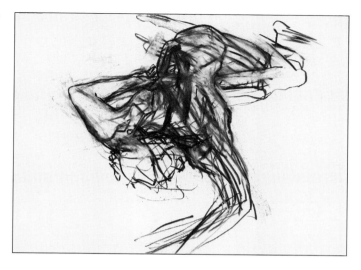

visual | 6–28 |

H. Stone, *Interconnectedness Drawing, Step 6.*

The finished drawing is shown in Visual 6–29. The right leg was finished with a contour line and a few mass tones. The darkest structures on the back were modified, and their edges were softened with an eraser to help maintain the consistent, **painterly** structure I was looking for. The head was finished with some slightly modified traditional modeling, and angular connectivity lines were added to the model's left shoulder. Why did I choose solid, angular lines? Simply because those kinds of lines seemed compatible with the character of the drawing.

Look at the Drawing

It is hard to draw conclusions about an abstract piece unless the viewer and artist share some of the same ideas about art. Because the drawing may not conform to common standards about what a life drawing should look like, it is particularly important to evaluate it with the same discipline and integrity that went into making it.

Quality standards related to how well the drawing is crafted will be the same for this piece as for previous drawings. If you used a contour line, it shouldn't be slack. Mass tones should be applied with skill and conviction. Your goal of using the media to show who you are is a constant in every figure drawing you do.

visual | 6–29 |

H. Stone, *Interconnectedness Drawing, final version,* pressed charcoal on paper, 22" × 30", 2006.

This drawing was an exploration of how the parts of this human body in this particular pose interacted to present a single structure. If there is one and only one identifiable human body in the drawing, you have accomplished this part of the plan.

To assess how well you integrated the parts into the whole, study the drawing and ask yourself specific questions about the structure:

- Is it clear from looking at the drawing whether you are looking at the front or the back of the figure?
- Can you tell which leg is the left one, and which is the right?
- If the torso was twisted, is the twist visible in your drawing? Is it clear how much of the structure is twisted?
- If the legs are crossed, or the arms folded, can you tell from looking at the drawing which one of them is in front of the other?
- Can individual structures be identified?
- Is the entire body clearly differentiated from the background?

Notice that these questions don't have to do with proportion, balance, anatomical accuracy, or the picture space. If you were able to answer "yes" to most of these questions, and your drawing is not primarily a contour, chiaroscuro, or traditional modeling drawing, your drawing was successful.

There are many ways to do figurative abstraction, and this exercise was just an introduction to it. Making real art in this idiom means practicing it until the drawings transcend the immediate intellectual problem and address the enduring questions: Who am I? How am I different from you? Who are we? How are we different from them?

CHAPTER SUMMARY

Modeling drawing is a way of rendering form analytically. In its traditional form, the surfaces of the figure that are parallel to the picture plane are left white on the drawing. These areas are called reference planes. As the forms of the body curve back away from a reference plane, they are made darker. Unlike chiaroscuro drawing, modeling drawing is concerned with the figure independent of its setting. Where chiaroscuro creates a unified structure for a picture by having its entire space share a common light source, modeling drawings create structure in a picture by describing the shape of the masses of the model's body. In a modeling drawing, often there is little articulation of the space outside the figure's immediate vicinity.

Modeling drawing and the theory behind it are compatible with explorations into new ways of defining the figure's forms. Using the analytical framework behind traditional modeling drawing, an artist can create personal methods of drawing the figure. Assessing these drawings requires an understanding of the thinking that went into them.

▶ *chapter questions*

Multiple Choice

1. The mechanics of drawing:
   a. Concerns the subject of the drawing.
   b. Concerns how the drawing is made.
   c. Concerns what the drawing means.
   d. Concerns what the drawing costs.

2. Structure in life drawing:
   a. Is the drawing's use of color.
   b. Is the drawing's use of value.
   c. Is how well the likeness works.
   d. Is the way the forms are organized.

3. Planar modeling:
   a. Is pretty much the same as chiaroscuro.
   b. Is not a form of conventional modeling drawing.
   c. Works pretty much the same as modeling with continuous gradients.
   d. Looks like an explosion in a shingle factory.

4. Skilled figurative artists:
   a. Never combine different techniques in a single drawing.
   b. Often combine different techniques in a single drawing.
   c. Use modeling most often.
   d. Use chiaroscuro most often.

5. In modeling drawing, a reference plane:
   a. Is the color of the bare paper.
   b. Is always parallel to the picture plane.
   c. Is always somewhere on the figure's abdomen.
   d. All of the above.

6. Traditional modeling drawings:

    a. Should not use contour lines.

    b. Should place equal emphasis on the figure and background.

    c. Began 300 years ago.

    d. Should be drawn using vine charcoal.

7. Nontraditional modeling drawings can be assessed by:

    a. Evaluating their anatomical accuracy.

    b. Evaluating their structure.

    c. Evaluating how much they look like those of other artists working on the same project.

    d. Evaluating how well their composition is balanced.

8. Traditional and nontraditional modeling drawings have in common:

    a. That they are both made by drawing a complete line drawing and filling it in with shading.

    b. That they are both realist drawing styles with few abstract elements.

    c. That they both render their forms according to an analytical method.

    d. That they are both concerned with placing the figure in a plausible environment.

9. A work of figurative abstraction:

    a. May not conform to common standards about what a life drawing should look like.

    b. Must be evaluated with the same discipline and integrity that went into making it.

    c. Is hard to draw a conclusion about unless the viewer and artist share some of the same ideas about art.

    d. All of the above.

10. A good reason to depart from the conventions of traditional figure drawing is:

    a. If you fail to understand the modeling drawing system.

    b. You lack control of the medium.

    c. Because working on a very loose drawing allows you t omit structures that are hard to draw.

    d. To create your own way of defining the body's forms.

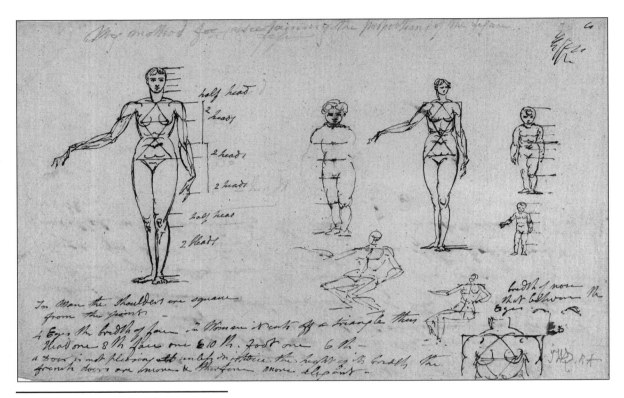

James Ward (1769–1859), *Studies of Anatomy with Measurements and Writing*, 7.8" × 12.5" pen and brown ink on paper, circa eighteenth to nineteenth century. *Private Collection / The Bridgeman Art Library*

CHAPTER 7

objectives

- Define proportion.
- Learn the standard proportions of the human body.
- Learn how anatomy and stance can affect the artist's perception of proportion.
- Understand ideal, objective, empirical, and internal proportions as they are used in life drawing.
- Learn twelve ways of measuring and verifying empirical proportions.
- Practice working specifically with proportion in a quick study and a finished drawing.

introduction

Proportion, the relationship of a drawing's elements with respect to size, is not simple. The complexity of the body's structure, variations in the artist's point of view, and differing theories of human proportion introduce ambiguities into one of the few quantitative processes in art. Mathematically, proportion is related to harmony in music, and in life drawing it is a complex and subtle organizing principle for both the construction of the drawing and the anatomy of its subject.

A few artists seem to have the ability to represent proportions correctly the first time they draw the figure. For most of us, it is the last skill we master and the first to get rusty if we abstain from drawing for a while. How important is it to get the proportions right? Orderly proportions establish an intimate connection between the viewer and the structures in the drawing. Working on proportion is a rite of passage for an artist, and mastering it is a technical achievement, but understanding the meaning of the choices about human proportions goes much deeper. Because it is a constant in life drawing, proportion is a way of connecting your work with enduring themes. An exploration of proportion is an inquiry into the assumptions you bring to art and an examination of how well they fit into the art you want to make.

CHOICES IN PROPORTION

In some forms of figurative art, drawing a correctly proportioned human body means figuring out which numerical ratios to use and sticking to them through thick and thin. For example, the **classical** standard, using the height of the head as a unit of measure, says that a man is 7½ heads tall. A heroic statue, which in the ancient world depicted an exemplary specimen of manhood, is 8 to 8½ heads tall, and many modern comic-book heroes are 10 heads tall, or taller. Some art disciplines, such as comic art and computer game animation, are self-contained systems that have rigid standards for body proportions. A human figure proportioned along these lines will be intelligible while running, flying, or fighting, but it may appear somewhat artificial out of context. For example, if we ask the question, "Does every hero have a small head?" in real life, the answer would have to be no (Visual 7–1).

visual | 7–1 |

Superheroes have very small heads. The scale on the right shows this individual to be 10 heads tall.

When the subject of our drawing is a person, and not a character in a story, proportion gets interesting. A real person doesn't necessarily conform to a standard design. How will you draw them? Will you make your subjects as beautiful as possible, will you draw their proportions as you know them to be, or will you draw them strictly as you see them? Your decision here will come from your values, and how you want to express them in art.

Classical Proportions

Classicism is concerned with the relationship between order and beauty. The original Classicists (in ancient Greece, 450–323 B.C.E.) believed that the proportions of the human body were the same set of perfect ratios that invisibly organized the universe. Because they believed that perfection was encoded into the human frame, they used the proportional ratios they derived from the body in their sculpture and architecture.

Classical proportions address the question, "What does an ideal person look like?" The Greeks didn't believe that everyone had perfect proportions. Their standard of perfection was the male athlete, so they took measurements of many athletes and made a composite figure from the best-proportioned parts. Polykleitos, a Classical-period sculptor, wrote a book called the *Canon* which defined the perfect proportions of the human body. His sculpture, the *Doryphoros* (Visual 4–10, 7–2), whose use of *contrapposto* was discussed in Chapter 4, embodies this set of proportions. Unfortunately, Polykleitos' book was lost. Almost 2000 years later, Leonardo da Vinci rediscovered this knowledge (Visual 7–3).

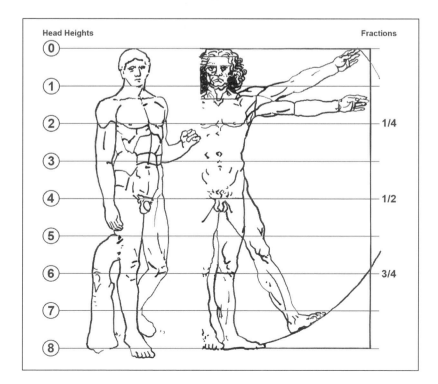

visual | 7–2 |

Objective proportions of Doryphoros (the Spear Bearer) with head heights shown.

visual | 7–3 |

Leonardo da
Vinci
(1452–1519),
Vitruvian Man,
pen and ink on
paper,
13.5" × 8.625",
1492. *Galleria
deli' Accademia,
Venice, Italy / The
Bridgeman Art
Library*

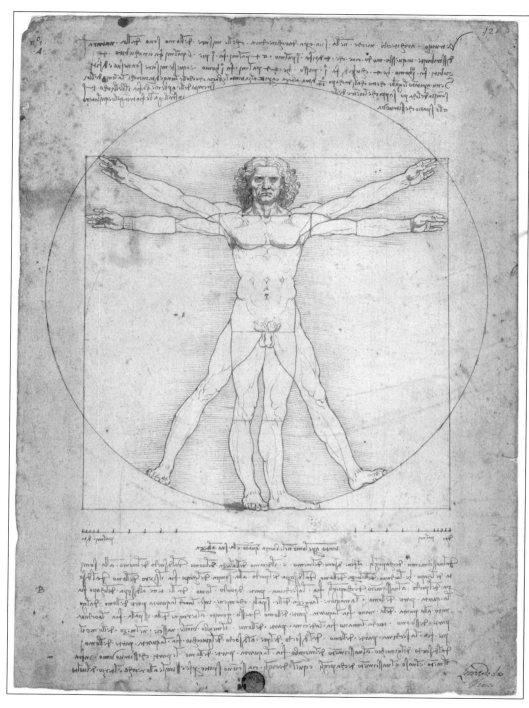

There are contemporary figurative artists working in a classical mode, and you may choose to be one of them. However, you don't have to immerse yourself in Classicism or adopt its attitudes about beauty to use its tools. It can be very helpful to know standard proportions when you want to quickly check for errors in your drawing.

The standard unit of measure for the human body is the height of the head. The standard adult human is 7½ heads tall (Visual 7–4). In practice, most men are that tall, with a few a little taller or shorter. Many women are not that tall, and it is very unusual to find a woman taller that 7½ heads.

Height errors in drawing are often due to poorly judging the height of the head. This usually occurs because of common preconceptions about the way the head looks. Most people believe that the face covers the front of the head, when it actually covers the lower half of the front of the head (Visual 7–5). If you draw a horizontal line at exactly the vertical midpoint of a level head (Visual 7–5, A), the eyes will overlap that line, with very few exceptions. Draw another horizontal line, this time halfway down the face from the first one (Visual 7–5, B), and you will locate the bottom of the nose. These two lines can also be used to locate the height and location of the ears, although individual variations in ear size make this useful only as a very general guide. Draw one more line, measuring one-third the distance from the bottom of the nose to the chin (Visual 7–5, C), to find the mouth, or more specifically the seam where the lips meet. The eyes are one eye apart (Visual 7–5, D). When a drawing of a face doesn't look right, the problem is almost always in one of these basic

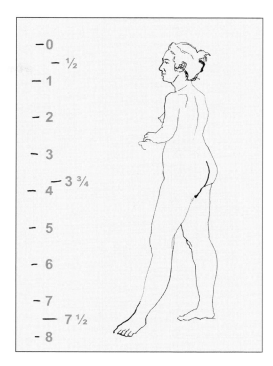

visual | 7–4 |

Standard standing height of 7 ½ heads tall. The eye line is half the height of the head, and the halfway point on the figure is 3¾ heads down.

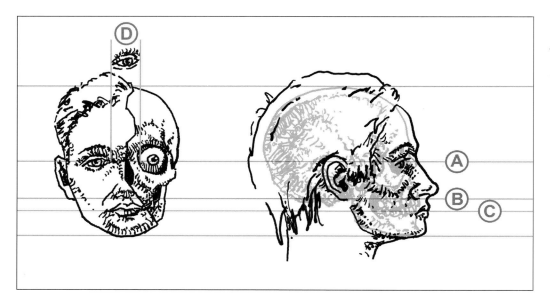

visual | 7–5 |

Proportions of the head, front and side view.

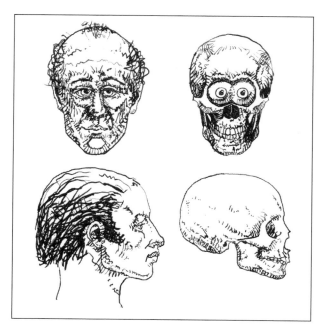

Head errors caused by objects occupying the same space. Top, the eyeballs are too big and too close together, so this face would only work if they occupied the same space behind the bridge of the nose. Bottom, the mandible could only be this shape if part of it was inside the skull.

proportional relationships, which, except for the ears, don't vary much from one person to another.

There are two common sources of error when drawing heads, and they both are caused by disregarding its bones. The first is allowing solid structures to occupy the same space (Visual 7–6), such as eyes so close together that they overlap, or a lower jawbone, or *mandible*, that is welded to the skull, rather than hanging from it on its hinge (called the *temporomandibular joint*). The second is misaligning the projections of the face and the bones that create them (Visual 7–7). The visible corners of the face must correspond to the location of the bones that protrude there. For example, if a cheekbone is drawn too high or low on the face, it contradicts the skull's structure.

As you draw, remember that the skin and muscle are layered together, like a quilt, and they are stretched tightly over the skull. The structure of the head is determined by where the bones of the skull are visible through these layers of external tissue. To visualize the head's structure, think about how a small skull stuffed into a large sock would look (Visual 7–8).

A head error caused by misalignment of external forms and the bones that create them. Left, the subject's right eye is lower on the face than it should be, causing the right cheekbone to be out of place. A face that looked like this would have the distorted bone structure of the skull on the right. *B* shows the eye line as it should have been drawn, perpendicular to the face's center line; *C* shows it as it was drawn.

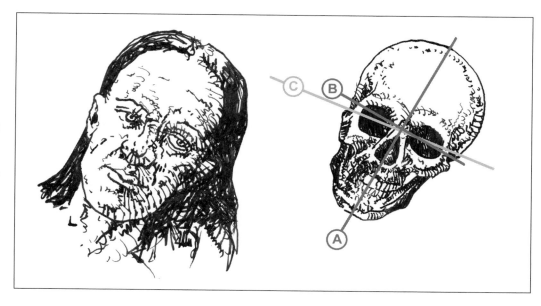

Unless anatomy fascinates you, it isn't necessary to know the name of every bone that you see in someone's head, but it will help you draw plausible, solid heads if you remember how a few of them look and fit together. The skull is shaped overall like an overlapping pair of ellipses (Visual 7–9). The upper two-thirds of the skull holds the brain, eyes, nose, and cheeks, and the lower third is where the mouth and mandible (Visual 7–9, *A*) are located. The cheekbones, or *zygomatic bones* (Visual 7–9, *B*), are a pair of frames on either side of the face that help hold the eyeballs in place and protect the temporomandibular joint. The zygomatic bones, also called the *malar* bones, hold the cheeks out and contribute to the overall shape of the face.

The base of the mandible is horseshoe-shaped (Visual 7–10, *A*). At the center of the horseshoe's bend is the tip of the chin, a ridge of bone called the *mental protuberance* (Visual 7–10, *B*). At each end of the horseshoe is a corner, called the *angle* (Visual 7–10, *C*), from which the remainder of the jawbone projects almost vertically to the *condoyle* (Visual 7–10, *D*), a rounded form that fits into a socket beneath the ear to form the pivot point of the temporomandibular joint (Visual 7–10, *E*). Remember that the eyeballs are spheres, the cornea is a smaller sphere, and the eyelids are draped over them and cast a shadow onto them (Visual 7–11). To get the corneas the right size and properly aligned, pay attention to the shapes of the whites of the eyes.

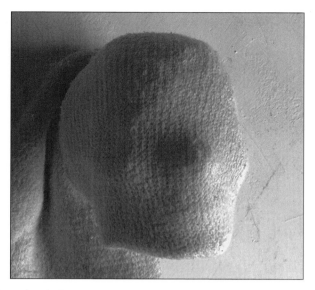

visual | 7–8 |

A half-size medical model skull and how it looks inside a sock. This is the basic structure of the head, which varies little from one person to another. An individual's unique face is determined by additions to this structure. These include how much it is padded with fat and muscle in various places and by the shape of the cartilage, muscle, and skin appended to it to make lips, nose, eyelids, and ears.

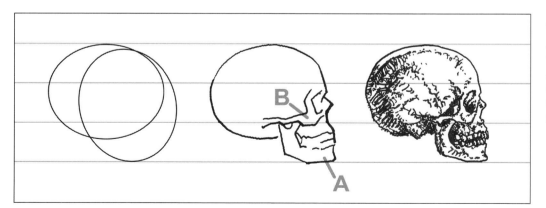

visual | 7–9 |

The simple construction of the human skull using a pair of ellipses.

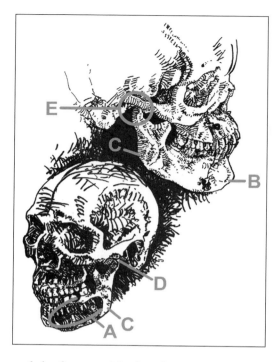

General specifications of the body, measuring from the top of the head, are as follows: The center of the breastbone is 2 heads down (Visual 7–12). The navel is 3 heads down. The vertical midpoint of the body is at the *pubic symphysis*, or tip of the pubic bone, for men, and usually a little higher for women; so the legs take up around half of the body's height.

The knees are roughly at the vertical center of the legs. When the arms hang relaxed, the fingertips reach to the middle of the thigh (Visual 7–13, *A*). It is a very common error to make the hands and feet too small. The foot is two-thirds the length of the lower leg, measured from the floor to the bottom edge of the knee (Visual 7–13, *B*). The same relationship holds for the hand and the forearm. The hand is about as tall as the face (Visual 7–13, *C*). The middle finger is half the length of the hand.

When you are using these measurements to check your drawing's proportions, remember that they are general guidelines rather than absolute rules. They are great for quickly tracking down major errors but less helpful in fine-tuning.

Objective Proportions

Objective proportions are the proportions of a particular person as you would directly measure them. Using calipers and a tape measure, you collect as much information as you can from the subject's body in order to address the question, "How is this person unique?"

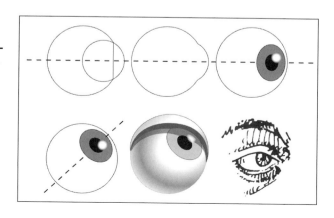

Objective proportions can be very helpful to figurative sculptors, but they are of little use in life drawing. Here's why: A sculpture occupies the same space that its subject does, and like its subject, it can be looked at from any point of view. You can use the same ruler to measure both the model and the sculpture.

A life drawing creates an illusion of space by rendering the subject from one point of view, in a frame of reference defined by linear perspective. In a linear perspective space, the size of an object varies, depending on how far away it is from the **picture plane**. An inch is always an inch in the real world, but in a perspective space, it is not. **Foreshortening** is the visual contraction of distance in a three-dimensional picture space, and the amount of foreshortening of an object depends on its location in this fictional space. Because the

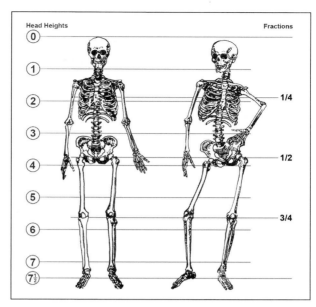

visual | 7–12 |

A human skeleton with good posture and in *contrapposto*. Changes in stance will cause many reference points to change location.

length of an inch in a drawing is not constant, you can not directly transfer a measurement taken from the real model to a drawing of the model.

Objective proportions have found a new application in 3D-modeling software. The model is

measured in the old-fashioned way, with calipers and a ruler, or automatically with a scanner, and the data are entered into the software. A replica of the model is created and rendered in a perspective space, and the software figures out where all the parts belong on the picture plane. The software can display something that can't be seen in the material world: an **orthographic** view of the model (Visual 7–14). An orthographic drawing shows an object as it would look with no foreshortening, often using more than one view. Orthographic views have been constructed manually for centuries to visualize buildings or objects to manufacture, but before computers, orthographic drawings of humans were rare.

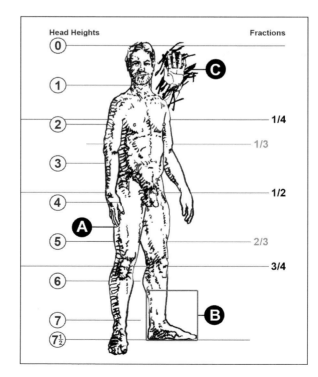

visual | 7–13 |

Standard proportions of the adult body, measured in head heights and fraction of total height.

Two orthographic views of a digital model of a human figure rotated 90 degrees. This model does not physically exist. *Model courtesy DAZ 3D*

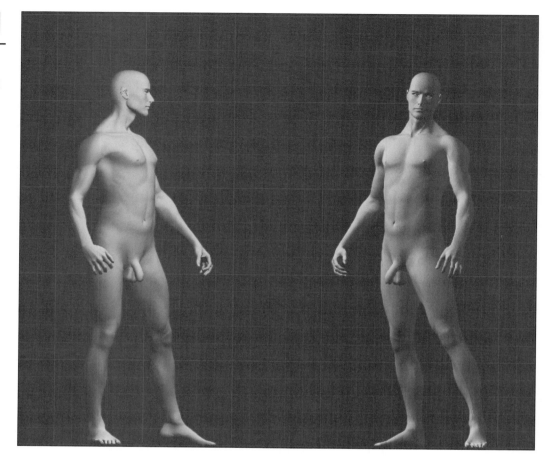

Empirical Proportions

All of the drawings you have seen in the previous chapters use empirical proportions. These are the proportions of a particular person as the artist sees them. Empirical proportions differ from objective proportions in that they are drawn as they appear from the artist's point of view, with the artist and model both in place. This approach to proportion does have as a goal showing the unique proportions of the subject, but it also takes into account the effects of linear perspective. Empirical proportions address the question, "What is my experience of this particular person, at this time and place?" When you draw from observation, you use empirical proportions because the subject's proportions will always be affected by your point of view.

Foreshortening is the key to understanding empirical proportions (Visual 7–15). If someone lies down so that we are seeing them from one end, they look shorter to us, but as long as they are more than ten feet away or so, their proportions are not affected much. As we get closer to the model, foreshortening starts to modify the proportions. The closer the artist is to the model, the more the proportions are distorted by foreshortening.

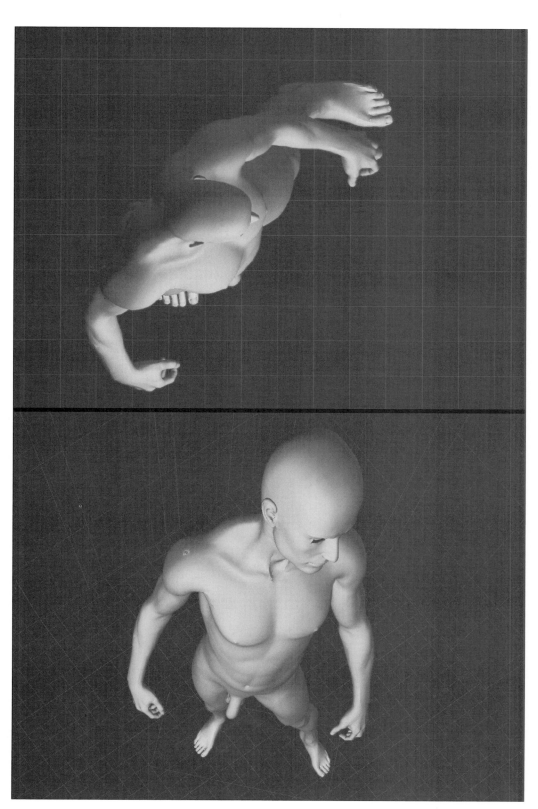

visual | 7–15 |

Foreshortening demonstration using an orthographic view and a perspective view of the digital model shown in Visual 7–14. Top: Orthographic view. Compare the length of the model's left foot with that of his head. In the physical world, we would expect the foot to appear smaller than we see it here because it is further away from us than the head is. In this picture, an inch of foot is the same length as an inch of head, even though the foot is deeper in the picture space. Bottom: Perspective view. The left foot appears much smaller than the head because we are seeing the figure in a three-point perspective space. This an accurate representation of the space that we occupy in the physical world. *Model courtesy DAZ 3D*

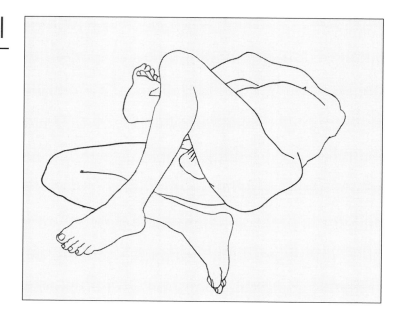

Foreshortened figure from ten feet away. H. Stone, *Untitled*, steel nib and India ink, 17" × 14", 2006.

We can see this effect in two similar drawings executed at different distances from the model. In Visual 7–16, the model was around ten feet away, or, more accurately, the model's feet were ten feet away, and his head was fifteen feet away or so. The distance from me to his feet was two-thirds the total distance, so his feet were closer to his head than they were to mine. Although the positioning of the body is unusual, the proportions appear consistent, with nothing conspicuously oversized. In Visual 7–17, I was sitting as close as I could get to the model, so her feet were around two feet away. Her head and feet were five feet apart, so her feet were closer to my head than they were to hers. Compare the size of the feet in the two drawings. At a short distance, foreshortening causes a pronounced distortion in scale between the closer and more distant parts of the model, making the model's nose look the same size as her left little toe. These effects make drawing a reclining figure viewed along its length a particular challenge in life drawing. When I drew Visual 7–17, I made the marks down the left side to help me draw proportions accurately. You can see that from where I sat, the foot was over one-fourth the height of the entire model.

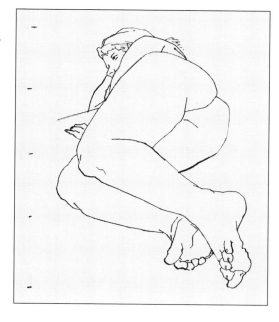

Foreshortened figure from two feet away. H. Stone, *Untitled*, steel nib and India ink, 17" × 14", 2006.

The closer the figure is to the picture plane, the greater the effects of foreshortening. The farther away the model is, the less the effects of foreshortening, and the closer the empirical proportions come to objective proportions. If the foreshortening is properly drawn as the artist sees it, the physical distance between the artist and the model will be clear to the viewer.

This is a simple statement with profound implications. The artist inhabits the same space as the model, and the drawing demonstrates that this is so. The artist is a participant in the scene rather than an objective reporter. A drawing from life is necessarily an interpretation by the artist, whose motivations may be immediately visible in the drawing. Does this imply that a skilled artist with a great heart will produce powerful life drawings? Yes, it does.

INTERNAL PROPORTIONS

Internal proportions are the proportions used in the construction of the drawing. Although they are not always immediately apparent to untrained viewers, internal proportions are important in communicating the emotional tone of the drawing and the personality of the artist. Internal proportions address the question, "How can I make a drawing that truthfully represents my unique vision as an artist?"

Here are some examples of internal proportions:

- The width of the contour line compared to the size of the figure.
- The width of the hatching lines compared to the size of the figure.
- The size of the figure compared to the size of the drawing.
- The size of the drawing compared to the size of the person looking at it.

The drawings in Visual 7–18 and Visual 7–19 are similar in subject and point of view but use different sets of internal proportions. On your first impression, which image seems:

- More energetic?
- Emotionally warmer?
- Quieter?
- More balanced?

A hand-drawn image is intimately connected to human scale. As a *haptic trace*, or record of touch, it manifests the movements that made it, whether they are motions of the artist's hand alone or a coordinated, expansive gesture of the entire body. A large drawing may require more physical effort and energy than a small one, and the small one may demand care and concentration suggesting a kind of devotion. All of these qualities can be seen in the internal proportions of the piece. The way that you choose to resolve the internal proportions of your drawings is an important component of your personal drawing style.

visual | 7–18 |

Line drawing of a seated figure using a thin contour line. H. Stone, *Untitled*, steel nib and India ink, 17" × 14", 2006.

Line drawing of a
seated figure
using a thick
contour line. H.
Stone, *Untitled*,
steel nib and
India ink,
17" × 14", 2006.

A DOZEN WAYS OF GETTING THE PROPORTIONS RIGHT

One of the hardest tasks in art is to make a line drawing of a large form on a blank piece of paper and get the proportions right. It is even tougher when the large form is a human body: your errors are apt to be recognized even by persons untrained in the arts, who may make unsolicited comments about them. Fortunately, there are many methods of observing, measuring, and verifying empirical proportions, so help will always be at hand. Practice these techniques, and pick three or four of them to use most of the time, and a couple of others to use when you get stuck. Verify proportions using more than one method whenever you can.

The first few times you work with these techniques, it may seem awkward and a little frustrating. Be patient and pretty soon they will start to work more smoothly for you. The larger goal here is to develop your ability to correctly see proportions and integrate it into your personal drawing process. With practice, you will often be able to correctly draw the proportions without interrupting the flow of your drawing, and you can save these techniques for special problems.

Measuring head
height with a
pencil.

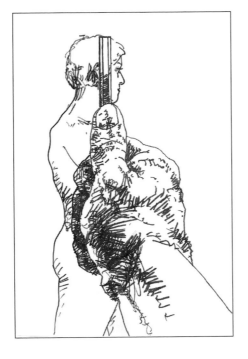

Construction Methods

These are procedures for planning the entire figure by mapping out its large structures before you start drawing. They can also be useful in checking proportions during the drawing's development.

Measuring Head Heights (1)

Measuring the model's proportions as they look from the artist's point of view is the traditional way of figuring out how to draw them accurately and fit the figure onto the paper. The height of the head is the unit of measurement. You hold a pencil as if it were an ice cream cone, stretch your arm out towards the model, and mark the height of the head with your thumb (Visual 7–20). Then you use that distance to measure the height of the rest of the figure. Mark off the head-height intervals on the paper, and construct the figure to conform to that scale. If you don't see the head from where you are drawing, use the same technique to measure the foot, and use that as your unit of measurement.

H. Stone, *Measuring Head Heights Demonstration, Step 1*: Constructing an operational head height. Measure from the chin to the eye line, and then double that measurement.

Demonstration 7-1: Measuring Head Heights

To construct an accurate drawing using head heights, measure the head first, measure the figure in head heights, and then mark off units on the paper to make a scale showing where you will put the figure. As you draw, use your head-height measurement to find landmarks on the body that correspond to the scale you have drawn.

With this method, you may go back to the head to find its height several times, and inconsistencies in measuring can cause drawing errors. A head height is the distance from the bottom of the chin to the highest point on the scalp as measured on a head being held level. Few models have perfectly bald heads, so we can't often directly see the crown to measure it, and few poses exhibit a perfectly level head. We can compensate for these ambiguities by constructing a head height by doubling the distance from the chin to the eyes (Visual 7–21).

When you are satisfied that you have a head height that you can replicate when you need to, use it to measure the figure. Rushing through this is another common source of error. Measure as precisely as you can, and measuring twice to be sure takes much less time than correcting a structure you have drawn at the wrong size. Keeping your arm stretched out, measure one unit down from the chin, take note of the location on the model's body, and carefully move the pencil down to that point. Repeat until you run out of body to measure.

Draw a scale on the paper by placing two marks to show where the figure will go, and subdivide that length by the model's size in heads, as you measured it from your point of view. As an alternative, you can determine the midpoint of your figure, and mark the head units outward. I used this method in Visual 7–22, starting by writing down the height of the model and making a mark to designate where her horizontal midpoint would be.

Measuring carefully, I constructed the scale outward from the center. This is a trial-and-error process; if you draw the units too big, the figure will not fit on the page. You will probably have to make some adjustments to your scale to get it exactly right before you start drawing. Erase the earlier erroneous scales, so you won't waste drawing time having to figure out which one

visual | 7–22 |

H. Stone,
*Measuring Head
Heights
Demonstration,
Step 2.*

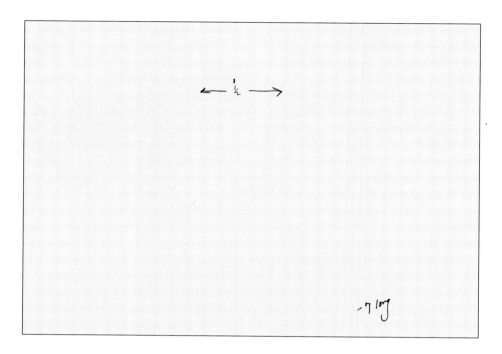

to use. Visual 7–23 shows the scale I wound up with. My first landmarks, the top of the head and the left big toe, were 6 heads apart. I measured 3 heads each way from center, and numbered them from right to left, starting at one. The right foot extended 1 head length right from mark number one, so I made a mark there to show the maximum right extent of the figure. That gave me a figure 7 heads tall, not including the right arm. It stretches to the left a little more than ½ a head, so I drew a reference mark for it also.

visual | 7–23 |

H. Stone,
*Measuring Head
Heights
Demonstration,
Step 3.*

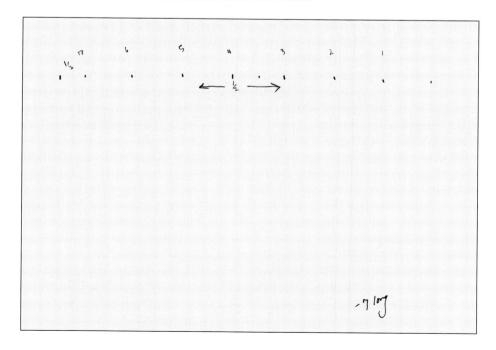

I drew the figure using the semiblind contour technique, starting at the halfway mark, approximately where the navel would be. If you look closely at Visual 7–24, you may be able to see the correction I had to make almost immediately. I did not draw one line all the way around the figure; I extended the contour line to one structure at a time as I determined its location. For example, I measured head heights right from her midpoint and found her right knee to be 2 heads away. I drew the right leg's upper contour to that point on the scale, and then used it as a landmark to draw its lower contour.

Drawing a figure this way, to an exact size, with established landmarks, can be difficult, but it is very effective as a learning experience. Practicing it is a good way to diagnose and remedy chronic problems in proportion like a recurring small or swollen head, or a figure that grows bigger and bigger the lower it is on the page. The measuring method can be used in any drawing session, but in my experience it builds skills best in a pose of fifteen minutes or longer. Work with charcoal, and correct errors as soon as you notice them. This may mean that the first few times you do this exercise, you will use all of the time correcting the proportions. Spend as much time as you need to get it right, and do not worry about the immediate product. The payoff will take the form of a gradual improvement in your sense of proportion.

Blocking in the Figure (2)

I am mentioning this method of establishing proportions even though I do not like it and never use it. Blocking in the figure involves drawing construction lines to show where the parts go, or sometimes using *primitive forms* such as spheres, cylinders, and boxes to create a rough version of the figure, to which details are added.

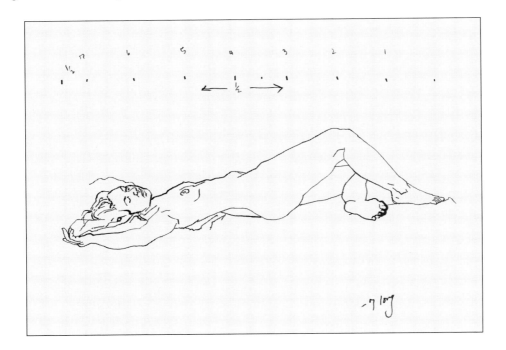

visual | 7–24 |

H. Stone, *Measuring Head Heights Demonstration, final version*, steel nib and India ink, 14" × 17", 2006.

It would be pretty hard to draw a comic book or an animation without using techniques like these, and in fact this method propagated as a means of drawing the same character over and over in different positions, or drawing a figure for a commercial application when there is no access to a model.

I disapprove of this kind of system for drawing from a live model for these reasons:

- It interferes with a direct response to what you are seeing. When you are drawing guidelines, it is easy to make your drawing conform to the guidelines rather than to the person you are looking at.

- Once the system is mastered, it does not build further skills. These systems were created to ensure a consistent product. If you rely on one, you will not get better because you do not ever have to figure out how to draw something new from scratch.

- It wastes drawing time. If you can draw a construction line where the eyes go, why not just draw the eyes there instead? Why erect a scaffolding around the figure that you will have to take down afterward?

If you get a job as a comic book artist, one of these methods is easy to adapt to your existing drawing skills. If you can draw well from life, you can draw this way; if you can draw this way, it does not mean that you can draw from life.

Demonstration 7-2: Blocking in the Figure

This demonstration is not a typical use of a blocking-in system. Artists who use these systems usually adapt one of them by using only as much of it as they need, and I am extravagantly combining a couple of systems here. I drew this demonstration in pencil, in one forty-five-minute session with a model. I started with the positioning structures and added details as the drawing developed. In cartooning and animation, an artist might go through a process like this to create a character but would probably use a much more abbreviated version of it to draw a character she was familiar with.

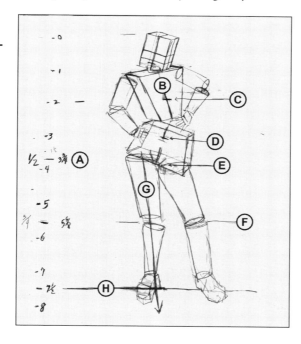

H. Stone,
Blocking in the Figure Demonstration,
Step 1.

Visual 7–25 shows the scale on the left with a halfway point, *A*. I decided to make this character 7½ heads tall because that was the height of the model. I set up the torso in an exaggerated *contrapposto*, which tilted the pelvis to the model's left and sank my halfway reference point, the *pubic symphysis*, E, below point A. Other landmarks are the **midline**, B, the center of the breastbone, C, the navel, D, and the knee, F. Line G is the axis that supports the weight, and H is the reference line for the floor. The measuring point for the foot is the point where G and H cross. The torso is set up as two trapezoidal solids. If I were drawing a man instead of a woman, I would invert them like an hourglass so that the wider one would be at the top.

Visual 7–26 shows the addition of an outer contour line to the body. The pose is a complex one, for the shoulders twist as well as tilt, and the hands rest at different levels on the abdomen. This prevents the arms from adopting a symmetrical position. The guidelines were erased as the body was developed.

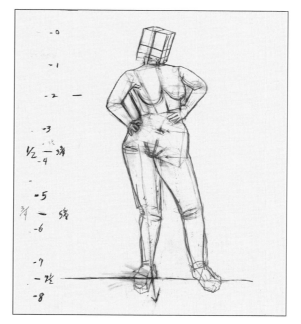

visual | 7–26 |

H. Stone, *Blocking in the Figure Demonstration, Step 2.*

Visual 7–27 shows how the head was developed using the box. The head box was a rectangle with a vertical midline and horizontal eye and nose lines. It was rotated to the right, relative to the body, and the chin was tilted slightly down. The eyes, ear, and nose were placed according to their reference lines, and the face's contour was drawn while keeping in mind that no part of it could be outside the box. The box was then erased and the hair added.

In Visual 7–28, I added some light hatching using the light on the model as a guide. A ring around her neck made her modestly clothed by superhero standards, and gauntlets, boots, a belt, a sidearm, and a logo over the breastbone added some detailing. The mask was added to preserve her secret identity.

Visual 7–29 shows the addition of a cape. In comic art, details like sidearms and insignia function somewhat like the details in architecture, to help provide a sense of scale for the main structure.

visual | 7–27 |

H. Stone, *Blocking in the Figure Demonstration, Step 3.*

H. Stone,
*Blocking in the
Figure
Demonstration,
Step 4.*

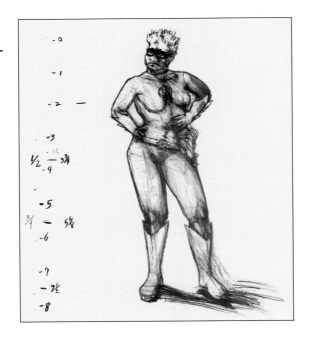

They also help fit a minimally drawn figure into the environment. Unusually cut gloves and boots clarify the position of the limbs in action, and the cape echoes the moving figure's forms and provides opportunities to draw dramatic negative space. Eagle-eyed readers will notice that the logo was lightened in postproduction, which means that I retouched the image on a computer to make it easier to see.

Visual 7–30 shows the final version of the drawing. The digital image was lightened overall; the logo on the chest was increased in size and lightened even more. The ray gun was also lightened.

Location Comparisons

Location comparisons are quick checks in which you compare the location of two elements you have drawn, or of a structure you have drawn with one you are about to draw. Get into the habit of checking locations frequently while you are drawing, and if one of these methods does not work for you, try another one.

H. Stone,
*Blocking in the
Figure
Demonstration,
Step 5.*

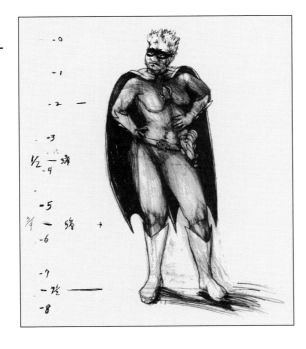

Pairs Method (3)

Many human body parts come in pairs, and when a pose causes one side of a pair to be higher or lower on the figure than the other, you have two reference points for how the pose affects the proportions. Comparing their locations is a good spot-check for errors. For example, in a **contrapposto** stance, the shoulders are tilted, as are the hips and the knees. By studying the three tilts, you can get a sense of the arrangement of the body's large forms. If you use the vertical/horizontal method (described below) to see how the three pairs vertically line up with each other (Visual 7–31), you can sensitively draw the subject's balance.

Once you are satisfied that the two sides of a pair are in the right places, you can use them to make a triangle to show you where the next element should go. For example, if you have drawn a pair of eyes, study the model's face and think about the triangle formed by the pupils of the eyes and the tip of the nose. Two thirds of that triangle is on your drawing, so all you have to do to locate the nose is visualize where the third point will be (Visual 7–32). Place a small dot on your drawing to complete the triangle, and assemble the nose around it. More triangles can help you place the nostrils, the center of the mouth, the corners of the mouth, and the chin. A triangle is a stable form

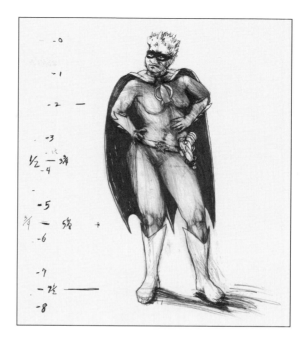

H. Stone,
Blocking in the Figure Demonstration, final image,
pencil on paper, 24" × 18".

because it cannot change shape without changing the length of its sides, so a series of triangles will serve as checks on each other, rather than compounding errors.

Vertical/Horizontal Method (4)

When one of the body's contours is close to being vertical or horizontal, it is easy to draw it tilting the wrong way. This is a subtle mistake in drawing a large structure, and it can throw your whole drawing out of kilter. Check the near-vertical and near-horizontal contours by holding your pencil in front of the drawing to figure out which way the line should tilt. Some artists use a plumb line to find a perfect vertical, but if you use your built-in vertical and horizontal sense to line up the pencil, you will do fine.

You can use the same technique to fine-tune the location of structures that are nearly vertically or horizontally aligned (Visual 7–33).

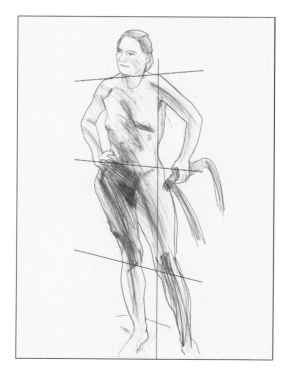

Using the pairs and vertical/horizontal methods to analyze a *contrapposto* stance.

visual | 7–32 |

Using one triangle to find a nose, and another one to locate the center of the upper lip.

Kinked-Line Method (5)

The kinked-line method is a way of finding the location of a structure by sighting along a straight line that already exists on the drawing. Where do you find a straight line on a human body? You find it connecting two points that you have drawn. Let's say that you are drawing a standing person, and you are trying to find the best location for the model's right foot. You study the pose and notice that if you extended the imaginary line between the left eye and the navel down to the floor, it would come pretty close to the right ankle. It is unusual for three structures of the body to line up exactly, so you can fine-tune the ankle's location by noticing whether it is to the left, or right, of the imaginary straight line you have constructed. If you can get a second sighting from the vertical/horizontal, or a measurement method, you will have a pretty good sense of where that ankle will go (Visual 7–34).

visual | 7–33 |

Checking vertical alignment with the vertical/horizontal method.

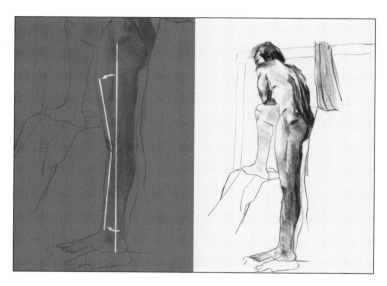

visual | 7–34 |

The kinked-line method. A line starting at the model's right eye and crossing his navel will make a close approach to his left ankle.

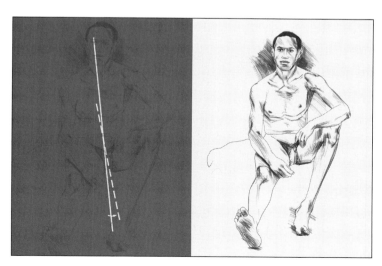

Two Triangles Method (6)

When you are immersed in a drawing, sometimes you can lose your ability to see the spatial relationships clearly, and you get stuck. It is like repeating a word over and over until it seems to lose its meaning. When this happens, it is time to use the industrial-strength solution. It is time to deploy the triangles.

These triangles are a pair of cheap, transparent plastic right triangles of the type used for drafting. One of them has two forty-five degree angles, and the other has a thirty and a sixty degree angle. Use one by holding it up, at arm's length, in front of the model. Rotate it until the bottom side is horizontal, and use it to evaluate the position of some familiar landmarks on the model, and the same landmarks as you have drawn them. For example, is the angle of the upper leg more than, or less than, one of the sides of the triangle (Visual 7–35)?

Because it provides a concrete reference, this is a very effective check on proportions. It is a little cumbersome, though, so it doesn't necessarily need to be used when everything is going smoothly.

Cloisonné Method (7)

Cloisonné is the art of enameling, in which an image is made up of many small, separate shapes of color. The *cloisonné* proportion method is based on the idea that it is easier to draw small shapes than large ones. Build the image up by drawing one complete shape at a time, figuring out each one's size and position based what you have drawn. At the end, you will have a figure composed of interlocking, properly proportioned shapes (Visual 7–36).

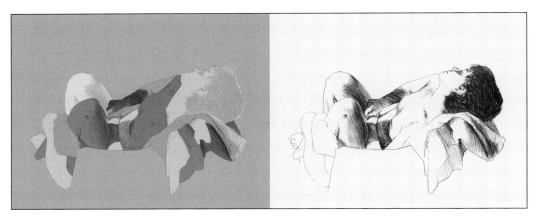

visual | 7–36 |

The *cloisonné* method.

This method is a matter of mentally reconsidering the figure as an assembly of many component forms, rather than as one large, complex unit. If you are drawing a pose with many overlapping forms that lend themselves to being assembled like pieces of a puzzle, this method is a natural.

Blink Comparison (8)

The blink comparison method isn't feasible with every drawing you do, but when it can be used, it is perhaps the most effective way of checking proportions. You do it by looking at the model, and then at your drawing. Position yourself so that you see both figures pretty close to the same size, and then flick your attention back and forth from one to the other. This process will literally animate the discrepancies in the drawing, so that they seem to hop out of position.

The blink method doesn't work well if there is a big difference in scale between the model and the figure in the drawing. It is not useful if you are working in ink and can't make corrections, and it does not work at all if you can not get your drawing to look enough like the model for your eye to relate them to each other. It is great for portraits, studies of hands and feet, and drawing groups of figures.

Negative Space Methods

In life drawing, positive space is the part of the picture corresponding to the figure, and negative space is the part corresponding to the background. Together, they interlock to form the composition of the piece. Drawing the figure first, and then the background, seems intuitively like the best way to make a life drawing, but there are advantages to developing them both at once, or even drawing the negative space first.

We've seen how preconceptions about how something looks can interfere with seeing it, and drawing it, objectively. Drawing the negative space instead of the positive space is a good way to prevent your ideas about a particular structure from getting in the way. For example, you know that the outline of a hand is a complex shape. If you draw the spaces between the fingers, you will draw the hand without letting your idea of its complexity distract you (Visual 7–37).

Chapter 5 demonstrated using negative space to quickly clarify a complex structure (Visual 5-15). Working simultaneously on the figure and the background has other tonic effects, which will be discussed in detail in Chapter 8.

The Figure's Negative Spaces(s) (9)

Sometimes, the model chooses to roll up in a ball, or stands rigid, with hands at sides, performing an impression of a two-by-four. In most other kinds of poses, the body will generate negative space (Visual 7–38).

These flat, negative forms are usually easier to draw than the figure that encloses them. If you start the drawing with the negative space, you often will be able to get the figure in position on the page, with substantial tracts of it in proportion, early in the drawing.

visual | 7–38 |

Negative space in a standing pose, with a diagram of the space.

Demonstration 7–3: Developing a Drawing with Negative Space

When you are working with media to which you can make corrections, such as charcoal or pencil, getting the proportions correct is usually a process of rubbing out and redrawing the image until it looks right. Sometimes, you may want to draw in ink, or you might just want to make a drawing without visible corrections. This demonstration, an uncorrected line drawing of an independent figure with no background detail, is a standard problem in life drawing. This one will use negative space to keep track of the proportions.

This is a twenty-minute pose, and I am drawing with a pointed felt-tip marker on cheap paper. When drawing with media as unforgiving as this, it's a good idea to proceed slowly, making frequent checks on the proportions, and budget for some of the drawings to not work out.

I started by carefully drawing the negative forms, using the semiblind contour technique. Visual 7–39 shows the drawing when those first forms were complete. This is a good point in the drawing to evaluate the proportions. I used the vertical/horizontal method to help me draw the forms, and I verified them with the blink technique afterward. If the drawing at this point has any errors other than very minor ones, either throw it out and start a new one, or draw better lines on the existing drawing.

H. Stone,
*Negative Space
and Proportions
Demonstration,
Step 1.*

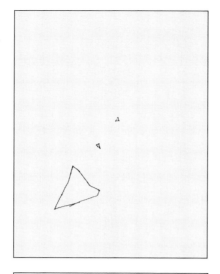

H. Stone,
*Negative Space
and Proportions
Demonstration,
Step 2.*

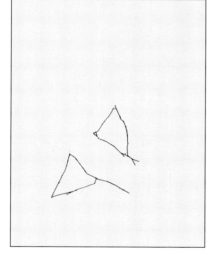

H. Stone,
*Negative Space
and Proportions
Demonstration,
Step 3.*

Visual 7–40 shows the placement of the second large negative space, using the previously drawn tiny triangles to locate two of its corners. Two contour lines were extended from the negative forms into the drawing.

Step 3, shown in Visual 7–41, shows how I continued the drawing with a semiblind contour line. To keep the proportions under better control than they usually are with that technique, I attached a new set of thoughts to that line, using the *cloisonné* method to develop the shapes adjacent to the negative forms. For example, instead of thinking of the line that would define the left edge of the leg as an independent structure in a wilderness of white, I thought of it as completing a form that already existed. I used the familiar line technique, but as I drew, I compared it both to reference points on the negative form and to the shape of the model's leg as I saw it. The left arm readily dropped into place above that leg because its back edge had been defined by the other negative form.

Once the areas immediately around the negative space had been developed, I finished by using the semiblind technique to draw the shoulders and back. I used the pairs method to find the location of the right shoulder (Visual 7–42).

Rectangles and Parallelograms (10)

It is not unusual to see an art student, accustomed to drawing with courage and vigor, become dispirited when confronted with a model sitting in a simple ladder-back chair (Visual 7–43). The chair has its own structure and proportions, and it is hard enough to figure out just the model's. How do you get the model and the chair the right size relative to each other? Where do you start?

When you are presented with this tableau, do not be discouraged; you are being handed the key to the drawing's proportions. Those evenly spaced boxes are easier to draw than the model. Just draw the boxes, draw what is in the boxes, and then draw what is around the boxes (Visual 7–44).

Unless you are drawing outside, there usually will be windows, walls, and corners interacting with the model. Study the shape of these background forms, and use them like a grid to establish the proportions of the figure (Visual 7–45).

Proprioception

Proprioception is your sense of where the parts of your body are in the surrounding space and relative to each other. If you close your eyes and touch your nose with your fingertip, it is proprioception that finds your nose for you. It is how you know where your hand is without having to open your eyes and look for it. This is also how your built-in sense of proportion works. A few people have this sense to such a degree that they can accurately draw proportions without seeming to have to think about it. The rest of us can work toward this ideal state by training or by enhancing our proprioceptive sense.

Training Proprioception (11)

You can get an immediate boost in your proprioceptive powers by standing up while you draw. Drawing is more like dancing than it is like typing, and you get best results when you engage your whole body in it. For the same reason, your proportions will be better if you draw with your whole arm, rather than just your wrist and fingers.

Any drawing practice improves proprioception, but the quick contour exercise from Chapter 5 (Exercise 5-1) seems to be especially useful for this. Do the exercise for at least forty-five minutes, and it will charge your proportion batteries. Do a forty-five-minute session five times a week for a month, and you will see a permanent improvement in your proportions.

visual | 7–42 |

H. Stone, *Negative Space and Proportions Demonstration, final version,* permanent marker on paper, 17" × 14", 2006.

visual | 7–43 |

H. Stone, *Model in a Ladderback Chair,* compressed charcoal on paper, 30" × 22", 2005.

visual | 7–44 |

Negative space from previous drawing.

H. Stone,
Untitled, charcoal
on Rives BFK
paper, 30" × 22",
1996.

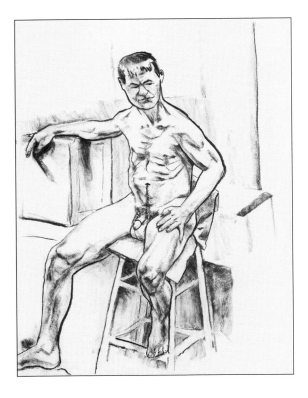

Enhanced Proprioception (12)

Sometimes, proportions can seem like the 100-yard dash, which you run again and again and see only a slight improvement in your speed. This exercise in enhanced proprioception will give you improved proportions on your very next line drawing.

Is there a catch? Of course there is:

- You need to have practiced enough at contour line drawing that you can do it without having to think about it too much.

- You need to work in a quiet enough place that you can concentrate.

Here's the secret: You are going to visualize drawing the line on your own body while you draw the model's. The first time you do this exercise, draw a standing pose, and use a sharp pencil. Stand at the easel, and pick a point on the back of the model's leg to start your drawing. Place your pencil point on the paper, and think about how that pencil point would feel at the same place on your own leg. Concentrate on how that sharp point would feel on your skin until you can almost feel it, and then start to make your line. You will use your semiblind exercise here, but in addition to keeping your hand and your eye moving together, you will also feel the bite of that pencil-point moving on your leg. Move slowly, and concentrate on keeping a perfect synchronization between the line that is being drawn on your paper and the fictional one that is being drawn on your leg. In your mind, maintain a mechanical connection between these two lines for the duration of the drawing.

This exercise is essentially putting a set of training wheels on your proprioceptive sense. As you get more practice with it, you will be able to use it in environments where there are more distractions and with drawing media besides pencil.

Exercise 7–1: Proportion Round-Robin

In this exercise, you will practice using some of the methods of seeing and drawing proportions described in this chapter. It is unlikely that you will need to use all twelve; you will experiment with several of them and pick out three or four that fit you well.

Materials

- Vine charcoal.
- A small piece of clean terrycloth, or a washrag or other cotton cloth to use as an eraser.
- Your eraser set.
- 18" × 24" drawing pad.

Procedures

1. Before starting this exercise, go through the proportion-drawing methods in the chapter and make a list of the six or so that seem most interesting to you. You may want to write down a short summary of the instructions for each one.

2. Do two twenty-minute line drawings, paying close attention to the proportions. Start your proportion checks by using the first method on your list. Use it for a while, and then go to the next one. Correct errors as soon as you see them. If one method doesn't seem to work for you, go to the next one. This process will be slow at first, but take as much time you need to master each of the techniques. If you can't get to all of them in these two drawings, pick up where you left off next time you do this exercise.

3. Do one forty-five-minute, detailed line drawing in charcoal. Use the measuring method, and mark the paper with head heights before you start. Rotate through the proportion-checking methods as you did in the twenty-minute drawings.

4. Before you do this exercise again, update your list with one or two methods you haven't tried. Keep track of the ones that are most helpful to you.

Look at the Drawings

Post your drawings where you can get back from them a few feet to look at them. Recruit some other artists to look at them with you, and evaluate the drawings for correct proportions. It may be helpful to use the standard proportions, described earlier in the chapter, as a set of general guidelines. If there is a consensus in your focus group on where the errors are, make a note of them and work on improving them next time.

We are looking for:

- As always, a single, confident, smooth, accurate line.
- A head that is twice as tall as the face and that is the right size with respect to the body.
- Hands that would comfortably cover the face.
- Feet that would be two-thirds the length of the lower leg, if they were seen in profile.
- A pair of properly proportioned arms that match each other.

- A matching pair of legs that take up half the height of the body.
- Consistent proportions throughout the figure.

We are not looking for:

- A figure that is not stably balanced. If the model could not assume that pose without falling over, there is an error in proportion somewhere.
- Uneven negative space. For example, if the model is sitting on a chair, the chair should appear to be structurally sound. If there is a window in the background, all of the rectangles in it should line up.
- A figure that grows or shrinks from the top of the page to the bottom.

When you have a set of proportioning techniques that work for you, get in the habit of using them whenever you draw. When you see a drawing or a painting of a person, evaluate its use of proportions. Are they classical, or empirical? Why did the artist choose that system? Are there errors? In time, and with practice, your proportional sense will work well as a natural part of your drawing ability.

CHAPTER SUMMARY

Proportion is the relationship of parts with respect to size. In life drawing, it is getting the parts of the body the right size and creating a set of internal proportions for the drawing. Internal proportions are the size relationships of formal aspects of the drawing such as the width of the line or the size of the figure on the page.

There are three frames of reference for understanding human proportions. The first, Classical proportions, is a method of making the proportions in a work of art conform to a traditional standard of beauty. The second, objective proportions, are the proportions of an individual as they are measured. The third is empirical proportions, which is drawing the proportions as they appear from the artist's point of view. There are many methods to help artists do this.

Proportion exercises are intended to develop proprioception, which is the body's sense of its position in space. Artists with a highly developed proprioceptive sense can draw proportions correctly by relying almost entirely on it. This sense can be trained, so every artist can, through practice, improve her ability to draw proportions by feel.

▶ chapter questions

In Visual 7–24, we can see that the model is seven heads tall from the top of her head to the tip of her right toe. Her right knee is bent. If we straighten out her right leg, it will add at almost a head height to her length, making her eight heads tall lying down, compared to 7½ heads standing up. Is this model taller lying down than she would be standing up? Why or why not? Discuss this.

H. Stone, *Rosalie*, charcoal on Rives BFK paper,
30" × 22", 2003.

CHAPTER

8

objectives

- Define figure–ground relationship and know where the term comes from.
- Understand how edge effects contribute to the figure–ground relationship.
- Understand contrast reversal and how it contributes to the figure–ground relationship.
- Draw a figure with an emphasis on edge effects and contrast reversals.
- Understand the relationship between positive–negative space and the figure–ground relationship.
- Create a finished drawing using a dynamic figure–ground relationship.

introduction

In the 1920s, psychologists started doing research on basic processes of visual perception. One of their interests was finding out how our eyes and brain pick out a shape from its surroundings. Like artists, they knew that when we look at an object, we do not see it by itself, isolated from its background. We see it as it appears in its environment, and the conditions there affect how intelligible it is to us.

To understand how their work connects to ours, imagine that we are seized with an inspiration to draw the figure in a natural setting. We leave early on a foggy morning and arrive at the site before daylight. As we take our positions, visibility is so poor that we cannot even tell whether or not the model is in place. We peer into the mist as the scene gets lighter. At some point, someone sees a few indistinct, neutrally-colored shapes, which soon organize themselves into a hazy image of the model. We start drawing. In an hour or two the sun is up, the fog has dissipated, and we can see the model well enough to draw every detail.

While we have been drinking coffee and drawing, a researcher has been standing behind us, watching, taking notes, and smoking a cigar. Like the sour smoke, questions hover in the air: When exactly did someone see a recognizable image emerge from the fog? What was it about the way the scene was organized that let us visually separate it into figure and background? When all that we could see was a few gray shapes, what made them represent a person (Visual 8–1) to us, rather than something else? When our researcher writes this project up, these questions will be grouped under the heading **Figure–Ground Relationship**.

H. Stone,
Untitled, graphite
stick on paper,
22" × 22", 1996.

THE FIGURE–GROUND RELATIONSHIP

The figure–ground relationship in art is the sum of the **formal qualities** that define a shape
and make it fit into a composition.

Formal qualities are objective facts about the way a work of art looks or is constructed. If you
wrote a complete list of a drawing's formal qualities, you would be writing a description of the
piece, without opinions or theories. Such a list for Visual 8–2 might begin:

- The drawing's dimensions are approximately 22" × 30".

- The drawing depicts a standing woman.

- The figure was drawn in sumi ink, using a sumi brush and bamboo pen.

If we listed the formal qualities related to the figure–ground relationship, we would get something like this:

- The head is drawn as a solid dark form on a white background.

- The torso is defined with contour lines.

- The torso is the same white as its background.

- The bottom half of the body is a white form on a black background.

- The figure is in the center of the picture.

Each of these observations describes a part of the figure–ground relationship. If we look at all five items at the same time, we can start to answer some basic figure–ground questions: How did the artist make the figure's shape separate from the rest of the composition? What did the artist do to connect this shape to the rest of the composition so that it looks like it belongs in this particular work of art? Was this figure–ground relationship created consciously, or did it fall into place by accident? The figure–ground relationship is not always a simple concept, but it is very useful to us as a way of thinking about one of the basic processes of art without getting entangled in standard formulas or dogmas.

visual | 8–2 |

H. Stone, *Figure–Ground Demonstration*, sumi ink with sumi pen and sumi brush, 30" × 22", 2004.

EDGE EFFECTS AND CONTRAST REVERSAL

Before there was a figure–ground relationship, there were edge effects. Traditional artists varied the **contrast** along the edges of the figure to merge the forms into the composition and create a visual center for the picture. Some edges had a hard contour, with black on one side and white on the other, whereas others were defined by blended or smudged charcoal, with one side only a little lighter than the other. Because the forms are clearer and more visible in the areas of higher contrast, the eye is attracted to these places.

Visual 8–3, by William Sommer, is a good example of the way that edge effects are used in traditional drawings. The drawing is a portrait in profile, done in a manner similar to Exercise 3-3, with the image developed against a middle tone. What is the hardest edge in this drawing? It is the contour of the face, where the lightest values in the drawing meet the warm gray background along a crisp, unblended boundary. This edge was crafted to designate the facial features as the drawing's center of interest. The clear articulation of forms continues down the chin, past the medallion the subject is wearing at her neck. Below that, the rendering of the forms seems less urgent, with her lower neckerchief having a softer transition to the background. Where the shoulder blades would be, the form is **open**, with no edge between the figure and the background. The edge emerges at the top of her back as a dark gray against a lighter gray, with a contour line providing guidance. The bun, and the back contour of her hair, has been carefully balanced so that it is clear to us what the shape of the edge is, but the

William Sommer (1876–1949), *Portrait of a Woman in Profile, Turned to the Left,* charcoal with stumping and erasure, 20" × 15.35", 1890. *© The Cleveland Museum of Art, Gift of Joseph Erdelac in memory of Ed Henning.* 2001.110

contrast is not so high that it distracts our eye from the face. Sommer achieved this balance by keeping the **mass tone** of the hair in that area a dark gray, rather than making it black, as it is over the ear and temple. He also blended and erased along the edge to maintain exactly the level of legibility he wanted.

There are many things to admire about this drawing, and one of them is its use of **contrast reversal.** In drawing, this term refers to inverting the relative brightness of a form and its background from one part of the form to another. To see it in this drawing, follow the edge of the face from the hairline down. The forehead and the bridge of the nose are light, and the background there is darker (Visual 8–4, *A*). The underside of the nose is dark, and the background is lighter (Visual 8–4, *B*). Below the nose, the figure is lighter again, with the lips a little darker than the background (Visual 8–4, *C*). On the underside of the chin, and the back of the head, the figure is darker than the background (Visual 8–4, *D*).

The human eye seems to savor contrast reversals, so using them creates an interesting visual dialog between the figure and the background. In this drawing, the dialog is heightened by the participation of the background as well as the figure. Compare the brightness of the forehead's background (Visual 8–4, *A*) with that of the mouth and chin (Visual 8–4, *C*). Which part of the background is darker? Measuring the brightness as seen on a digital image of the drawing, the background of the forehead is eighteen percent darker than the background of the chin. Rather than leaving the background blank, filling it with generic shading, or drawing literally what he could see behind the model, the artist varied it to define the figure more clearly.

Discussion key to William Sommer's drawing, Visual 8–3.

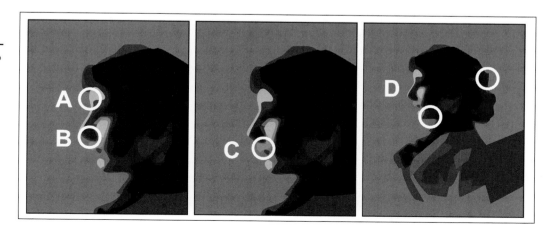

In the old days, edge effects were considered as a way of fine-tuning the structure of the drawing. Now, we more often think of edge treatments in the context of the larger idea of the figure–ground relationship, where they are incorporated into the drawing's sense of structure from the start. Visual 8–5 shows us how this can work. Does the drawing have a center of interest? Clearly, it does. Our eye is pulled toward the face from anywhere in the drawing. Is the face the region of highest contrast? No, it is not. There are many places of higher contrast, where the boundary between figure and background is a gray against black, or a black against white, along a hard contour. The drawing's center of interest is the model's face, framed by the V formed by her

visual | 8–5 |

Richard Diebenkorn, *Untitled*, charcoal on paper, 17" × 14", circa 1960–1963. © *Estate of Richard Diebenkorn*

fingers and thumb (Visual 8–6, *A*). Our eyes are also drawn to the figure by a large X implied by the diagonals in the piece (Visual 8–6, *B*). Most of the picture plane is subdivided into simple, interlocking shapes called **cloisonné forms** that fit together like the pieces of a puzzle. If

we think of structure as the drawing's way of organizing its elements, then the structure of this drawing is established by cloisonné forms and implicit triangles.

This figure has none of the careful gradations of value seen in the previous drawing; like the drawing's background, it is composed of mostly hard-edged forms. The only open forms in the drawing are on the figure, at her right temple (Visual 8–6, *C*), and the merging of the model's hair with her black dress (Visual 8–6, *D*) and the shadow behind her (Visual 8–6, *E*). These visually porous edges provide a bridge from the figure to its setting, as

visual | 8–6 |

Discussion key for Richard Diebenkorn's drawing, Visual 8–5.

they would in a traditional drawing, but they also prevent the viewer's attention from being distracted and, in effect, trapped, by a self-contained figure. The drawing provides no place for the eye to settle. A traditional drawing subordinates edge effects to the descriptive function of the drawing, but this drawing uses them to keep the viewer actively engaged with the composition.

Is the Diebenkorn drawing an advance in drawing technique over the Sommer piece? No, both drawings were created by accomplished artists, but with different intentions. A better question might be, "How well does each drawing achieve its goals?" Thinking about how a drawing uses its figure—ground relationship can show us some of the thinking behind the drawing and help us answer that question.

Here are some values about edge effects that contemporary and traditional figurative artists share:

* The treatment of the edges of forms should be the result of conscious decisions by the artist, rather than according to a formula.
* The viewer's eye is attracted by areas of higher contrast.
* Elements in the darker areas normally have softer edges.
* The less important areas of the image can have softer edges.
* A soft edge can be created by a near match of the values on either side of the edge or by blending the medium along the edge.

visual | 8–7 |

Julia Trops,
Marks on paper,
charcoal on
paper, 24" × 18",
2005.

* Contrast reversals can make an edge active by giving the figure a variable relationship with the background.

Sometimes you will see a drawing in which the figure seems to emerge as if by magic from a very abstract set of marks. Such drawings can be exciting to look at and thrilling to create. This illusionistic, pull-a-rabbit-out-of-a-hat quality comes from an understanding of how to use edge effects to develop forms with economy.

Julia Trops' drawing (Visual 8–7) is a good example of how a drawing can suggest structure and detail through the way its edges are crafted. It is immediately clear what the stance of the figure is, even though the drawing's execution is loose. The contour is defined by narrow, ribbon-like **mass tones** outside the figure, and the form opens in a couple of places. Look closely at the model's left foot. The outer edge is solid, and the inner one is open, which is to say that the foot merges with the background there. As you study the area, you may start to see a foot with the heel raised slightly off the floor, with the body's weight carried on the ball of the foot and the toes. You might even get a sense of the stress in the ankle, or what that missing contour along the inside of her ankle looks like. This foot's position gives the figure an almost balletic sense of balance, transferring the weight so that it gently rocks on her right foot. Looking at the foot another way, you might only see a few gestural marks on paper. The particular manner in which the outside edge implies the form allows the piece to swing between representation and abstraction.

Gotthard Schuh uses a contrast reversal to enhance the three-dimensional form of the figure in his quick study (Visual 8–8). The front of the figure is light against a dark background; the back is dark against a light background. The drawing has a rough finish and little detail, but it can serve as an object lesson in what is really important in a life drawing. The drawing's speedy, extemporaneous use of the medium could seem almost casual if its sense of form were not so clear. We could create a pretty good clay model of the figure from what Schuh has given us here, so we know that the forms are good.

Exercise 8-1: Edges and Contrast Reversal Exercise

The best way to develop your own way of handling the figure–ground relationship is to construct it along the edge of the form. This exercise is an introduction to this process. You won't use contour lines, and you won't use value in exactly the same way that you have before. The exercise is an experiment to see how much of the figure's sense of form can be created by edges alone.

Materials

* Compressed charcoal, soft grade. Square sticks or blocks of it are best for this exercise.

* Your set of erasers.

* A drawing pad, at least 11" × 14". You do not need to use an expensive grade of paper for this exercise, especially for the quick drawings.

visual | 8–8 |

Gotthard Schuh, *Study of a Young Girl,* charcoal on white paper, 17¾" × 11¼", 1922. *Minneapolis Institute of Arts.* © *2007 Artists Rights Society (ARS), New York / ProLitteris, Zurich*

Procedures

1. Apply the charcoal using the side of the charcoal stick. Do not use it to make contour lines. Create the contours by making one side of the edge darker than the other. You will always be drawing on the figure, or on the background, but never straddling the edge.

2. Focus your attention on any place on the edge of the figure, and notice whether the figure or the background is darker at that location.

3. Start drawing by applying mass tone (a solid area of gray or black) to the dark side of the edge.

4. Continue the drawing by following the edge around the figure, applying charcoal to match the contrast relationship as you see it. Pay close attention to which side of the edge is darker, and if the relationship reverses, show it in your drawing.

5. If you choose to develop the inside of the figure, do it by continuing to emphasize edges, instead of by modeling or chiaroscuro.

6. If you see that you have made an error, erase it and draw the area again.

7. Do several two- to five-minute drawings, and a few ten- to fifteen-minute drawings. Work quickly, and try to get the figure's entire contour drawn.

8. Try at least one thirty- to forty-five-minute drawing using this exercise.

visual | 8–9 |

H. Stone,
Ten-Minute Demonstration, compressed charcoal on paper, 30" × 22", 2006.

Demonstration 8-1: Edges and Contrast Reversal

I did this ten-minute exercise (Visual 8–9) after warming up with a sequence of shorter ones. I did the fast drawings to calibrate my sense of proportion and make sure that I was doing the exercise right. On this drawing, I intentionally shifted to a more deliberate use of the medium than is natural for me, so that the focus of the exercise would not be diluted by an overly textured surface. The result is a drawing that is a little more austere than I like my work to be, but I did it as a learning exercise and not a finished piece.

Some of the points of interest are the contrast reversals on the foot, the thigh, and the right hip. The one on the right hip is particularly important. It is not as conspicuous as the others, but it is an example of how close observation of an edge can clarify a larger form. The right side of the torso is a dark form (Visual 8–10, *A*) against the white **negative space** it makes with the chair back (Visual 8–10, *B*). Follow the edge down, and the contrast relationship reverses where the hip overlaps the chair (Visual 8–10, *C*). The hip continues as a white form down to the cushion. This form opens to the background in two places (Visual 8–10, *D, E*), but the contrast reversal defines the edge so strongly that the eye tends to see it as continuing through the open areas. This implied edge is able to suggest the structure of the hip with just a few black shapes on the paper, and no chiaroscuro, modeling, or contour line.

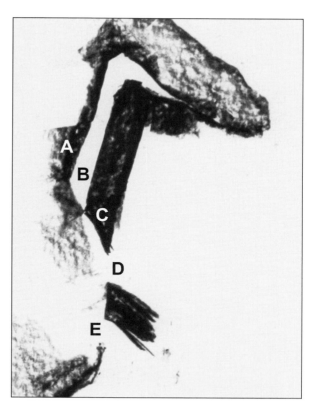

visual | 8–10 |

H. Stone, *Detail, Ten-Minute Demonstration.*

I started the forty-minute version of the exercise after the ten-minute one, so I was fully warmed up. I found a view of the model that showed her in front of a typical studio background of easels, tables, artists, and a dark floor. This variegated background provided many opportunities to observe contrast reversals around the edges of the figure.

Visual 8–11 shows an early stage of the drawing. I started with the nose, placing it after thinking about where the figure would go on the **picture plane**. What you see at this point is the hair, the nose, the back of the right hand, and the right forearm. The small form like a flag extending from the wrist is at the location of the first contrast reversal. This is the only place on the edge so far in which the background is darker than the figure.

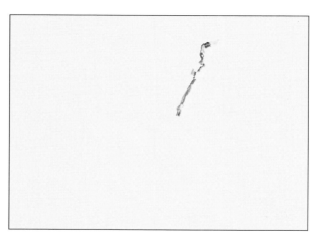

visual | 8–11 |

H. Stone, *Forty-Minute Edges and Contrast Reversal Demonstration, Step 1.*

H. Stone, *Forty-Minute Edges and Contrast Reversal Demonstration, Step 2.*

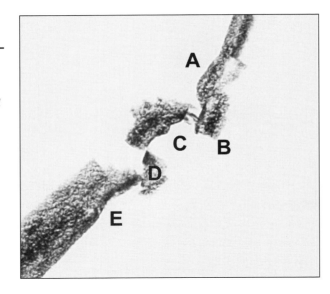

H. Stone, *Detail, Forty-Minute Edges and Contrast Reversal Demonstration.*

H. Stone, *Forty-Minute Edges and Contrast Reversal Demonstration, Step 3.*

Step 2 (Visual 8–12) shows the first set of contours for the bottom half of the body. I was working slowly and using some of the proportion methods to reduce the need for corrections later. There are a couple of areas of detail that were a little tricky. The first was the model's left hand, and the second is the lower legs. The key to the lower legs was the dark, irregularly-shaped negative form between them, at the bottom of the page. That very productive form established the relative positions of the lower legs and a created a contour for each one.

The left hand as shown at this stage (Visual 8–13) is an area of detail with several contrast reversals. It would be easy enough to simplify it, but that would not be in the best interest of the drawing. I drew the edges as accurately as I could see them, trusting that the somewhat abstract result would contribute later to an aggregation of detail that would help bring the drawing to life. The dark form at *A* is the lower part of the arm as seen in the previous drawing. *B* shows the elbow pressing into the back of the model's left hand, *C*, which will be a white form defined by surrounding dark forms. *D* is the fingers, and *E* is the contour of the upper leg.

Visual 8–14 shows the construction of the back of the model's head, left shoulder, and upper arm. The back of the hair is darker than the background, the top of the shoulder is lighter, the form opens, the shoulder gets darker again, and the back of the arm is lighter than the black chair behind it. In that short passage the contrast relationship changes five times. This picture also shows some tweaking of the edge of the model's right shin and the addition of a small black triangle to complete the rectangle behind the model's lower leg.

visual | 8–15 |

H. Stone, *Forty-Minute Edges and Contrast Reversal Demonstration, Step 4.*

Step 4 (Visual 8–15) shows the completion of the body's outline. The contrast relationship shifts often all the way down the subject's left side, to the bottom of her left leg. In a possibly overly pedantic interpretation of the exercise, I left some openings for the chair's dowel struts when I drew its leg.

We now have a figure present on the page, in reasonably accurate proportion. In a typical drawing, we might want to start developing the figure's interior forms using conventional techniques such as modeling, chiaroscuro, or contour lines. For this exercise, an exploration of edges, I chose to continue by completing the chair (Visual 8–16). This was partly to prevent the model from hovering in midair because the support never got drawn (see Visual 8–9) and partly because I thought that using this technique to draw the chair would be an interesting challenge. I inserted the two dowel struts into the holes I left for them, drawing each one in an end-to-end contrast reversal. The rest of the chair was black, as I saw it against the background of the floor. I kept in mind the rectangles and parallelograms method from Chapter 7 and paid attention to where the chair intersected the figure. This helped me validate the proportions for both elements.

Step 6 (Visual 8–17) shows the development of the interior structures of the upper body: the face, the left shoulder, and the right arm. Some details were also added to the area under the chair. I was still working primarily with edges, but I added a contour line or two to clarify some structures. The right hand came in a little too big, which can be verified by mentally straightening it out and laying it up against the face. If I had had more time, I would have fixed this. Minor errors in proportion are not unforgivable crimes in an exercise such as this, where restrictions in technique make you draw, in effect, with one cognitive hand tied behind your back.

visual | 8–16 |

H. Stone, *Forty-Minute Edges and Contrast Reversal Demonstration, Step 5.*

visual | 8–17 |

H. Stone, *Forty-Minute Edges and Contrast Reversal Demonstration, Step 6.*

With the addition of the last few interior forms (Visual 8–18), the drawing was finished. I concentrated on edges and intentionally tried to use as few marks as possible in drawing these forms. With a little adjustment to the contour of the upper leg, the left hand fulfilled its promise. The left arm's structure is pretty clear, even though its inner contour is largely implied by the simple shapes at the elbow joint.

Look at the Drawings

In order to explore what edge effects by themselves can bring to the drawing, the exercise prohibits many beautiful and persuasive drawing techniques, such as contour line, chiaroscuro, and modeling. As a consolation prize, this technique of creating contours by using mass tones excels at implying more detail than is actually drawn.

In this exercise, we are looking for:

- An unambiguous sense of what is figure and what is background. You should be able to touch any part of the drawing and name whether it is figure or ground.

- In the quick drawings, a general sense of what the pose was.

- A clean contour with no ambiguities. This project seeks to create a sense of three-dimensional form through the accuracy of the contours, so it should be obvious from the drawing exactly where the edge is on any part of the figure.

visual | 8–18 |

H. Stone, *Forty-Minute Edges and Contrast Reversal Demonstration, final version,* charcoal on paper, 22" × 30", 2006.

- Implied forms. If you have a large expanse of bare paper inside the figure's outline, and it doesn't stand out as needing more work, you are in the right ballpark. If the figure has open contours that read as if there is an edge present, pat yourself on the back. If the drawing has a region of random-seeming marks that resolve into a detailed structure, give yourself a gold star.

We are not looking for:

- More than a few contour lines. Almost all of the marks you make should be clearly on one side of the edge, not centered on it.

- Gross errors in proportion.

- A good sense of where the light is coming from. This would mean that the drawing is using chiaroscuro as its main strategy for defining form. Some shadows may be visible as a product of your edge work, but the drawing should not be held together by light and shadow.

- Modeling. Modeling is rendering shape, and this exercise renders edges. You shouldn't apply any mass tones that your eye does not see.

FIGURE, GROUND, AND NEGATIVE SPACE

We know that **positive space** is the part of the picture that corresponds to the object, and **negative space** is the part that corresponds to the background. Positive and negative space and figure and ground refer to some of the same characteristics of a composition. How is the positive–negative space interaction different from the figure–ground relationship?

Positive and negative space exist as concrete components of the piece, whereas the figure–ground relationship is part of the meaning of the piece. The figure–ground relationship is the picture's strategy for differentiating an object from its background and integrating it into the composition. The positive–negative space interaction is one of the tools an artist uses to create a figure–ground relationship.

Positive and negative forms are not ideas, they are parts of a drawing that can be touched and named (Visual 8–19). Positive and negative space interact as solid, flat, interlocking shapes on the surface of the picture plane. The concept of positive and negative space concerns the **mechanics** of a drawing more than its meaning, and it is helpful for addressing questions such as:

- Is the drawing accurate?

- Does it convey a clear sense of form?

- Does it contain any inarticulate areas?

The figure–ground relationship is not a structure drawn by the artist; it is a process that the picture sustains. A figure–ground relationship is either static, with the figure existing as a simple

visual | 8–19 |

Guercino, *Study of a Seated Young Man*, oiled black chalk with white chalk highlights, 22⅞" × 16¾", circa 1619–1920. This drawing uses negative space in a way that would be familiar to a modern life-drawing class. *The J. Paul Getty Museum, Los Angeles*

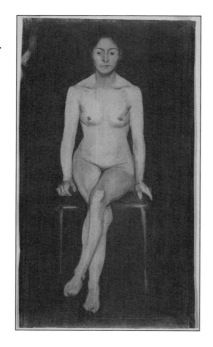

Paula Modersohn-Becker (1876–1907), *Seated Female Nude (Self-Portrait?)*, charcoal with stumping, 24.5" × 13.34", 1899. © *The Cleveland Museum of Art, Purchase from the J.H. Wade Fund. 1973.35*

silhouette or reverse silhouette (Visual 8–20), or **dynamic**, with many interactions between figure and background in the use of negative space, hard and soft edges, contrast reversals, and whatever other devices the artist can think of (Visual 8–21). The figure–ground relationship connects the mechanics of the drawing to its meaning and addresses questions such as:

- Does the drawing have a visual center?

- In this piece, is the subject more important or the manner in which the subject is drawn?

- Does this piece pay more attention to the forms of the figure or the organization of the picture plane?

- What did the picture gain by the particular figure–ground choices that the artist made?

Edge effects contribute to the figure–ground relationship by manipulating the transitions from one to the other. The figure and ground can be made to visually merge by matching the values on either side of a contour or by blending the drawing media to soften the edge. We use the idea of positive and negative space to think about the way that interlocking forms can subdivide the picture plane. A figure–ground dialog using positive and negative space is an interaction of shapes, in the same sense that a building is an interaction of masses and voids. Positive and

John Singer Sargent (1856–1925), *Sketch for the Judgement - One Study, rough - Boston Public Library Murals*, charcoal on paper, 10¼" × 16⅛", late nineteenth to early twentieth century. *Museum of Fine Arts, Boston. Sargent Collection. Gift of Miss Emily Sargent and Mrs. Violet Ormond in memory of their brother John Singer Sargent. 28.813. Photograph © 2007 Museum of Fine Arts, Boston.*

negative space are part of a drawing's **tectonic** features, the logic by which the drawing's space is organized.

There is an axiom in design that says that positive space and negative space are equally important to the success of a composition. Positive and negative space do their part for the figure–ground relationship by, in effect, uncompressing each other. They reach into each other, support each other, take turns being in front, spread each other out, and in the process open up the picture plane.

Imagine that you have created a masterpiece. It goes to the gallery, and two art critics stand before it, awed and little humbled. As trained professionals, they are able to point to and describe some of the features that make the drawing a life-changing experience. It is the play of light in gentle chiaroscuro across the model's back. It is the deep, velvety blacks and the concise, austere whites. The critics agree that your use of negative space is masterful; one of them is overcome with feeling and needs to be helped. But what exactly is it about the negative space that makes it so great? The critics do not agree, and they do not feel the need to. Like a melody that moves you in a way you cannot explain, positive and negative space, as part of the bones and structure of the drawing, can reach past the drawing's descriptive functions to directly persuade the emotions.

As an experiment, study Visual 8–22 and Visual 8–23. They are quick studies done during the same drawing session, both are standing poses, done in the same media, and they both use contrast reversal. Think about these questions:

- On first impression, which drawing do you prefer to look at?
- In which drawing is it clearer which leg is supporting more of the model's weight?
- Which drawing is more dramatic?
- Which drawing is more balanced?

It is easy to see which drawing uses more negative space, but it is not always easy to spell out why one use of negative space is better than another. In life drawing, the effect of negative space is influenced by the handling of the edges, the sense of space in the picture, and the arrangement of the model. Like visual balance, a good positive–negative space interaction is a subjective quality that most people recognize when they see it. Your mission as an

visual | 8–22 |

H. Stone, *Ten-Minute Drawing*, sumi pen and brush on paper, 17" × 14", 2006.

H. Stone, *Ten-Minute Drawing*, sumi pen and brush on paper, 17" × 14", 2006.

artist is to practice applying the idea until it is built into your eye, so that you will see it before others do.

Exercise 2: Dynamic Figure–Ground Exercise

The purpose of this exercise is to attach new thoughts to some of the skills you have been practicing. This does not require an overhaul of your normal way of drawing, but it does involve some thinking about how to connect your formal vocabulary to artistic values that are important to you.

Urgency, intentionality, engagement, and inner necessity are terms for the authority present in a master drawing. This quality is the visible command of the medium that comes from using it skillfully and truthfully. We have been working with an operational definition of drawing skill, which is that it is the ability to accurately define three-dimensional form on a flat surface. What does it mean to draw truthfully? You are drawing truthfully if your drawing process is connected in some way with your inner emotional machinery. When you draw without sentimentality, artifice, or cynicism, you are drawing truthfully.

Before you start drawing, think about the kinds of drawing you have practiced and the general look you want the finished piece to have:

- Will the drawing emphasize one visual center, or will it have many forms of equal importance to the composition?

- Do you want it to use a wide range of values, from very dark to very light, or are you more interested in working mostly light, mostly dark, or in the middle?

- Do you want to use hatching, smooth shading, or a painterly erasing and scrubbing?

- Do you want to practice with **silhouettes** or **reverse silhouettes** (Visual 8–24)?

- Do you want to use any **open forms** (Visual 8–25)?

Notice that this list presents choices for constructing the drawing. Don't worry about figuring out a pose or costume for the model, or implying that some kind of activity is taking place in the picture. You do not need to tell a story to create a profound work of art. Let the drawing communicate by how it looks and how it is made.

Materials

- Charcoal, either vine or compressed.
- A small cloth for blending the charcoal.
- Your set of erasers.
- A piece of good drawing paper at least 18" × 24". This will be a long pose, so don't use cheap paper.

Procedures

1. Make some notes summarizing your ideas about how the drawing should look, and keep them on hand while you work.

2. Consult your notes, and start the drawing in a way that will help it meet its goals. For example, if you want to work against a middle tone, as in Visual 8–25, you may want to start by covering the surface with gray.

3. Build the image by first drawing negative forms and edge effects, and then developing interior forms. Use any techniques you want to build the interior forms. It is not mandatory to draw every edge before you work on interiors; let the drawing grow across the picture plane if you want.

4. Improve the drawing by making adjustments to the figure–ground relationship. If you are not sure whether a change will make the drawing better or worse, you will never know unless you try it.

5. Draw for at least one forty-five-minute sitting.

6. If the drawing looks finished before the time is up, stop working on it and start another one.

I planned that my drawing would be a set of cloisonné forms drawn in high contrast. The particular challenge would be to create transitions between the dark forms and the white background. I started by drawing a dark negative form (Visual 8–26). I was

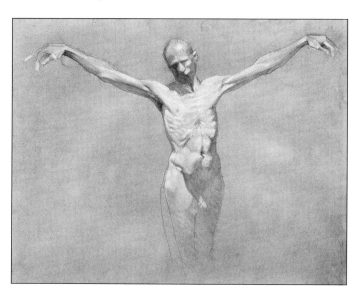

visual | 8–24 |

Loren Klein, *Reading Nude*, charcoal on newsprint 24" × 18". The head is drawn as a silhouette. *Courtesy of Loren Klein*

visual | 8–25 |

Douglas Malone, *l'Oiseau*, charcoal and graphite, 18" × 24". The slow transition from hard edges at the top of the picture to an open form at the bottom helps establish the head and torso as the drawing's centers of interest. *Courtesy of the Artist*

visual | 8–26 |

H. Stone,
*Dynamic
Figure–Ground
Demonstration,
Step 1.*

visual | 8–27 |

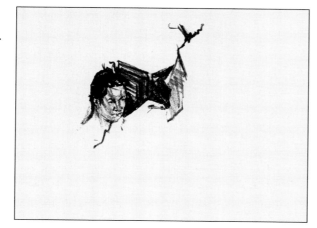

H. Stone,
*Dynamic
Figure–Ground
Demonstration,
Step 2.*

visual | 8–28 |

H. Stone,
*Dynamic
Figure–Ground
Demonstration,
Step 3.*

lucky enough to have two models to draw, which was another reason to start with negative space. The proportions of one human body are hard to get right, and getting two bodies correctly drawn and proportioned with respect to each other can be one of the more difficult problems in life drawing. Drawing the shapes between the models is the easiest way to put everything in the right place.

Step 2 (Visual 8–27) shows the first recognizable body structures. I put them in early so that I could establish the positioning of the two figures. Because it is easy to make errors in placing two models, I wanted to get it figured out early in the drawing, before there was very much to correct. I was working pretty quickly, because I only had one forty-five-minute session to finish the drawing.

Step 3 (Visual 8–28) shows further development of the figure on the right. I made an exaggerated contrast reversal down the contour of the back. The background at the lower back was not that dark in the setup, but I exaggerated it to make the white shape on the figure a little brighter. I drew the head in silhouette and let it run off the edge of the paper. Although I did not think this over before I did it, in retrospect, I think it was a good decision because it stabilized the composition by anchoring the floating dark masses to the edge of the paper.

Visual 8–29 shows some development of the figure on the left and the completion of the one on the right. The right torso was darkened considerably, and the lower edge of the leg was defined by making the leg gray and the adjacent background black. This edge could be made harder or softer by lightening or darkening that gray on the leg. I chose to make it fairly dark, for a soft edge, because I wanted to reserve the hardest edges for the highlight areas on the figures. The hand on the left leg was drawn with a loose three-tone technique. There is a light contour line defining the top edge of the hand, and it would have been interesting to see how legible the hand would be if that line had been omitted.

visual | 8–29 |

H. Stone,
*Dynamic
Figure–Ground
Demonstration,
Step 4.*

Step 5 (Visual 8–30) shows both figures in place. My plan for this drawing was to get to this stage as early as possible so I could make sure that the composition was something I could live with, and so that I could find and correct any problems in proportion. At this point the two figures do not live in the same space. You can see how each figure inhabits its own drawing by comparing the white on the left figure's shoulder with the one on the right figure's buttocks. Because both of the whites are the color of the bare paper, it would make sense for them to be of equal brightness in the drawing. The right one seems a little brighter because the edges are harder and it is surrounded by darker tones. The left figure lives in a more atmospheric place composed mostly of middle tones, and a finished drawing created for her would be held together by the overall soft tonality and the transitions along the edges. The right figure's drawing would be built on solid blocks of light and dark. Which way would I go with this drawing? I looked at my notes….

The hard, crisp blacks were adequately participating in defining the contours of the right figure, but beyond that they did not seem to have any reason for being where they were, floating in a field of white. If this drawing were primarily about that figure, the blacks would be fine the way they were, but I was trying to create a composition, and those dark forms were not pulling their weight because they were isolated from the rest of the picture plane. Particularly bothersome was the black, butterfly-shaped mass between the two people. It seemed to collect the energy from the rest of the drawing and dam it up. At this stage, it is the only form on the drawing

visual | 8–30 |

H. Stone,
*Dynamic
Figure–Ground
Demonstration,
Step 5.*

visual | 8–31 |

H. Stone,
*Dynamic
Figure–Ground
Demonstration,
Step 6.*

that is completely static, with no transitions into the background. I could have started a vigorous program of erasing on the right side, but I did like the drama of the solid blacks, I just did not think they were consistent with the rest of the drawing.

Visual 8–31 shows how I addressed this problem by renegotiating most of the edges. I added some forms, such as the loosely drawn table at top center, and I softened its edges with some loose hatching to ease the transition from the tabletop into the background. I also darkened the shadows below the right figure's arm. I think the white drapery under the right figure works well now; in some ways it's too bad that I eliminated it in the finished drawing. I did this because even though it is well drawn, it goes with the hypothetical drawing that would suit the left figure and not the right. At this point I was getting a pretty good idea of how I wanted the highlights to look. I would summarize this idea now as "broken pieces of light floating on a black surface."

The last set of additions, shown in Visual 8–32, consisted of further darkening the drawing, fine-tuning the transitions from the dark forms to the background, and adding two verticals on the right. These created some negative forms and interacted with the right edge in a kind of visual rhyme. I did not make them up; they were visible in the scene. Without them, I would have had

visual | 8–32 |

H. Stone,
*Dynamic
Figure–Ground
Demonstration,
final version,*
charcoal on
paper, 22" × 30",
2006.

to figure out some other way to resolve that region of the piece. Turning the left figure's neck into a dark mass, and compromising the contrast reversal that was there, strikes me in retrospect as kind of a daring step. That figure worked pretty well before I did this, and if you say that you like the drawing in Step 6 better than the finished one, I cannot say that you are wrong. There is no objective rule that we can cite to prove that the second one is better.

Look at the Drawing

When you wrote down your notes about this drawing, you crossed a line. You declared your intention to make a work of figurative art that reflects your own values. We evaluate the success of such a drawing in two stages: first, we look at how well it is made; second, we ask how well it follows through on its premises. The first stage asks some familiar questions:

- Are the figure's three-dimensional forms clearly defined?
- Are there unarticulated areas in the drawing?
- Is it clear in every part of the drawing what is figure and what is background?
- Are there any elements in the drawing that seem arbitrary or that otherwise do not seem to belong?

The second stage is a little more complicated because you may not know exactly what the artist was trying to accomplish with the drawing. You can draw some preliminary conclusions by carefully looking at the piece and considering these questions:

- Is the drawing internally consistent? Does it have the same mood, surface finish, and style throughout?
- Does the drawing have a single point of emphasis? If it does not, is it because the artist wanted one but could not make it happen, or is the drawing not meant to have one?
- Is the drawing finished, or do parts of it need more work? The intentionally incomplete life drawing has been done so much that it has worn out its metaphor. You have seen from the demonstration that knowing when to declare the picture finished and leave it alone is as important as any other decision you can make about the piece. Did the artist make the decision responsibly? Should it have been made earlier?

Much of life drawing is a process of looking and learning. Its methodology of finding out what a structure objectively looks like, and drawing it accurately, is one of the most demanding disciplines in art. You could spend the rest of your life discovering forms that you never noticed before and converting them into art, but you will never discover a figure–ground relationship. It does not exist unless you create it.

CHAPTER SUMMARY

The figure–ground relationship is the process by which an object is differentiated from its background and integrated into the composition. The figure–ground relationship is constructed by the artist and is part of the meaning of the picture. It is a clue to the thinking that produced the drawing and thus is key to evaluating how well the drawing realizes its intentions. Contrast reversals and the positive and negative space interaction are two tools used to create the figure–ground relationship. To create a contrast reversal, adjust the values on either side of a figure's edges so that the figure is lighter than the background in some areas and darker in others. A positive and negative space interaction is created by making figure and background shapes interlock with each other. It is a part of the structure, or architecture, of the drawing.

The figure–ground relationship is a place for an artist's inventions. It is the collection of attributes that causes the figure to be recognizable, and it is a process by which the picture's composition is made active.

▶ *chapter questions*

Contrast Reversals

Which of the following pictures use a contrast reversal?

1.

visual | 8–33 |

   a. Uses a contrast reversal.

   b. Does not use a contrast reversal.

2.

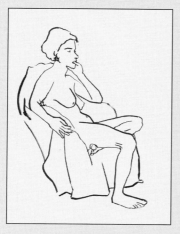

visual | 8–34 |

   a. Uses a contrast reversal.

   b. Does not use a contrast reversal.

3.

a. Uses a contrast reversal.

b. Does not use a contrast reversal.

4.

a. Uses a contrast reversal.

b. Does not use a contrast reversal.

5.

visual | 8–37 |

a. Uses a contrast reversal.

b. Does not use a contrast reversal.

6.

visual | 8–38 |

a. Uses a contrast reversal.

b. Does not use a contrast reversal.

7–9. List three ways of making a figure–ground relationship more active.

10. Is it always desirable for a drawing to have an active figure–ground relationship? Why or why not?

Sangram Majumdar, *Hidden*, charcoal on
paper, 50" × 38", 2002.

CHAPTER 9

objectives

- Define composition and explore compositional issues unique to figurative art.
- Define picture-plane-based composition and compare it with figure-based composition.
- Define illusionistic space.
- Define flat space, shallow space, and deep space and understand how they can be made to interact to make a more interesting drawing.
- Create a figure drawing with an integrated composition using a spatial dialog.
- Experiment with different ways of creating an illusion of deep space in a life drawing.

introduction

Composition is both the process of organizing the space in a work of art and the visible organization of the completed piece. For some artists, the word **composition** means geometry: a set of procedures using rectangles and diagonal lines to create a **structure** for the picture. For others, composition is more subjective. These artists rely on their personal sense of order and supplement it with useful folk wisdom such as the **rule of thirds**.

You will acquire both kinds of knowledge as part of your continuing study of art. A good design textbook will show you how to subdivide a picture plane, and practicing your drawing will give you a visual intuition you can trust. These will give you the methods of organizing a picture that come from common culture, and if you are impatient to just get on with drawing the model, these broad guidelines may be all you need. At some point, though, you may be seized by a different ambition: to make sure that everything in the drawing is the product of your intentional choice. A picture conforming to this standard would have no **unarticulated space** or extraneous elements. All of its parts, and their interactions, would cooperate to create the meaning of the piece.

In life drawing, where the human figure is the center of interest, there is always the temptation to arrange the figure first and then flip through the mental card file to find the best composition to showcase it: make your choice, draw it in, and your picture is finished. Drawings of this type treat composition as architecture for the figure to occupy or as a kind of display case for it. In other words, the composition is separate from the subject. Work on one, and then work on the other. This formula lacks a certain adventurousness, doesn't it?

In the Chapter 8, you learned how to prevent a figure from becoming separate from its background. Instead of drawing the figure and applying a background to it, you created an active figure–ground relationship by developing the figure and the background at the same time, with interactions between them taking place along the figure's contour (Visual 9–1). In such a drawing, the figure cannot exist independent of its background. If you remove the background, the figure falls to pieces (Visual 9–2). What if we treated the entire composition this way, so that the figure was inseparable from it? This would mean creating the figure and its environment in concert, so that the **picture plane** has integrity throughout the development process. The entire picture would be the product of the artist's attentive choices, with none of it taken for granted. It would grow through invention, maintain a resistance to formulas, and manifest the artist's voice at every stage.

THIS TIME, IT'S PERSONAL

There are many kinds of order in art, and there is no unacceptable way of creating it. To create order is to detach oneself from the impetuous rush of life and take time to think things over. This is not always easy to do when there is a naked person in the room who expects you to

draw them. Composing a life drawing can never be a purely intellectual exercise because the presence of a human in the work challenges the viewer to make an emotional connection to it. In addition, when the composition has a tenant, the picture has a natural center of interest, which colors the artist's **design** decisions. Fortunately, when we compose a life drawing, we do not have to figure out all of the profound content in advance. We just have to draw as honestly and intelligently as we can, and the drawing will speak for itself. The **rendering** skills that we build through regular drawing practice will help us to always tell the truth, and a large body of knowledge is standing by to help us move more intelligently from the figure to the space surrounding it. You have probably absorbed a good bit of this lore looking at paintings, movies, and magazines, or you may have studied it formally in a design class.

Design and figuration have been walking hand-in-hand for 2500 years, and they share some preoccupations, such as proportion and balance, which originated with the first detailed studies of human anatomy. Other design concerns are not as intimately connected to the body, but they frequently surface in life drawing:

- The predominance of round forms or angular forms, and transitions from one to the other.
- Using triangles to organize the picture.
- Scale: Does the drawing use big forms, medium-sized forms, and small forms, or are the most apparent forms pretty close to the same size?
- The **Tree Model**.
- Use of **symmetry** or **asymmetry** as an organizing principle. In design, symmetry is order based on repeating elements. These repeating structures can be superimposed, or arranged in a line, around a circle, or to mirror each other.

After looking at the list, you may be thinking that you know more about composition than you thought you did. In fact, you have applied these topics in earlier chapters of this book.

In the old days, before Impressionism (1860–1900), a figurative artist would compose a picture using traditional design practices. In contemporary art, artists more often rely on a well-trained sense of visual balance, sometimes challenging it with new thinking. Composition is no longer a set of policies; it is an opportunity to create art with personal meaning and to invent a way to communicate that meaning to others.

The Two Temperaments

When you attend a life-drawing session, are you there to draw the model or to make a picture? If you quickly answered "both," think a little more about what holds your attention while you are drawing. What are you trying to accomplish when you draw? Which of the exercises in this book have felt most natural to you?

Most artists who draw from life tend to be more interested either in rendering the figure or organizing the picture plane. I believe that a natural affinity for one or the other is a basic expression of artistic temperament. Identifying your own preference, and respecting it, is a good way to begin to discover what will be uniquely yours in drawing.

H. Stone,
Untitled,
compressed
charcoal on Rives
BFK paper,
30" × 22", 2004.

Composing the Figure

If drawing the figure is your primary interest, you will want to spend your limited drawing time capturing exactly what that person looks like right then. To you, the meaning of the drawing comes from showing the uniqueness of your subject. Errors in proportion, or a face that does not look quite right, are apt to bother you quite a bit. On the other hand, if you are happy with the way the model is drawn, you may not notice that, for example, she seems to be sitting on an antigravity device of some sort (Visual 9–3). It is not unusual for your life drawings to have this kind of implausibility in them, but your viewers often do not pay any more attention to it than you do because they are carried along by the intensity you bring to the figure.

Figure people find skeletons and anatomy textbooks fascinating and are interested in the way faces look. If you often find yourself studying a stranger in a public place, and hoping they won't notice, you are probably a figure person.

To a figure person, the word "balance" refers to literal physical balance: the complex and subtle way that human anatomy works to allow someone to remain standing. "Structure" means the anatomical structure of the body. This kind of artist can build an entire art career around the idea of contrapposto.

Figure people will humor the instructor who tells them to draw something in the background, even though it seems arbitrary and superfluous to them. They may believe in their hearts that a beautifully drawn figure on a bare piece of paper represents a kind of perfection in art. Accordingly, the life drawings they like best emphasize a figure sensitively and accurately observed, and drawn in a straightforward manner (Visual 9–4).

Composing the Picture Plane

If you are a picture-plane person, you approach the easel with the intention of creating a great-looking work of art. You often start your drawing by quickly laying in some marks on every part of the paper. To you, the figure you are drawing does not mean much by itself, but it is necessary as a component of the work you are creating. It is the figure's context that gives the drawing meaning, so when you see a figure floating on a white background, you may want to make tactless remarks on the drawing's unfinished state.

Picture-plane people may be impatient with figure-drawing exercises because they see the integrity of the work of art as more important than an exact likeness of the model. If you belong to this crowd, you will work for hours with charcoal and an eraser, crafting the surface so that every bit of it contributes to the drawing. If your completed drawing shows a figure inhabiting a plausible space that has been subdivided in an interesting manner, it is not a problem for you that it could never be used as a police sketch. Unarticulated places in the drawing do bother you, and you may secretly believe that an artist who does not address them has a character weakness. You often do not respond to drawings that lack logic. You want the person in the drawing to have a reason for being where they are (Visual 9–5).

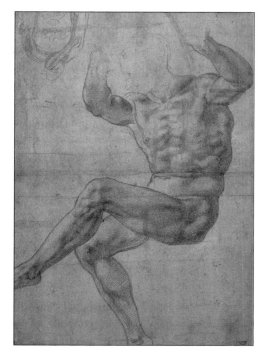

Picture-plane people are likely to see life drawing as an intellectual problem. This group will use the word "balance" in reference to the **formal** aspects of the drawing. They are interested in such tasks as balancing an abstract, painterly surface with a convincing illusionistic space, balancing the use of hard edges and soft edges, and balancing large forms and smaller forms while managing the transitions between them.

To a picture-plane person, "structure" always means the architecture of the piece: how the picture plane is organized, how solid the forms are, and how the drawing defines space.

If you recognize yourself as one of these two artistic types, you have identified one of your natural talents. Respect it, cherish it, and then practice working the other way until you are comfortable doing that kind of drawing, too.

THREE KINDS OF SPACE

A drawing is a film of carbon on a sheet of paper. Life drawing is arranging the carbon to persuade a viewer to see a person when they look at it. If we see the person, then the drawing has expanded from the literal carbon on the surface into a fictional space. This space that the figure inhabits is not subject to physical laws. It does not have to be realistic, or even consistent; it only needs to look the way you, the artist, want it to. This degree of freedom is a strong tonic. Can you handle it without losing your way?

It is not easy to compose a drawing that is true to your personal artistic compass, but you can identify some directions to take if you classify picture space as flat, shallow, or deep.

Flat Space

In a drawing that uses a **flat space**, all of the action takes place on the surface of the picture. In other words, the drawing makes little or no attempt to create an illusion of three dimensions. A figure drawn with a contour line may remain on a flat space, but other uses of flat space are necessarily a break with life-drawing tradition. An artist's decision to use a flat space is itself an important part of the content of the piece. Making this choice establishes the premise that the drawing should be considered on its own terms, and not necessarily evaluated according to conventional figure-drawing standards.

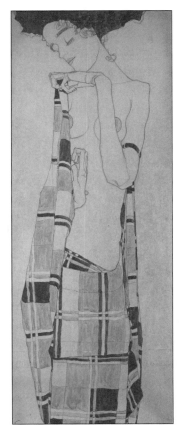

visual | 9–6 |

Egon Schiele
(1890–1918),
*Gerti Schiele in a
Plaid Garment*,
charcoal and
tempera,
52⅜" × 20⅝", circa
1908–1909.
*Minneapolis
Institute of Arts,
The John R. Van
Derlip Fund and
gift of funds from
Dr. Otto Kallir.*

In Visual 9–6, Egon Schiele uses a flat space in a line drawing of a standing, partially draped woman. There's no attempt to define the figure with chiaroscuro or modeling. The figure is used as a design element, interacting with the sides of the drawing to create interesting negative shapes and contributing a set of interlocking flat forms to the composition. The figure is as flat as the drawing's rectangles and stripes, yet it is drawn with such sensitivity that it is somewhat at odds with the cooler emotional tone of the rest of the drawing. This tension is part of what makes the picture interesting.

In Julia Trops' drawing (Visual 9–7), the composition is dominated by a large, reclining torso, seen from behind, and rendered lighter than its background. This central form is a figure-ground jam session in a flat space, **open** in some places, and defined by a loose collection of black strokes in others. These marks, which vary in width and density, are applied with *brio* and give a movement to the piece that is in some ways incompatible with the model's position of repose. This is a small contradiction, as if the artist were working with such intensity that she could not slow down to draw the resting figure in a more relaxed style. Is this a problem? No, it is not. The artist is using the surface as a performance space to build the larger metaphor of the piece. The marks document her moment-by-moment process of making sense of what she is pre-

Julia Trops, *Marks on Paper*, charcoal on paper, 22" × 30", 2006.

sented with and responding to it out of emotional necessity. This piece uses life drawing to construct a subjective representation of experience itself.

Tomi McLellan, in Visual 9–8, uses a flat space to juxtapose literature, calligraphy, and the human figure. The figure is drawn very loosely, in middle tones on gray paper, without obvious modeling or chiaroscuro. Three handwritten lines from Shakespeare are horizontally superimposed in white over the figure. The text does not refer to the figure, and the inversion of the top and bottom lines is an impediment to reading it in a straightforward way. The picture's surface is used as a kind of stage, where the elements function as references to shared culture and interact to create poetic associations without a single, fixed meaning. There is not a right or wrong way to interpret the piece. The drawing invites viewers to create a connection to the artist and her culture by constructing their own response to the drawing's content. This connection is the true subject of the drawing.

These three drawings use a flat space to establish that they are not intended to express their meanings according to life drawing traditions. By working outside of conventions each artist offers view-ers the opportunity to construct without pre-conceptions a meaning for the drawing.

Shallow Space

A shallow picture space is a type of **illusionistic** space. An illusionistic picture space treats the picture plane as a win-dow in which we can see

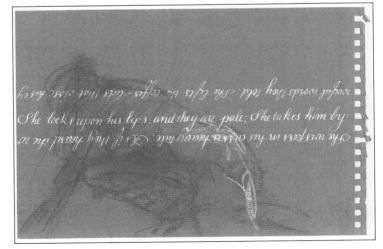

Tomi McLellan, *Untitled*, red chalk and white ink on gray paper, 6¼" × 9¼", 2006. The figure is drawn in red chalk in the original.

a believable depth. In most illusionistic art, the sense of space is created by using the familiar devices of linear perspective, **atmospheric perspective**, and overlapping forms. These are seldom used to create a shallow space in life drawing.

To say that a shallow life-drawing space is not difficult for an artist to create is true, but it misrepresents the problem because a shallow space is seldom created intentionally. If we use modeling or chiaroscuro techniques, a shallow picture space grows around the figure as we draw it, so it is usually a byproduct of rendering the figure, rather than a goal for its own sake.

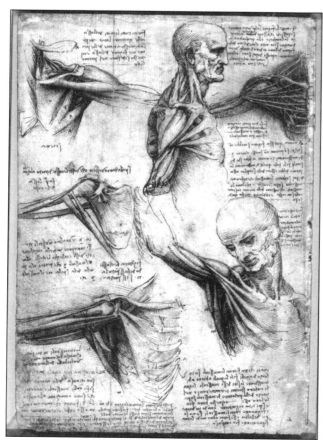

Most of the exercises presented so far in this book have used a shallow space, in which we draw the figure's three-dimensional forms as well as we can and let the space take care of itself. Visual 9–9 is an example. The three-dimensional form of the figure is described with modeling, and the background is mostly undefined. The solidity of the figure implies the space immediately surrounding it. As long as the drawing's point of view is fairly close to the model, the space will be convincing.

A drawing intended to show what someone looks like, either to demonstrate something (Visual 9–10) or as a portrait (Visual 9–11), often uses a shallow space.

The shallowest illusionistic space is a **relief space**, in which the image seems to project a little way from a solid background (Visual 9–12). In Visual 9–13, the picture space is considerably deeper. It is a drawing of a man in a toga lying on his back in a stage-like space. Is this a shallow space or a deep space? Gérôme has drawn this model with such accuracy and completeness that he not only shows us the projections and hollows of the figure, but he also defines the shape of the small caves generated by the overhanging drape. Focus your attention on the model's head and the shady area just to its right. Do these structures seem be firmly resting on a solid, flat surface? Study the negative shape this region makes with the bottom edge of the picture. Does this read as

visual | 9–11 |

H. Stone, *Portrait*, compressed charcoal on paper, 17" × 14", 2004.

flat, blank paper, or as part of the surface the model is lying on? Now look at the left side of the figure, where the cloth is bunched up and casts a shadow on the floor. Let your eye move into the background. At what point does the background stop seeming like a part of the floor, and start looking like the paper the artist was drawing on? You may find that the illusionistic space in this drawing dissipates at some small distance from the figure. It is the figure that articulates the space, and the regions of the drawing outside the figure's influence are undefined. This drawing uses a shallow space.

Exercise 9-1: Giving Caesar Some Space

As an informal experiment, let's see what it would take to transform the space in Gérôme's drawing (Visual 9–13) into a deep space.

Materials

* Six photocopies of Visual 9–13.

* A pencil.

* An eraser.

* A straightedge.

visual | 9–12 |

Hope Lobner Cahill, *Savonarola*, charcoal, 24.9" × 18.9", 1914. *Fine Arts Museums of San Francisco, Gift of the artist, 1976.2.17*

Procedures

1. Look at the drawing, and think of Caesar's cadaver as lying in the desert, on a flat, infinite surface. Is it easy to visualize this?

2. Now draw a horizon line on one of your working copies. How does this affect the impression of space in the drawing?

3. Make five more of these studies, varying the position of the horizon. Draw one low enough that it crosses the model's left big toe.

4. Compare the drawings. Which one creates the most believable deep space? How does the placement of the horizon line affect the picture's point of view?

Deep Space

Exercise 9-1 demonstrates some of the characteristics of deep picture space as it is used in life drawing:

* A deep space is an illusionistic space that organizes the entire picture plane.
* It is created with the intention of showing the figure in an environment, rather than in isolation.
* It is defined independently of the figure.
* It creates a context for the figure and thus modifies its meaning.

In a shallow space, the figure's background may have no other purpose than to hold up its end of the figure—ground relationship; the background is subsidiary to the figure and exists only to help define it. A deep space is an independent invention that does not need a figure to exist. In life drawing, a deep space presents some interesting formal problems: the space needs to be constructed, which may require skills from outside the life drawing studio, and the figure needs to be fitted into the space, which often involves reconciling the figure—ground relationship with an uncooperative setting. More difficult is figuring out how the space will function in the drawing. What kind of scenery are you going to place the model in? A deep space must be the product of an artist's intentional thinking, and one negligently created can turn even the best-drawn figure into an unfortunate learning experience.

There is nothing wrong with making a deep space by drawing the background and foreground of the model as you see them. This is a good way to learn how to work with deep space, and there is an exercise using this method later in the chapter. If you want to pursue figurative art as a profession, you may want to plan the picture space even more comprehensively:

- What will the space look like? Will it be indoors or outdoors? Will it be a recognizable place?

- What mood do you want to achieve, and how will you draw the space so that it contributes to it?

- How big will the figure be? Consider an inspiring landscape with a tiny person in it. If we zoomed in so that the figure took up most of the picture plane, how would that change the meaning of the drawing?

- What point of view do you want to have?

- Will the space be drawn in as much detail as the figure?

Let's look at how two drawings address these questions. I drew the first one (Visual 9–14) in a life-drawing session. I am a figure person, so I was most interested in getting the best likeness of the model that I could at that time and place. The background was my studio. I wanted to show the light and air that was present during the session, so I drew the window with a slight draft pulling at the curtains. This is not something I made up; I noticed it and drew it, but as unobtrusively as I could so that the figure would be more solidly defined than anything else in the drawing. The subject is large and in the center of the drawing. I avoided extreme

visual | 9–14 |

H. Stone, *Portrait*, black crayon on Rives BFK paper, 30" × 22", 1998.

points of view. I intended to imply a collegial relationship between the artist, the model, and the viewer, so I placed the model so that his eyes would be at the same level as ours.

The figure in the landscape in Visual 9–15 is not recognizable as a particular person, and in fact she seems to be intentionally hiding her face. The background is a very deep illusionistic space and it is developed to the same level of detail as the figure. The beach is deserted, but the tire tracks are evidence that it has seen some recent heavy use. If we imagine the woman straightening up and adopting good posture, her eye level would be pretty close to the horizon line. We know that the horizon line is a line constructed for the purpose of defining eye level, so the drawing places us as standing on the same beach as she is. Do you feel that you are part of the action, or watching it? Do you feel welcome there?

THE SPATIAL DIALOG

How can you use the three picture spaces to create drawings that are interesting to look at? Let's look at what we know so far:

- Flat space uses the literal surface of the paper.
- Illusionistic space treats the picture plane like a window.
- The content in a flat space is shapes, textures, or other features that are interesting because of how they are made or the associations they elicit in the viewer.
- The content in an illusionistic space is interesting because of its resemblance to reality as our eye sees it.

The role of the flat space in a work of figurative art received a radical reconsideration approximately a century ago with the introduction of the cubist style. In Cubism, the human figure

Graham Nickson, *Expulsion I*, charcoal on paper, 31" × 61¼", 1991. *James Dee. Courtesy of Graham Nickson, Salander-O'Reilly Galleries, NY*

is taken through a set of transformations outside the concerns of traditional life drawing. The result is a set of textured geometric forms that indirectly reference the way the subject looks, instead of representing it in a straightforward way (Visual 9–16). The conventions of illusionistic space are irrelevant to these pictures, which declare their intention to hold the viewer's interest by the action on their surfaces. On the other hand, in a relief-space drawing such as Visual 9–12, the illusionistic space is created with so refined a use of the medium that you can look at the drawing and barely think of the surface at all. This type of careful drawing is interesting because of how well it is able to suggest visual reality as our eye sees it. Both of these drawings treat their choice of picture space as an inflexible premise, to be consistently followed

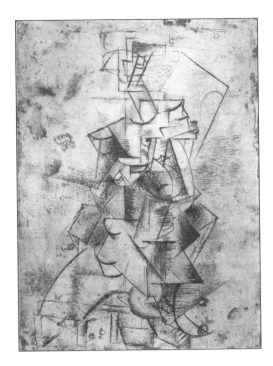

visual | 9–16 |

Pablo Picasso (1881–1973), *Mademoiselle Leonie dans une chaise longue (Miss Leonie in a Chaise Longue),* etching and drypoint on Van Gelder paper, 7¾" × 5½", 1910. *Fine Arts Museums of San Francisco, Gift of R. E. Lewis, Inc., 1966.83.6.* © 2007 Estate of *Pablo Picasso / Artists Rights Society (ARS), New York*

to a logical conclusion. They stay in the space they have established. Studying one of these drawings, it is easy to forget that a flat space is not the opposite of an illusionistic space. The two kinds of space can coexist in the same drawing.

If maintaining life drawing's traditional practices is part of the meaning of your work, you will probably want to use the three spaces one at a time, when they are called for: line drawings operate in a flat space, life studies in the studio create a shallow space, and complex pictures use a deep space. If tradition is less important to you than finding your own way to draw, you may want to think of the three picture spaces as referring to areas of interest in a drawing,

instead of being mutually exclusive choices. A flat space and an illusionistic space do operate in different ways, but they can do so in the same drawing. The key to making them work together is to let each one obey its own rules and keep them out of each other's way.

Visual 9–17, by San Francisco artist William H. Brown, shows us a drawing of a woman in a relaxed moment. She is sitting at a small, round table, having a

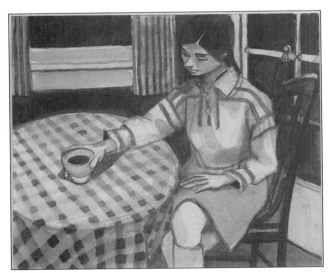

visual | 9–17 |

William H. Brown (1931–1980), *Seated Figure with Checkered Tablecloth,* charcoal, black and grey wash, 15" × 17.75", 1964. *Fine Arts Museums of San Francisco, Gift of Mr. & Mrs. Edgar Sinton, 1964.61*

cup of coffee. There are windows behind her, but the panes are black, which keeps us from being distracted by any activity taking place outdoors. The drawing establishes a deep space that places us, the viewers, close enough to the subject that we are looking down at her and the table. Relative to the subject, the tabletop is tilted toward us. This is not a jarring error in perspective. The table fits comfortably into the drawing because it obeys the rules of the flat space more than the illusionistic space. If we read it as an oval instead of a table, it is one of several flat forms that interlock almost like the pieces of a puzzle to form the picture plane.

Study the parts of the drawing other than the figure. There are rectangular shapes, diagonal forms that resemble parallelograms, some well-defined negative space, and the single large oval of the table. Many of these forms are solid black. The interaction of these forms on the picture plane gives the drawing a satisfying visual balance that complements the emotional content carried by the figure. The table, which can be read both as an illusionistic object and a flat geometric form, serves as a bridge between the deep space and the picture plane. The black windowpanes call our attention to their presence as abstract forms, but they also are consistent with this drawing's practice of making the forms lighter as they get closer to us in the illusionistic space. In this drawing, the flat space and the illusionistic space are each interesting in their own way. Working together, they create a complex, sophisticated drawing.

In Visual 9–18, Nathan Oliveira uses a different set of tactics to set up a spatial dialogue in his drawing. The subject reclines on a bed, or a model stand that looks like one, and she is looking right at us. She is positioned high on the page in a deep space, with the bed taking up most of the foreground. This picture's illusionistic space was organized to create a point of view close to the model, and fairly low, so that our eyes are at the same level as hers. The previous drawing, with its solid, flat forms and high point of view, approached its subject with a reserve that this missing in this picture. This drawing is not intended to present us with an intellectual problem. It was made to show us how it felt to be there.

Nathan Oliveira, *Model with Arm over Face,* graphite, 17.79" × 19.1", 1966. *Fine Arts Museums of San Francisco, Gift of the artist, 1969.30.8.* © *Nathan Oliveira, Courtesy of the artist and John Berggruen Gallery, San Francisco.*

The Oliveira drawing's surface is covered with **hatching** lines. They are vigorous scribbles in the bottom half of the picture, and dark, matter-of-fact horizontal lines in the trapezoidal negative form at the top. The hatching is applied more deliberately when describing the model, approaching softness in some places. This repertoire of hatching effects activates the surface and reinforces the sense of immediacy in the drawing.

Building the forms in this way, with a personal calligraphy, creates a surface covered with the trajectories of the artist's hand. This continuing reminder of the artist's presence, which takes place on the flat space, is consistent with the physical closeness to the model implied in the organization of the deep space.

INTEGRATED COMPOSITION

An integrated composition is a complete composition. It is achieved when nothing can be added to the drawing or taken away from it without diminishing it in some way. Achieving this condition of unity in a deep-space composition is a particular challenge in art. It is an even more interesting one when you are doing it with the minimal tools used to draw the figure.

If the model is indoors, there will probably be some visible **linear perspective**, in which some of the parallel lines of the building converge on a **vanishing point**. If you were making an illustration, you might want to construct the scene's perspective using a straightedge. In life drawing, linear perspective is more often drawn from observation, as David Rich did in Visual 9–19. If you align a ruler with the perspective lines in this drawing, you will find that they do not perfectly converge on a single vanishing point. To get an exact linear perspective, Rich might have constructed it in advance and added the model when he took his seat. This would have separated the figure from the development of the composition and violated the intent of this drawing. By using **empirical perspective**, the artist created and balanced the picture plane as a single construction and thus made the figure integral to the composition.

If the model were outdoors, you would probably use some atmospheric perspective, in which the forms in the more distant areas would be lighter and their edges softer. Visual 9–15, earlier in the chapter, is an example. Atmospheric perspective effects depend on lighting conditions and the amount of haze in the air. Like empirical perspective, getting it right is a matter of careful observation.

Atmospheric haze is such a handy indicator of depth that it is too bad we have to leave it outside. Some artists, such Sangram Majumdar (Visual 9–20) are able to bring visible air, or something like it, into the studio with them. In this drawing, he creates an improvisation on the surface whose cumulative effect is to assign a character to the space in the room. It is as if he is able to draw a portrait of the particular mass of air inhabiting the room he is working in. Atmospheric perspective is created by varying

visual | 9–19 |

David Rich, *Michael*, charcoal and eraser on paper, 22" × 30", 2002.

visual | 9–20 |

Sangram
Majumdar,
Pyramid,
charcoal and
graphite on
paper, 32" × 40",
2006.

the value and softness of forms to demonstrate how space looks outdoors. Majumdar repurposes these drawing conventions into a visual metaphor for indoor space.

There is no recipe for using an atmospheric background to integrate picture space. Using this method successfully depends on how well you can apply your energy, alertness, and wit to create a balance between observation and improvisation. Are you ready to try it?

Exercise 9–2: Integrated Composition Exercise

In this exercise, you will practice developing integrated deep-space compositions in the studio. You will work on building the figure and the picture plane at the same time and coordinating the figure—ground relationship with the drawing's illusionistic space.

Materials

- Vine charcoal and compressed charcoal. Some of the compressed charcoal should be the softest grade.

- Your eraser set. Remember that you can use the white polymer eraser to remove the charcoal completely, the cheap pink rubber erasers to push the medium around and create the surface you want, and a kneaded eraser to lighten an area without rubbing.

- Some good paper at least 18" × 24". It should be 100 percent rag to stand up to repeated erasing. Larger is better because that will challenge your improvisational skills more.

Procedures

1. Create at least four drawings, working for a minimum of forty-five minutes on each one. If you can spend more time, up to three or four hours on each drawing, you will have a better chance of creating a masterpiece.

2. Arrange the studio so that you see space in front of and behind the model. If many people are working, this may mean placing the model in the center of the room.

3. If you are a picture-plane person, this project will be a natural for you. If you are a figure person, here is an opportunity to practice working the other way. Early in the drawing, work as quickly as you can and get some preliminary forms in the background as well as in the figure. If you want to, you can start by covering the surface with charcoal, and working against the gray with soft charcoal and an eraser as shown in Exercise 3-3 in Chapter 3.

4. Remember the space is as much a participant in this drawing as the figure. You may have to consciously interrupt your work on the figure from time to time to develop the background. Define the space as completely as you do the model, with no unarticulated areas. Have some recognizable structures in the foreground, the middle distance, and the background. In this drawing the foreground will be defined as the space between you and the model.

5. Although this is a deep space exercise, keep the flat space in mind as you work. Create a spatial dialog by using hatching, erasing, or interlocking forms to call attention to the picture plane at the same time as you are developing the illusionistic space.

6. Proportion the entire drawing as a unit. This means that you are not going to work on the figure's proportions without reference to the objects outside the figure. If a corner, a window, or some object in the room is out of place with respect to the figure, fix it. Draw perspective lines as you see them, using structures on the figure as landmarks.

7. You probably will not see actual atmospheric effects in the studio, but you can use some of the techniques used to draw atmospheric perspective to heighten the sense of space in the piece. For example, make the foreground lighter than the background, or vice versa, and soften the edges in the background. Do not be afraid to experiment.

Demonstration 9-1: Integrated Composition

I made several drawings in order to get the one I am using for this demonstration. I started by spending a four-hour drawing period doing twenty- and twenty-five-minute versions of the assignment. I recommend a tune-up session like this if you can fit it into your schedule. These drawings were practice, on cheap paper, done primarily to get my drawing speed to a point where I felt I could complete the final drawing in forty-five minutes. I could have simply decided to take longer on the final drawing, but I figured that working under time pressure would keep me moving fast and give my marks more vigor. This would, I hoped, make the surface **painterly** and ensure that it does its part for the spatial dialog.

The drawing you see in this demonstration was one of four done in a second four-hour segment, in which there were two models. One of the models was seated on a black stool, and the other was sitting on the padded model stand, which was covered with a white cloth. These gave me the opportunity to draw some solid, crisp geometric forms near the figures. Using hard edges and few mid-tones here would make the foreground seem clearer and more focused, and the background softer and less distinct in comparison. This atmospheric invention would, I hoped, be complemented by the empirical perspective of the mostly empty room. How did I have so many happy inspirations about organizing the space in this drawing?

H. Stone,
*Integrated
Composition
Demonstration,
Step 1.*

They came, one by one, during the first four hours of work on this project. That tune-up session really paid off here. I have no plans to show you those first working drawings.

My foreground strategy required me to hold out the whites and prevented me from starting by blasting a charcoal **imprimatura** over the picture plane. Instead I took note of a place near the center of the scene where the two figures overlapped, and located it on the paper with some pale gray forms and a few contour lines (Visual 9–21). This would be my first reference point, which I would use to proportion the figure and position other elements.

H. Stone,
*Integrated
Composition
Demonstration,
Step 2.*

Step 2 (Visual 9–22) shows the beginning of the figure–ground relationship. My plan was to establish it early in the drawing so it did not get overlooked. I wanted to build the figures from the edges, so the figure–ground relationship would be a dominant structure in the drawing that I could merge with the illusionistic space later. I thought that this would be more logical than drawing the deep space first and grafting a figure–ground relationship in the drawing during its last minutes. I quickly drew the closer figure using a very light version of the edges and contrast reversal project, Exercise 8-1 in Chapter 8. The second figure did not get as much attention because its proportions would be drawn with reference to the first figure, and I was not sure yet the first one was correct.

I did want to make sure the placement of the figures did not cause the second one to extend off the paper, so I located it with a contour line before continuing (Visual 9–23).

Step 4, in Visual 9–24, saw the placement of the first background forms. The first one was the dark parallelogram outlining the model's head. This existed in the room as a drawing board leaning against the wall. I drew this to define the contour of the face, so that I could use the tip of the nose as a position reference for the rectangular forms to the left of the model's head. These corresponded to canvases, shipping crates, and other rectangular objects that make art studios good environments for this exercise. On the right side of the drawing, I drew the baseboard in as an empirical perspective line and made a few marks with the side of the charcoal to indicate an easel and the drawing board leaning against it. I omitted the artist who was drawing there.

One of the things I learned from the practice drawings was that the deep space would not be convincing unless the floor read as a continuous surface. My plan for this was to extend mass tones across the floor from the model to the rectangles in back, which were in a hallway, and work with an eraser until the surface emerged. In the lower third of the drawing, the floor surface would be defined by the model stand's figure–ground relationship. Visual 9–25 gives an update on this process and shows additional work on the closer figure. I drew interior forms such as the back and left arm by continuing to develop edges. I wanted to keep the emphasis on the figure–ground structure for as long as possible.

Step 6, shown in Visual 9–26, shows how working along the contours develops two structures

visual | 9–23 |

H. Stone, *Integrated Composition Demonstration, Step 3.*

visual | 9–24 |

H. Stone, *Integrated Composition Demonstration, Step 4.*

visual | 9–25 |

H. Stone, *Integrated Composition Demonstration, Step 5.*

H. Stone,
*Integrated
Composition
Demonstration,
Step 6.*

at once. From my point of view, one model is in front of the other, so to firm up the forms on the first one's back, I darkened its background, which was the figure of the second model. Other examples of this two-for-the-price-of-one effect can be seen at the closer model's knee, left shoulder, and arm. The left leg was resized to fit the rest of the figure.

H. Stone,
*Integrated
Composition
Demonstration,
Step 7.*

Step 7 (Visual 9–27) shows the first figure nearly finished. The left leg was narrowed, the right leg was created with the other model's right hand on it, and details were added to the head, back, and legs. The figure on the right received some articulation in the face and torso.

Visual 9–28 shows the completed figure on the right. I abandoned the figure–ground technique in favor of chiaroscuro because much of that figure was hidden, and defining it with just edge work might not provide enough information to make it look solid. The brute force of chiaroscuro worked well enough that the body is recognizable even though it is drawn loosely in many areas. I added some sketchy dark forms as a cast shadow on the model stand, and in the background to connect that figure to the easel to the right. I also drew another dark cast shadow under the left model's leg.

H. Stone,
*Integrated
Composition
Demonstration,
Step 8.*

The final version of the drawing, in Visual 9–29, shows the black, angular form at the bottom center of the drawing, and the floor after erasing and reworking it. These changes were part of the atmospheric perspective plan for this drawing, which called for the more distant forms to be lighter and softer than those in the foreground. The baseboard was made black, and the drawing board leaning against the easel on the right was darkened with hatching lines. A cast shadow was extended to the right from the bottom of that form.

visual | 9–29 |

H. Stone, *Integrated Composition Demonstration, final version,* charcoal on paper, 22" × 30", 2006.

Look at the Drawing

Study the drawings you made for this assignment, evaluating them according to the criteria below. In this exercise, we are looking for:

- A well-defined, consistent, deep illusionistic space, with some room both in front of and behind the model. To test for how consistent the space is, imagine that the model stands up and starts walking around the room you have drawn. Are there any areas where she is conspicuously too big or small? Alternatively, you should be able to touch any part of the completed drawing and say where in the room that point is: is it above or below the model? Is it in front of, or behind the model?

- A spatial dialog that comes from an assertive flat space. Did you use hatching, erasing or some other painterly technique? Are the marks recognizable as yours? Is the surface of the picture attractive or interesting for its own sake, independent of how well the image is drawn? Turning the picture upside down may help you evaluate this without being distracted by the image.

- Every portion of the picture plane contributing to the unified impression presented by the drawing. In other words, are there unarticulated spots in the picture? You can test for this by having a friend point to different places on your drawing and ask you what is represented there. It may be a recognizable structure, or it may be a squiggle or smudge whose purpose is to sit on the surface in a provocative way. It could even be bare paper if it is a part of a construction, such as a geometric form, that you intentionally created. If you cannot answer the question in a way that makes sense to your interrogator, it is a signal that the designated spot may not be pulling its weight.

We are not looking for:

- Unarticulated areas.
- A shallow picture space that is consistent only in the area immediately surrounding the figure.
- A flat space that is so stimulating that it detracts from the sense of deep space in the picture.
- Excessive attention to the figure at the expense of the rest of the composition.
- A very smooth, refined surface.
- Unintentional awkwardness in the placement of the figure, the subdivision of the picture plane, or the way the deep space is organized.

My demonstration holds up pretty well according to these criteria, but I showed you the pick of the litter. Anyway, I'm a figure person.

CHAPTER SUMMARY

In life drawing, there can be a tendency to draw the figure first and surround it with the rest of the composition afterward. Many artists draw the figure's background in a perfunctory way, and some have a strong natural inclination to leave it out altogether.

It is possible to draw the figure and the background at the same time, so that each one influences the other at all stages of the drawing process. This creates an integrated composition, in which the artist's considered choices determine how all parts of the picture will look and interact.

Picture space can be classed as flat, shallow, or deep. Shallow space and deep space are illusionistic spaces, in which the drawing maintains the convention that it is a window that looks into a three-dimensional space. Illusionistic picture spaces in life drawing have historical precedents in which each type of space was used in particular kinds of pictures. The picture spaces are not mutually exclusive, however, and by thinking of them as areas of interest in a picture instead of fixed systems, they can be made to work together in a spatial dialog to create life drawings that avoid conventional formulas, are personal expressions of the artist, and are interesting to viewers.

▶ *chapter questions*

1. Is Sangram Majumdar's drawing at the beginning of the chapter an example of flat space, shallow space, or deep space?

2. In Visual 9–19, do you think David Rich is more interested in the picture plane or the figure?

3–4. Give two reasons for your answer to Question 2.

5. In Visual 9–20, do you think Sangram Majumdar is more interested in the picture plane or the figure?

6–7. Give two reasons for your answer to Question 5.

8. How specifically would Graham Nickson's drawing in Visual 9–15 look different if he had chosen to draw it with the sun directly overhead?

9. How would that change have affected the sense of space in the picture?

10. How do you think that change would have affected the mood of the drawing?

H. Stone, *Drawing from Intimacy Series*,
graphite on Rives BFK paper, 30" × 22", 1994.

CHAPTER

objectives

- Use a drawing inventory to identify your life-drawing interests and strengths.
- Draw a finished portrait using value techniques.
- Define narrative, and compare some strategies used in narrative art.
- Understand some ways that abstraction is used in life drawing.
- Plan and execute a finished drawing using your drawing inventory.
- Compare your finished portrait to the benchmark drawing you made in Chapter 1.

introduction

Most of the exercises in this book are means to an end. You created them as part of a learning experience, and they are valuable as a record of your growth as a figurative artist. I always enjoy looking at this stream-of-consciousness narrative of an artist in progress, but these exercises can look pretty mysterious to uninitiated observers. Even if you would not cheerfully exhibit more than a few of these pieces in an art gallery, you probably have some thoughts about how you can use the skills you acquired as you drew them. In this chapter, you will apply what you have learned to make a drawing that is a complete work of art. This is called a finished drawing, and it represents your best thinking, work ethic, and skill.

THE ART OF LIFE DRAWING

A finished drawing is the best drawing you can make, with no excuses. It is the drawing that you send out into the world. You can declare any drawing finished if you have done as much with it as you can, but that does not by itself make it a finished drawing. It is possible to create a finished drawing in life-drawing class, but most of the drawings you make there will not meet the standard. How can we differentiate a finished drawing from the mass of drawings we generate? Although the line between a life-drawing study and a finished life drawing can be a smudged one, the finished drawing does have some distinctive characteristics:

- Intention: A finished drawing is created as a serious work of art that can hold its own in an exhibition with other artists' best work.

- Ambition: A finished drawing reaches outside of itself to address concerns larger than technical issues such as composition or rendering. These could be enduring, universal themes or a contemporary art dialectic.

- Quality: A finished drawing meets an artist's personal standards and represents those standards to the audience.

Listening to the Drawing

The idea of distilling the best parts of one's being into a work of art that will hang on a wall can elicit a certain amount of performance anxiety. It is not as if you are writing a paper that someone has to track down and read. Your drawing will hang where even the most jaded passerby can see it and make invidious comments. What if they don't get what you are trying to say? Even worse, what if they understand it too well and conclude that you are not a person to be taken seriously?

This unpleasantness is part of being a serious artist. With practice, you will learn to disregard the noise provoked by your art, but the sneakier danger to your artistic integrity may not be as easy to ignore. This menace is the Art Judge.

The Art Judge is much smarter than you and reads all of the art magazines. This individual has access to better information about art than you do, can see that you are just kidding yourself, and will explain in subtle, complex language why your ideas are not really that profound. The Art Judge is especially suspicious of drawing skill and is a member of a powerful art-world clique who objects to figurative work on philosophical, moral, political, and aesthetic grounds.

The Art Judge is such a formidable enemy that it is lucky for all of us that no such person actually exists. This is a mythical character more malicious than anyone in real life: a personification of every objection anyone could have to the way you want to make art. Unfortunately, this fictional voice can cause real trouble for artists when they allow it to stampede them into mistrusting their own work. Trusting your work means believing that over time, your work is smarter than you are. The art you make is an improvement on the thinking that goes into it, and making it not only builds your skills, but it also will give you valid information about directions you could take with it.

You may have noticed that a drawing you are working on sometimes bothers you. It may seem incomplete, or it may have an area that conspicuously fails to fit in well with the rest. At other times, the drawing will surprise and delight you because it is so recognizably yours that it feels like finding something you had misplaced. This kind of experience, when the work of art seems to have a life independent of your plans for it,

visual | 10–1 |

David Park, *Sketchbook, page one*, various media, 11.8" × 9", circa 1960. *Image courtesy of the David Park papers, 1917–1973, in the Archives of American Art, Smithsonian Institution*

is your own artistic voice finding an outlet in the work. As you continue to practice, your drawings will be come more articulate both in how well they describe what you are seeing and in how well they tell you what they need. In the same way that practice teaches you how to listen to the drawing, it will also teach how to learn from your process.

Visual 10–1 through Visual 10–4 are drawings from a single sketchbook that David Park created in 1960, near the end of his life. We know that he reviewed these drawings and used them to plan paintings because many of them are stained with coffee and artist fingerprints; dust and studio debris are glued to some pages with drops of oil paint. The sketchbook contains page after page of life drawings, most of them executed with ink and a brush, in three values, using simplified contour lines. Unlike many artists' journals, Park's contains little writing; they are primarily drawings done using a method that a censorious critic might call obsessive and repetitive. What was he up to? The answer is in the work. He trusted it when he

visual | 10–2 |

David Park, *Sketchbook, page nineteen*, various media, 11.8" × 9", circa 1960. *Image courtesy of the David Park papers, 1917–1973, in the Archives of American Art, Smithsonian Institution*

visual | 10–3 |

David Park, *Sketchbook, page twenty*, various media, 11.8" × 9", circa 1960. *Image courtesy of the David Park papers, 1917–1973, in the Archives of American Art, Smithsonian Institution*

made it, listened to it when he needed to, and became the pioneer in a new style of painting that came to be known as Bay Area Figuration. This movement grew directly out of a life-drawing group that Park organized in the 1950s.

RECOGNIZING YOUR DRAWING STYLE

When you visit an artist's studio, often the walls will be a disorderly collage of the occupant's work. The room may be cluttered with sketchbooks, notebooks and piles of drawings. As an interior design motif this may leave quite a bit to be desired, but keeping all of this material visible helps the artist reflect on recent work and figure out what to try next. What have your drawings done for you lately? A review of your drawings will help you identify which techniques you are most articulate in and give you some ideas about how your own style is emerging. When you are planning an independent project, studying your recent work can show you how you might want to approach it.

Exercise 10-1: The Drawing Inventory

In this exercise, you will look at and think about your recent drawings. Set aside enough time that you can do it without feeling rushed.

visual | 10–4 |

David Park, *Sketchbook, page twenty-four*, various media, 11.8" × 9", circa 1960. *Image courtesy of the David Park papers, 1917–1973, in the Archives of American Art, Smithsonian Institution*

Materials

- All of the life drawings you have produced in the last three months.
- Push pins.
- A bare wall.

Procedures

1. Go through all of your drawings one at a time. Look at and briefly consider each drawing. Do not evaluate the quality of the drawing. Instead, think about what the drawing means to you:

    a. When you were making the drawing, did you feel like you were doing something important?

    b. Did you feel a sense of satisfaction when you were finished with the drawing?

    c. Did you learn something from creating the drawing?

2. Pick out no more than six drawings that you feel particularly connected to according to the criteria above. Pin them to the wall and study them.

3. Write down a few **formal observations** about each drawing. These will be factual statements describing the way the piece looks or is constructed. These statements should be objective, so that anyone would be able to agree with them regardless of how they feel about the piece. For example: "The drawing is a single image of a standing man, drawn with a thin contour line. A few light gray mass tones were added in the figure. The model casts a dark shadow onto the surface he is standing on."

4. Write down a few statements describing what these drawings have in common that is distinctively yours. In other words, what is it about the way those drawings look that makes them recognizable as something you created?

5. Save the notes to use in Exercise 10-4.

SPEAKING THROUGH THE FIGURE

Probably the closest you will ever come to perfect freedom is in your choice of what kind of art to make. Visual art is the most ecumenical of the arts, encompassing diverse media and levels of skill, and assimilating techniques from theater, music, literature, and philosophy. In this environment, it is not difficult to produce an object that others will agree is art. The hard question is, how do you make the very best art you can?

Making a finished life drawing refines your personal preoccupations into art using the human figure as a catalyst. If someone can look at your drawing and understand what these concerns are, the piece has achieved a measure of success. If it persuades the audience to care about what they are seeing, it has power in the real world. How can you create a figure drawing that meets this standard?

One usual way of tackling this problem is for the artist to make a short list of the most profound concepts he knows or believes, figure out which one to make a drawing of, and connect the idea to an image. Select the drawing style that is most compatible with the message, draw a few studies, and the finished drawing practically draws itself. This is a standard procedure for visual problem solving, and it is a very productive one in many art settings. There is a problem, though, with using it to plan finished life drawings.

Each variety of art finds a natural jurisdiction over particular regions of human experience. The strength of life drawing is in showing what we as individual persons have in common, despite differences in background or belief. Being in the same room with someone, studying them without making judgments, and striving to represent who they are in a drawing is a meditation on being human. It is a project that by its nature has clear intentions, integrity of process, and a potentially profound result. Introducing content originating outside the process can sometimes compromise the drawing's power and engender work that is awkward, preachy, or patronizing to the viewer. A life drawing is most powerful when its content grows from exploring the implications of drawing another person rather than from applying drawing skills to illustrate a theory or make a point.

The drawing shown in Visual 10–5 is an example of this kind of disconnect between high-minded content and the technique used to express it. This drawing of Joséphine, Empress of France from 1804 to 1810, is not entirely satisfying to modern eyes. The content is not at issue: a person in a private moment of prayer is a standard motif in Western art, and it has often been drawn with honesty and feeling. The problem with this drawing is that the coolness of its presentation is at odds with the intimate moment it is depicting. The most beautifully drawn structure in the picture is the Empress' elaborate, brocaded train. It has more character than any of the humans in the picture, whose faces are so generic as to be interchangeable. The two ladies behind Joséphine seem to be more important to the drawing as curators of the heavy

Jacques Louis David (1748–1825), *L'Impératrice à genoux, avec Mme de La Rochefoucauld et Mme de La Valette*, black crayon and graphite, 10.2" × 14.3", early nineteenth century. *Thierry Le Mage. Reunion des Musees Nationaux / Art Resource, NY, Louvre, Paris, France*

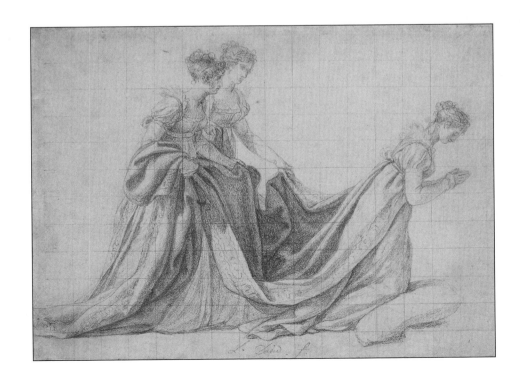

fabric they are holding off the floor than as companions to the Empress. Is Joséphine's costume more important than she is? It is in this drawing because it identifies the subject of the piece as royalty itself, rather than this particular royal person. Here, Joséphine's personality and inner life are irrelevant. This drawing is a simple play expressing an equivalence between royal status and moral virtue. We don't have to know anything about Joséphine to feel manipulated by it.

Studying this picture, we might well wonder where the artist, Jacques Louis David, is. The drawing's surface is smooth, and the media are used in the consistent, thorough way that a modern person might describe as professional. If the word also implies a certain emotional disengagement, that usage is valid here as well. Is David simply being properly deferential to authority by using a drawing technique so neutral that it gives him no visible presence in the drawing? Maybe he is he letting us know that he is no more than a hired hand here, telling a story whose honesty he cannot personally vouch for.

David made a different kind of drawing more than a decade earlier (Visual 10–6). This is a portrait of his friend, Jean-Paul Marat, one of the more radical participants in the French Revolution. Marat was assassinated in 1793, and David drew his corpse to make this picture. The face is the subject here, and it is framed twice; first, by the corner diagonals, and second, by the cloth wrapped around Marat's head. The soft, directional lighting creates a gentle chiaroscuro used to show us the structure of Marat's face. As in the previous drawing, David's treatment of the surface is refined and precise, but this time he uses short, fine hatching lines. Instead of functioning as a distancing device, here the carefully crafted surface has a tender, contemplative quality that makes his musings on death, and his friend, inseparable from the descriptive function of the drawing. With only slight changes in technique, David conceals his presence in one drawing and establishes himself as a trustworthy narrator in another.

Is the moral here that a portrait is more authentic than a narrative? No, it is to respect your own voice and pay attention. Start with the things you know: A life drawing will depict at least one person. It can express itself by showing what the figure looks like, using the figure to present facts or tell a story, or through abstraction: a use of forms or media in an interesting way. You may want to use all three of these strategies in the same drawing, or you could emphasize one at the expense of the

visual | 10–6 |

Jacques Louis David, *Head of the Dead Marat*, pen, black and brown ink, 10.6" × 8.27" 1793. The inscription on the four corners says *To Marat, the Friend of the People, David*. Marat's newspaper was named *The Friend of the People*.

other two. The next step is to figure out how you will use these strategies to express what is most important to you. In other words, the goal is to construct your own life-drawing methodology. If you have been practicing, you have made some progress toward this, and your drawings are already answering some questions the world might have about you:

- Do you find ambivalence interesting?
- Would you be a good motivational speaker, or is understated self-assurance more your style?
- Are you more interested in the process of drawing or in the completed piece?
- Do you stand up for your convictions by intense argument, or patient reasoning?

These are components of your voice as an artist: the personal authority you are able to express in your drawing. Becoming articulate in this nonverbal form of self-disclosure is the hard part of life drawing. Now that you have an artist's voice, let it lead the way as you develop your finished drawing. This means that instead of starting with a message and figuring out how to draw it, start with the voice and figure out what it excels in saying.

PORTRAITURE

The purpose of a portrait is to express the uniqueness of its subject. This book approaches life drawing as a form of portraiture in that its exercises emphasize drawing the structures of the body from observation, instead of according to a formula or method. Because drawing a portrait from a living person is so similar to a life-drawing session, you won't have to make many changes to your usual way of working in order to draw a finished portrait. Like a life-drawing exercise, a portrait has an intrinsic harmony between intent, planning, and drawing technique.

Exercise 10-2: Drawing a Finished Portrait Using Value

For this exercise, you will use value drawing techniques (Chapter 3) to create a finished portrait. You will not use contour lines in this drawing. I decided on this restriction for a couple of reasons. First, value drawing is the technique for drawing reality as it presents itself to the eye, so it fits well with the goal of achieving a likeness, as Stuart Pearson Wright did in his portrait of Christopher Lee (Visual 10–7). Second, portraits done on commission tend to use value much more than line, so if you practice this project enough that you can consistently do it well, you can make money with it.

An individual's distinctive look, or likeness, is determined by the person's **facial set**, or habitual facial expression, and the way it interacts with the physical features of the face. A good way to see how facial set works is to find someone who cannot see well without their glasses and draw the person with glasses on and then again with them off. Usually, without their glasses, people lose some of their attentiveness, and you will see their facial features with little personality inhabiting them.

Drawing a facial likeness is a subspecialty of life drawing which usually requires dedicated practice, so do not feel too frustrated if you are not great at it right away. To learn how to do it, commit yourself to making corrections until the face starts to look familiar. Often, the resemblance will start to feel right intuitively before it begins to look right. Do your best to draw what you are seeing and the likeness will start to happen in time.

This exercise will be done over a span of three to four hours. You will not be using any skills you haven't practiced, but try to apply them in a more sophisticated way by being conscious of the figure—ground relationship and making frequent checks on the proportions as you work.

Stuart Pearson Wright, *Christopher Lee*, pencil, charcoal and ink on paper, 2003. © *Stuart Pearson Wright. Courtesy of the artist.*

Materials

- A good grade of paper, such as Rives BFK or Arches Cover, at least 18" × 24". Although good paper costs more, it stands up better to erasures, and it does not deteriorate over time the way cheap paper does.

- Your eraser set. If you want a clean, refined surface, as created by Wright in Visual 10–7, you may want to start with new erasers.

- Vine or compressed charcoal, whichever you prefer.

Procedures

1. Use directional lighting such as a spotlight or a window. If the model will be lit from a window, remember that the sun will move quite a bit during a long pose. North light will keep the shadows fairly stable over the span of the drawing. Move around the room to find a point of view you like, keeping in mind that you need to see both light and shadow areas.

2. Work from the general to the specific. Start out drawing loosely, and gradually bring the image into focus. Before you draw, visualize where you are going to place the figure on the paper. Study the model to locate the largest areas of gray. Place these shapes on the paper, evaluate their position, and use your eraser to make corrections as necessary. Do not add details until you are satisfied that the figure fits on the page the way you want it to.

3. Do not use contour lines or construction lines. Use hatching lines if you want.

4. Trust the value exercise. Everything you draw should be a shape you have directly observed.

5. Correct errors as soon as you notice them.

6. Here are some tips on drawing a likeness:

   a. The most important point of likeness is the jaw line. Pay close attention to it from the earliest stages of the drawing. If you cannot see even a little resemblance to your subject in the jaw line, fix it before you continue the drawing.

   b. The second most important point of likeness is the hair line. When the jaw line and the hair line have been established, you have defined the shape of the face. If you have drawn this contour and it is not satisfactory, study it and note where it is rounded and where it is more angular. Matching the angular and round forms is a good way to strengthen a sagging likeness.

   c. The eyes are the third most important point of likeness. It is interesting how far out of place an eye can be before the subject starts looking strange. Before you start drawing details, make sure the **midline** of the head is in the right place, and place the eyes using a light **mass tone**. Then make your proportion checks. Are the eyes too high on the head? Is one above the other? Are they too far apart or too close together? To get the eyes aligned and pointed in the right direction, draw their negative space, that is, the whites of the eyes, instead of the irises.

   d. The mouth is the next most important point of likeness. The most common error in drawing the mouth is to focus on its details, failing to show its basic structure. If you draw it in three tones, the structure will emerge. If you want details, add them after the structure is established.

   e. Draw the nose after the other features are in place. When the eyes and mouth are right, they will imply the shape and location of the nose, so you can usually finish the nose quickly by adding a few dark accents in the right places.

Demonstration 10-1: A Finished Portrait

I did this demonstration in four hours with compressed charcoal on 22" × 30" Rives BFK paper. One of the goals of this exercise is to fit the model on the paper, so you should turn your paper to match the view you have of the model. In this setting, I intentionally chose the conventional format for a portrait, which is a seated model viewed from the front.

I started by very quickly placing the shadow masses of the face and neck (Visual 10–8). It does not really matter where you start, as long as you keep moving and do not commit yourself by drawing details too early.

In Visual 10–9, you can see my preliminary three-value study of the figure. I spent about a half hour on this stage of the drawing. A traditional portrait emphasizes either a person's place in the world (see Visual 10–5) or his personality. I want this picture to give a sense of what the sitter is like as a person, so the drawing had to be large enough that I could draw her face in some detail. The roughed-in figure as shown is a little more than two feet tall. I asked the subject to wear a simple, dark dress, so that her clothing would not distract from the details in the face and hands.

Another reason to have the model wear something simple in a **psychological portrait** such as this, is that it keeps the drawing from being locked in the present. As the drawing marches into the future, its focus will remain on the person in the picture, rather than the fashion sense of the early twenty-first century. This, of course, is also a reason to draw people naked.

visual | 10–8 |

H. Stone,
*Drawing a
Finished Portrait
Using Value,
Step 1.*

In Visual 10–10, I have started to develop the forms of the head and upper torso in more detail. Everything you see here is drawn using something pretty close to the three-value technique. It is a paradox that in order to get the best likeness, you need to forget what you know about the person you are drawing and just respond to the lights and darks that you see.

Sometimes a presentable face will happen quickly, as it did in this drawing, and you will be tempted to leave it alone. This is a time to look carefully and think about how you can transform a "good enough" drawing into the best one you can make. At this point in this drawing, there is a severity in the face that didn't reflect the real face I was looking at. The model's right eye is a little too high, and the jaw line is a little jowly. It is perhaps true that most of the drawing's audience won't notice these small errors, but your drawing skills will stop improving

visual | 10–9 |

H. Stone,
*Drawing a
Finished Portrait
Using Value,
Step 2.*

H. Stone,
*Drawing a
Finished Portrait
Using Value,
Step 3.*

if you get in the habit of letting inaccuracies lie. Visual 10–11, two hours into the drawing, shows the changes I made to the face as well as some much larger edits. Compare the position of the model's right arm in Visuals 10–10 and 10–11. It is possible that she did not get exactly into position after one of the breaks, or I may have not seen it right the first time, but the negative space between her hands told me it was time for a change. To fix it, I pulled most of the structure out with the vinyl eraser and started again with the three-value exercise. I also worked on the figure–ground relationship on the model's right side and used soft charcoal and an eraser to develop the torso as revealed by the dress.

With less than half an hour of drawing time left, the drawing in Visual 10–12 could be called finished. The last hour and a half were spent making fine adjustments. Compare Visual 10–12 to the previous one.

- The model's right forearm and hand have been further developed. I darkened the shadow that the right arm was submerged in, lightened the forearm, and clarified the structure of the hand.

H. Stone,
*Drawing a
Finished Portrait
Using Value,
Step 4.*

- The lower legs were developed starting at the edges. I used the eraser quite a bit in this passage.

- Grays and blacks were added to the background to develop the figure–ground relationship and fit the figure into the composition better. I will want the background to reflect what I see, but not in so much detail that it distracts from the sitter's face and hands.

Now let's find fault with the drawing. What still needs work?

- Can we tell where the light is coming from? Yes, but it does not identify the drawing's center of interest as well as it could.

The cast shadow on the couch, on the left side of the drawing (the model's right), is a real shape that I could see, but it has a hard edge that emphasizes a structure that is of only peripheral interest to the drawing, unlike the more important ones on the model's left arm and on that side of her face. Also, the flat expanse of white there is inconsistent with the surface treatment of the other articulated parts of the drawing.

- The subject's left leg contradicts itself. We can see where the knee bends, but it does not look like part of the same structure as the lower leg.

The final version of the drawing (Visual 10–13) shows my attempts to remedy these problems. The left side of the drawing is much darker, which softens the edges on that side of the figure. Although this cost the drawing some detail in the lower legs, it contributes to a consistent sense of light in the drawing. The local color of the couch was black, so the changes had the effect of softening the cast shadow that was problematic in Visual 10–12, rather than eliminating it. I used an eraser to firm up the model's left knee.

Look at the Drawing

In this exercise, we are looking for:

- A consistent, directional light on the figure.
- A figure that comfortably occupies the picture plane without crowding the sides.
- A figure that fits into its illusionistic environment, without underdeveloped or awkward edges.
- A figure without major errors in its structure.
- A face that resembles the subject.

visual | 10–12 |

H. Stone, *Drawing a Finished Portrait Using Value, Step 5.*

visual | 10–13 |

H. Stone, *Drawing a Finished Portrait Using Value, final version*, charcoal on paper, 24" × 18", 2004.

Ann Piper, *Jess Tells Me Her Terrible Secret*, charcoal and gesso on paper, 29.25" × 40.5", 2003. *Courtesy of Ann Piper*

We are not looking for:

- A figure floating on an expanse of white.

- A figure not positioned in or on an identifiable structure. The drawing should provide a reason for the figure's stance or positioning.

- An ill-considered figure–ground relationship. The figure–ground relationship falls short if it contains no contrast reversals, or if it is not clear whether an edge of the figure is intended to be hard or soft.

- A generic face, which was obviously not drawn from observation.

- A face with major structural problems, such as the eyes too high or too low.

I would judge my drawing as successful based on these criteria. The forms are clear in most areas of the figure, with only a few problems. The model's left knee is better than it was, but it still is not exactly right. The dress hangs implausibly over the model's left shin, so the shin does not look straight and solid. The model's right inner elbow is a little darker than it needs to be. The dark background on the left side of the drawing does not show the arm of the couch as well as I would wish. This would be a good place to flatten the kneaded eraser and use it like a rubber stamp to lift some of the charcoal off. That way, I could firm up the structure of that area without having to renegotiate its surface by rubbing it with an eraser.

This drawing is not perfect, but it does what I wanted it to do in most places, and the things that are wrong with it do not compromise it very much. I had to give the model the drawing in return for sitting for me, so I do not have the original around to make improvements to.

Louis Lafitte
(1770–1828),
'Le Vengeur du
Peuple' Sinking at
the Battle of
Ouessant, 1st June
1794, graphite on
paper, circa early
nineteenth
century.
Bibliotheque
Nationale, Paris,
France / Giraudon
/ The Bridgeman
Art Library

NARRATIVE

A narrative is a story in which action takes place and the condition of the subject is changed in some way. The term may remind you of a literary or cinematic narrative structure, where the story's events, and the order in which they occur, are described in a clear and orderly manner. Louis Lafitte's *'Le Vengeur du Peuple' Sinking at the Battle of Ouessant, 1st June 1794* (Visual 10–15) is an example of a drawing that tells its story cinematically. The event is the sinking of a French battleship in the first major naval battle of revolutionary France. Lafitte might have shown the French ships in line, sailing against the British; or this ship's four-hour engagement with HMS *Brunswick*. Instead, he chose to emphasize the struggle for survival that took place as the ship sank. He is obeying the literary rule that a scene should be started at the last possible moment in the action of the event being depicted.

Lafitte uses edge effects to present the narrative to us. The region of the drawing of greatest contrast is at the center, where a few gesticulating characters have been heightened with white, and with details added in black. Our eye is drawn to this area, where the image is sharpest. Behind these central characters is a monochromatic mob of sailors whose individual struggles are not as clearly articulated. The slanting deck of the sinking ship creates the setting, but it is a contour line drawing with no variations in value, and thus is harder to recognize than the first set of figures. As our eye slides down the deck, we see sailors in the water, also drawn with contour lines. A broken mast at left points to the *Brunswick* in the background, which provides an audience for the disaster. This picture could easily be broken into four movie shots or cartoon panels: activity on deck; listing, sinking ship; struggling figures in the water; and aloof observers on the *Brunswick*.

In Lafitte's drawing, the story is the subject, and the human figures are actors in it. Robert Benney's drawing (Visual 10–16) is a portrait in which action is implied, rather than shown sequentially. Like the previous drawing, it documents the aftermath of an assault during wartime. Without knowing exactly how the subject was wounded, we still can guess some of the recent events in his life. This is a remarkable drawing because it is straightforward and unself-conscious at a time when serious injuries, and particularly missing limbs, were almost never viewed or discussed except by medical personnel. The drawing is not calculated to shock us or to evoke easy feelings of patriotism or pathos. The injured man is shown simply as himself. This piece has no editorial agenda except commitment to showing the dignity of the subject.

Narrative art is not always limited to depictions of events that are, or could be, literally true. The story you choose to tell is limited only by your imagination and wit. Some of the best contemporary figurative artists work in a comic-book format, where the frame-by-frame plot development parallels the shot-by-shot narrative used in moviemaking (Visual 10–17). Comic art emphasizes well-differentiated characters and clearly defined action over strictly accurate **rendering**. Exaggeration of proportions, an emphasis on gesture, and the use of unusual compositions are standard cartooning strategies for telling a story with clarity and drama.

A graphic novel with an ambiguous plot would be pretty unsatisfying, but in other forms of narrative art, it is not always important for viewers to know exactly what is happening. Sometimes the meaning of the piece depends on their not knowing. Giorgio De Chirico's drawing in Visual 10–18 is an example of Pictorial Surrealism, which uses the conventions of visual storytelling to assemble unlikely narratives with obscure meanings. The premise behind Surrealism is that the subconscious is an authentic reality that operates according to its own logic, and therefore the forms that percolate out of it are significant. Surrealist pictures are

visual | 10–16 |

Robert Benney, *Amputee Awaiting Evacuation on Plane Flight to Eniwetok*, graphite, 14" × 18.6", 1944. *Fine Arts Museums of San Francisco, Gift of the artist to the M.H. de Young Memorial Museum, 46.27.2.* © *Robert Benney / Licensed by VAGA, New York, NY*

intended to bypass the conscious, rational mind and speak to the viewer's subconscious, but you do not need to accept the theory to appreciate one of them. The invented images and implausible narratives in these drawings are often interesting for their own sake.

Some characteristics of Surrealist narrative are:

* Use of unexpected image juxtapositions.

* A mood of mystery.

* A sense that time is suspended.

* Imagery from dreams, mythology, and other regions outside everyday reality.

visual | 10–17 |

Frank Miller, *Sin City: A Dame to Kill For*, comic art, 5¼" x 5¼", 2005. © 2007 Frank Miller, Inc. All Rights Reserved. Sin City and the Sin City logo are registered trademarks of Frank Miller, Inc. Published by Dark Horse Comics, Inc.

Although few artists are still preoccupied with the subconscious, the narrative devices of Surrealism are so useful that they have become part of the grammar of contemporary narrative art. Like Surrealist narratives, Kay Ruane's drawings are not intended to be taken literally, but they are poetic where Surrealism is analytical, and they are concerned with images that are personal, rather than universal. We can list the elements in *Witness* (Visual 10–19) and catalogue the action implicit in it without being much closer to its meaning. Where do we start with this drawing? We start by looking. The drawing's distinctive finish and attention to detail tell us two things:

visual | 10–18 |

* It will take time to see it all.

* The artist felt that the drawing was important enough to deserve her best effort.

Giorgio de Chirico (1888–1978), *Solitude*, pencil and wash on paper, 8¼" × 12⅝", 1917. Gift of Abby Aldrich Rockefeller (by exchange) and Purchase. (112.1986), Digital Image © The Museum of Modern Art, New York, NY / Licensed by SCALA / Art Resource, NY. © 2007 Artists Rights Society (ARS), New York / SIAE, Rome.

This drawing is not a riddle with a single answer that completes its meaning. It gives you permission to look and to keep looking; instead of figuring it out, you get to know it. Is there a payoff for spending time with this drawing? Through patience and craft, Ruane gently persuades us that there is.

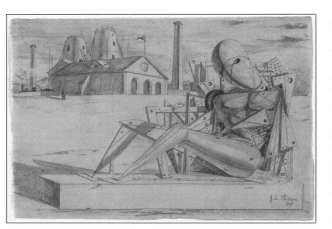

Kay Ruane,
Witness, graphite,
17" × 27", 2005.
*Courtesy of Kay
Ruane*

Abstraction

What is abstraction? In the context of the mechanics of life drawing, abstraction is a visible emphasis on the processes used to make the image. In other words, the drawing may use forms that are themselves interesting, or the medium may be used in a compelling way, independent of how well the picture resembles its subject or tells a story. In order to receive what the drawing offers, the viewer must suspend the expectation that the purpose of the drawing is a realistic depiction of its subject. This book contains several exercises in abstraction:

- In Chapter 2, the blind contour exercise produces drawings that are interesting to look at but hard to understand unless you know how they were made.

- In Chapter 3, hatching is an abstract drawing device. When we study an object we want to draw, we do not see hatching lines on it. On the other hand, it would not be hard to make a drawing consisting of nothing but hatching lines, with no recognizable human image.

- In Chapter 4, the palimpsest drawing was an exercise in gestural abstraction, in the tradition of **action painting**.

- In Chapter 5, the developed gesture drawings were abstract in that they integrated your own personal marks into recognizable drawings of the figure.

- In Chapter 6, the improvisations were explorations into developing a personal graphic language for expressing the body's three-dimensional forms.

These are all examples of **figurative abstraction**, in which the human figure is the armature, or foundation, for personal inquiries into picture-making. I hope that one of the things you take away from this book is that a drawing communicates through the way it is made, as well as by what it depicts. Your formal choices have significance. An abstract drawing foregrounds its construction, which carries the content and meaning of the piece.

Exercise 10-3: A Finished Drawing

In this exercise, you will create a finished drawing consistent with your own intentions, ambitions, and standards.

Materials

- Your choice of drawing media. This can be material you have used in earlier exercises, such as charcoal or ink, or it may be any other monochromatic medium that you have some experience with.

- A good grade of white paper at least 22" × 30" for the final drawing and a lesser grade to practice with.

- Erasers as needed.

visual | 10–20 |

H. Stone, *Drawing from Intimacy Series*, pencil on paper, 18" × 24", 2000.

Procedures

1. Assemble the drawings and notes from your drawing inventory.

2. Create a plan for the drawing by writing down the answers to these questions:

   a. Will the drawing be mostly contour line, mostly values, or will you balance the two?

   b. Will it have only one figure in it, or more than one?

   c. What kind of finish do you want the drawing to have? Will it be smooth and refined, or do you want to use hatching or erasing to create an active surface?

   d. Will the drawing be primarily a portrait?

   e. Will the drawing use narrative? If so, is the purpose of the drawing to tell a story, or will the action be implied?

   f. How important will abstraction be to the drawing?

3. Make the drawing. Either draw some studies from the model to use as source material, or work directly from the model on your final drawing.

4. When the drawing is done, evaluate it for how well it meets your personal standards for quality. If you are not generally pleased with it, you may want to rework it, or start it over.

Look at the Drawing:

Look at the written plan you made for the drawing. You won't evaluate the drawing according to how well it implemented the plan because the plan was a way of organizing your exploration, not anticipating your destination. Take note of departures from the plan as points of interest, which you can incorporate into the next plan.

You have diagnosed problems and addressed them as a part of the process of creating this drawing. After a finished drawing is complete, there is only one assessment question left: Is this a drawing that you would exhibit?

Exercise 10-4: Benchmark Comparison

Procedures

1. Find the benchmarking drawing you did in Chapter 1 (Exercise 1-1), and compare it to one of the two finished drawings you completed in this chapter.

2. Write down four formal observations about each drawing. These should be statements about characteristics, rather than shortcomings, of the work. For example, it won't be helpful if you make the statement, "The work fails miserably in its figure–ground integration."

3. Write a couple of paragraphs on how the two pieces are different. Be specific when you do this, avoiding general statements such as, "The second piece is a big improvement over the first."

4. Can you see yourself in the first drawing? In other words, did you make distinctive, personal marks when you drew it, or is it in some other way consistent with the way you do things? If the answer is yes, what do you see in the drawing that you recognize as your own? If the answer is no, what is missing?

CHAPTER SUMMARY

A finished drawing is a work of art that you would exhibit. A finished drawing requires your best thinking, planning, and drawing skill. Reflecting on your work is an important part of thinking and planning because your work will give you clues about your strengths as an artist and directions you might take in your art.

Finished drawings are the best work that you are capable of. It is possible to develop a finished drawing as you would a commercial design, with a brainstorming phase, connecting the best idea to an image and drawing it, but illustrating a theory or belief in this way may not be the best way to use life drawing to express a deep theme. The discipline of life drawing has a natural compatibility with themes related to interpersonal experience, so to find its power, let the content grow from what your drawings are telling you.

▶ *chapter questions*

1. Artist studios frequently are cluttered places, with drawings pinned everywhere. Why is this?

    a. Because artists have a poor work ethic and are too lazy to clean the studio up.

    b. Because artists have little or no pride in their environment.

    c. So the artists can study their work and think about it.

    d. So customers can see the work.

2. Which of these items is not a characteristic of a finished drawing?

    a. Marketability

    b. Ambition

    c. Quality

    d. Intention

3. To make a finished drawing:

    a. You should be humble before the process.

    b. You should be free of performance anxiety.

    c. You should mistrust your own work.

    d. You should respect your own voice and pay attention.

4. What is the hard question for an artist?

    a. "How can I master drawing?"

    b. "Am I good enough to be an artist?"

    c. "How do I make the very best art I can?"

    d. "Do I find ambivalence interesting?"

5. If a drawing is important to you:

    a. You felt a sense of satisfaction when you finished it.

    b. You learned something from creating it.

    c. You felt like you were doing something important when you made it.

    d. All of the above.

6. You have written a short plan for a drawing. When you evaluate the drawing:

   a. Take notes of departures the drawing made from the plan.

   b. Evaluate how well the drawing implemented the plan.

   c. Disregard the plan; the drawing should stand on its own terms.

   d. Vow to follow the plan better in your next drawing.

7. A plan for a drawing:

   a. Should be very detailed.

   b. Should be theoretical, rather than concrete.

   c. Should anticipate the drawing's destination.

   d. Should organize the drawing's exploration.

8. A person's likeness is determined by:

   a. Facial set.

   b. Facial features.

   c. Both facial set and facial features.

   d. Facial expression.

9. The best drawing technique for drawing a portrait is:

   a. Value drawing.

   b. Contour line drawing.

   c. Blind contour drawing.

   d. Modeling drawing.

10. The most important point of likeness is:

   a. The eyes.

   b. The jaw line.

   c. The hairline.

   d. The nose.

glossary

abstract: The use of elements or media in a work of art in a manner that is interesting for its own sake, independent of any recognizable image that may be in the work.

action painting: A method of abstract painting originating with Jackson Pollock, in which the medium is applied spontaneously with the intention of creating a record of the artist's movements.

ant trail: Also called a *cross-contour line*, an analytical line created by visualizing drawing across the surface of the body, instead of along a contour. The line shows the trail an ant would take walking across the body. Ant trails are usually drawn in sets, to show a particular structure.

asymmetry: An absence of symmetry. Lacking repeating elements.

atmospheric perspective: Creating the appearance of deep space in a work of art by softening the contours and lightening, or cooling, the colors of the forms in the more distant areas.

barrier cream: A nontoxic ointment applied to the hands that dries to an invisible film and protects the skin from irritants.

calligraphy: Beautiful writing, or making beautiful marks.

canon of proportions: A set of standardized proportional relationships for the human body. *The Classical Canon* was written by *Polykleitos* (5th–4th B.C.E.), and his sculpture

Doryphoros embodied this standard. *Leonardo da Vinci* (1452–1519) also constructed a set of idealized proportions in his drawing *Vitruvian Man*, sometimes called the *Canon of Proportions*.

chiaroscuro: In a drawing or painting, describing three-dimensional form by rendering the effects of light on the form.

Classicism: A style of art and architecture that started in ancient Greece circa 450 B.C.E. The classical style emphasizes balance, order, unity, and clarity.

cloisonné forms: Solid, closed shapes of color.

closed form: A form that is clearly distinguished from its background at all points along its edge; a hard-edged form.

composition: The organization of the elements in a work of art.

contour: The edge of a form.

contour drawing (contour line drawing): A drawing in which each edge is defined by a line that follows it. Contour drawings have little or no use of value.

contour line: A line that defines an edge.

contrapposto: The *weight-shift* stance discovered during the *Greek Classical* period (450–323 B.C.E.). Contrapposto is a relaxed standing position in which one leg is straight and bears most of the body's weight, and the other is bent. This causes the hips to laterally tilt and the shoulders to tip in the opposite direction.

contrast: The proportion of dark and light tones to middle tones in a work of art. A high-contrast image has few middle tones, and a low-contrast image is mostly middle grays, with few values either very dark or light.

contrast reversal: A condition in which a form is darker than the background in some places and lighter in others.

design (noun): The intentional organization present in a work of art.

design (verb): The process of planning how a work of art will be organized.

dynamic figure–ground relationship: A dialog that occurs between the figure and the background in a work of art. This can take the form of *edge effects*, *contrast reversals*, or interlocking *positive* and *negative forms*, although these are not the only methods for achieving it. Also called an *active* or *flexible* figure–ground relationship.

empirical perspective: Linear perspective as it is observed, rather than constructed.

figurative abstraction: A style of art that uses abstract techniques to create a composition that contains a recognizable human image. Also called *abstract figuration*.

figure: In art, any self-contained form; in life drawing, an image of a person.

figure drawing: The art of drawing another, usually unclothed, person. Also called *life drawing*.

figure–ground relationship: A picture's specific strategy of differentiating a figure from the background and making it fit into the composition.

flat space: A type of nonillusionistic picture space in which the action takes place on the picture plane.

foreshortened: The visual contraction of an object as it is seen in a perspective space. Foreshortening is most apparent when the object is viewed from one end.

formal: Relating to the way a piece of art looks or is constructed.

formal observation: A factual statement describing the way a work of art looks or is constructed. A formal observation is objective, so that anyone would be able to agree with it regardless of how he or she feels about the piece.

formal qualities: Concrete characteristics of a work of art concerned with its appearance or construction. Formal qualities are independent of the meaning of the work.

ground: The background of a drawing or painting.

hatching: A network or arrangement of lines used to create areas of value in a drawing.

horizon line: In linear perspective, a construction line that designates eye level.

illusionistic: In a work of art, resembling or intending to resemble space or objects in the physical world.

illusionistic space: A picture space that uses the convention that the picture plane is a window looking into a three-dimensional space similar to the one we inhabit. An illusionistic space implies a fixed point of view.

imprimatura: An initial layer of middle value in a drawing or painting.

life drawing: The art of drawing another, usually unclothed, person. Also called *figure drawing*.

linear perspective: Creating the illusion of depth on a two-dimensional surface by drawing receding parallel lines so that they converge on a *vanishing point*.

local color: The color of an object independent of effects of lighting and atmosphere.

mass tone: A solid shape of gray.

mechanics: The formal use of drawing or painting media to create structure in a work of art.

midline: The imaginary vertical line down the middle of the human body; the body's mirroring axis.

modeling: Describing the body's three-dimensional forms analytically, using a method of mapping them to a two-dimensional surface. Modeling works independently of chiaroscuro.

negative space: The parts of the background adjacent to the figure.

open form: A form that is not clearly distinguishable from its background at every point on its edge. An open form may have the figure and background at the same value in some areas, or it may have an incomplete contour line.

orthographic: A representation of a space or object without foreshortening. A three-view architect's drawing is an example of an orthographic drawing.

painterly: An application of drawing or painting media in which strokes are visible.

picture plane: The *construction plane* perpendicular to *perspective lines* and corresponding to the surface of the picture.

planar modeling: Defining a figure's form in a drawing by subdividing it into planes and giving each one its own value.

positive space: The portion of the composition corresponding to the *figure*.

proportion: The relationships of a drawing's elements with respect to size.

psychological portrait: A portrait that depicts the subject's personality, emotions, or state of mind.

reference plane: A surface on the figure that is parallel to the picture plane.

relief space: A shallow illusionistic picture space in which forms extend out of a reference plane near the picture plane.

rendering: The physical process of using drawing media to create an image.

reverse silhouette: A solid light form against a dark background.

rule of thirds: A method of composing a picture by dividing it into a grid of nine units and placing the center of interest at one of the corners of the rectangle in the center.

silhouette: A solid dark form against a light background.

smooth shading: Applying drawing media in an even, unbroken film to create mass tones and gradients.

structure: Unambiguous spatial relationships in a drawing or painting.

symmetry: Order in a picture based on repeating elements. The three most common forms of symmetry are *bilateral symmetry*, in which the forms are mirrored along a central axis; *rotational symmetry*, in which forms are arranged in a circle; and *translational symmetry*, which uses repeating modules along a line.

tectonic: The organization of the large masses and voids in a composition.

three-value drawing: A drawing executed with mass tones of black, one gray tone, and the white of the paper. A three-value drawing uses no gradients or contour lines.

tone: A level of light or dark in a drawing. Also called *value*.

Tree Model: A method of organizing a picture originating in the *Italian Renaissance* (1400–1520) using the structure of the tree as a hierarchical model. The largest form, the trunk, is represented by linear perspective. The large branches are the large masses and voids in the perspective space such as buildings. The bigger limbs on the branches are groups of people, and the smaller limbs are individual people, with the leaves and twigs represented by the postures and facial expressions.

unarticulated space: Ambiguous space in a drawing that shows no evidence of being the product of intentional thinking.

value: A level of light or dark in a drawing. Also called *tone*.

value drawing: A drawing without *contour lines*, rendered with levels of light and dark.

vanishing point: In a one- or two-point perspective space, a point on the horizon line where straight lines perpendicular to the picture plane are made to converge.

visual memory: A type of eidetic memory in which an image can be accurately recalled when it is no longer visible.

name index

subject index